THE GREEN SABBATH AND THE LAST VISTA OF HOPE

CHINEDU DANIEL OBASI

World rights reserved. This book, or any portion thereof, may not be copied or reproduced in any form or manner whatsoever, except as provided by law, without the written permission of the publisher, except by a reviewer who may quote brief passages in a review. The author assumes full responsibility for the accuracy of all facts and quotations as cited in this book.

Unless otherwise indicated, all scripture quotations are taken from the King James Version.

The ESV® Bible (The Holy Bible, English Standard Version®). ESV® Text Edition: 2016. Copyright © 2001 by Crossway, a publishing ministry of Good News Publishers. The ESV® text has been reproduced in cooperation with and by permission of Good News Publishers. Unauthorized reproduction of this publication is prohibited. All rights reserved.

Scripture taken from the New Century Version®. Copyright © 2005 by Thomas Nelson. Used by permission. All rights reserved.

THE HOLY BIBLE, NEW INTERNATIONAL VERSION®, NIV® Copyright © 1973, 1978, 1984, 2011 by Biblica, Inc.® Used by permission. All rights reserved worldwide.

Copyright © 2019 Chinedu Daniel Obasi
Copyright © 2019 TEACH Services, Inc.
ISBN-13: 978-1-4796-0997-0 (Paperback)
ISBN-13: 978-1-4796-0998-7 (ePub)
Library of Congress Control Number: 2018913560

Scripture taken from the New King James Version®. Copyright © 1982 by Thomas Nelson. Used by permission. All rights reserved.

Good News Translation® (Today's English Version, Second Edition)

Copyright © 1992 American Bible Society. All rights reserved.

TABLE OF CONTENTS

Foreword v
Preface vi
Introduction vii
Chapter 1—The Frightening Reality 1
Chapter 2—Global Consciousness 17
Chapter 3—The Green Sabbath 25
Chapter 4—God's Covenant with Mankind 34
Chapter 5—The Law of the New Covenant 47
Chapter 6—The Real Earth Day 60
Chapter 7—The Apostolic Tradition 74
Chapter 8—History in Outline 85
Chapter 9—Breaking the Secret Code 96
Chapter 10—America in Prophecy 105
Chapter 11—The Drunken Harlot 122
Chapter 12—The Abomination of Desolation 142
Chapter 13—The Kings of the North and South 157
Chapter 14—Dousing Allah's Torch 170
Chapter 15—The Time of Trouble 184
Bibliography 195

FOREWORD

What is the meaning of these times? What comes tomorrow? Here, at last, is an authoritative answer that probes the persistent realities of this tense age. Now, at last, you will recognize the clear-cut issues involved.

From chapter to chapter, page to page, in bold strokes this volume takes you behind play and counter play of world politics as you view the final struggle for world supremacy.

The masterful volume you hold in your hand will keep you spellbound from cover to cover as you are carried into the most thrilling drama of the past, present, and future.

This could well be the most important book you have read. Chinedu Daniel Obasi's *The Green Sabbath and the Last Vista of Hope* is filled with thoughtful insights, sure to reveal hidden truth that will cause you to live the blessed life.

Pastor Gaius A. Umahi, PhD
Associate Professor, New Testament Studies and Gender Issues, Babcock University
WAD Biblical Research Committee Member

PREFACE

Countdown to the end! The clock is now ticking as the world races to the finish at the speed of light. With multiple problems facing our world today, many people are asking, "Is the world really coming to an end?"

Climate and weather disasters have hit nearly every continent—flooding and monsoons in South Asia, hurricanes and major earthquakes in North America and Europe, landslides and drought in Africa, and a tsunami threat to Central America. Commentaries from experts seem to indicate that our planet is in danger and life on earth is itself severely threatened.

The idea of observing an environmental "green sabbath" and having it enforced is not only being urged to deal with the issue of preserving the environment, but it is also associated with saving mankind. Will this be the last vista of hope?

This book presents the commentary of one of Christianity's most prolific and respected writers the world has ever known—Ellen White—whose classic, *The Great Controversy*, is the framework of this effort.

The Green Sabbath and the Last Vista of Hope has the straightforward answers to these and other questions that you want and need to know. May God bless you in your journey of truth!

CHINEDU DANIEL OBASI

INTRODUCTION

The end of all things is stealing upon us stealthily and imperceptibly, like the noiseless approach of a thief in the night. For more than ten years, calamities have been ravaging the entire world. Droughts, floods, hurricanes, cyclones, volcanoes, and earthquakes have followed one after another in steady succession. Tens of thousands have lost their lives in accidents by land, sea, and air. Mass shootings, senseless murders of various kinds, and crashes of large jetliners have become the norm. **Could all this be the result of the worldwide disregard for the law of God?**

Every day brings fresh revelations of strife, bribery, and fraud with its heart-sickening record of violence and lawlessness, indifference to human suffering, and brutal, fiendish destruction of human life. We are indeed standing on the threshold of great and solemn events, not just for one nation, but all nations. The evidence is overwhelming.

This book is written to lead us along an incredible path behind the scenes so we can get a shocking glimpse of what is coming and become prepared. And what this book sees coming is not based on guesswork; it is based on a source of predictions that has never yet missed in its prophecies.

Chapter 1

THE FRIGHTENING REALITY

Everywhere today men and women are worried by the startling events now taking place all around the globe. These include terrorism, political instability in many countries, strife among the nations, escalating hostility in the Middle East, nuclear tensions, arson, looting, vandalism, lawlessness of every kind, accidents and calamities by land and sea, conflagrations, fierce tornadoes, terrific hailstorms, tempests, floods, cyclones, tidal waves, and earthquakes. These and more are happening in quick succession in various places and a thousand forms.

What is really coming upon the earth today? The relationship between mankind and nature has become the acutest global problem. The scientific community has warned that if greenhouse gas emissions keep increasing, the planet will reach a point of no return. Global warming will become catastrophic and irreversible. The Bible speaks of this: **"Men's hearts failing them for fear, and for looking after those things which are coming upon the earth"** (Luke 21:26).

The above text perfectly describes our time. This brings us to the following question: Does the Bible in any way predict climate change as one of the signs of Christ's second coming? This is an important question. If the Bible, our most reliable source of wisdom and guidance, says something about climate change, that could inform our discussion. Getting reliable guidance would have tremendous implications. However, before we look at what the Bible says, let's define the term "climate change."

What is Climate Change?

Climate change is defined as "a change in the global or regional climate patterns, mostly due to the burning of fossil fuel." In the opinion of many scientists, human-induced changes in the earth's atmosphere and ocean are the major causes of climate change.

"According to the Intergovernmental Panel on Climate Change (IPCC), we need immediate and aggressive solutions. Without them, natural ecosystems—and the services they provide to all of humanity—are at risk of dangerous impacts, such as:

- **rising sea levels**
- **melting glaciers and ice caps**
- **increasingly frequent instances of drought**
- **heavy precipitation causing flooding**
- **changes in timing of wet/dry seasons (seasonality)**
- **intense tropical cyclone activity**
- **changes to the lakes, rivers, streams and hydrological systems that supply fresh water**
- **shifts in species habitat ranges**
- **alterations and disturbances to agriculture**
- **heat-related mortality**
- **increased outbreaks of infectious diseases**

"Given the magnitude of this threat, we must urgently deploy all available measures—and nature provides many of the most immediate" (Conservation International, http://1ref.us/o3, accessed 9/5/2018).

While some others agree that the earth is warming, they are uncertain of both the causes and consequences. Human activities may be a factor, they say, but not necessarily the primary one.

Natural Disasters and God's Judgment

The Bible has a lot to say about natural disasters linked to God's judgment. He proclaims how He sometimes deals with sin. **"If I shut up heaven that there be no rain, or if I command the locusts to devour the land, or if I send pestilence among my people; If my people, which are called by my name, shall humble themselves, and pray, and seek my face, and turn from their wicked ways; then will I hear from heaven, and will forgive their sin, and will heal their land"** (2 Chron. 7:13, 14).

From the above text, we see that some natural disasters are often designed by God to lead people to humble their hearts and repent of their sins. For instance, it was an earthquake that caused the jailer at Philippi to exclaim, **"Sirs, what must I do to be saved"** (Acts 16:30)? It was a famine that sent King Ahab searching everywhere for the prophet Elijah (see 1 Kings 18:10). It was a plague that brought Pharaoh to his knees, confessing before Moses, **"I have sinned against the LORD your God, and against you. Now therefore forgive, I pray thee, my sin only this once, and intreat the LORD your God, that he may take away from me this death only"** (Ex. 10: 16, 17). Disasters can have a sobering effect upon the human mind. It can serve as a wakeup call to repentance. Please note that natural disasters are not natural to God's creation.

> *Disasters can have a sobering effect upon the human mind. It can serve as a wakeup call to repentance*

The Origin of Natural Disasters

When God made the earth, it was exceedingly beautiful. Creation was complete and perfect. The rivers, vegetation, flowers, fruit trees, birds, fish, and animals all lived harmoniously together in a peaceful, stable, and idyllic environment. Missing from God's creation was disease and death. There were no hurricanes, floods, earthquakes, or tsunamis. Adam and Eve lived happily in an unspoiled paradise, cultivating an intimate relationship with their Maker who visited them in the cool of every day (see Gen. 3:8).

It was sin that put natural disasters in place. When Adam and Eve transgressed God's law, the peace and tranquility of Eden were shattered. **"[C]ursed *is* the ground for thy sake; in sorrow shalt thou eat *of* it all the days of thy life; Thorns also and thistles shall it bring forth to thee; and thou shalt eat the herb of the field; In the sweat of thy face shalt thou eat bread, till thou return unto the ground; for out of it wast thou taken: for dust thou *art*, and unto dust shalt thou return"** (3:17–19).

The entire creation was subjected to the curse and corruption resulting from the entrance of sin into this world. As you all know, before this time, everything in the world, including the weather, was perfect, but after humanity's sin, the climate began to change. Death entered the world, and some animal kinds became predatory. The land no longer yielded its abundant. Thorns and thistles sprung up. People would have to work the ground to grow their food. Childbirth would be painful. Life itself became more of a struggle.

As people continue to live in sin, everything around them keeps changing. From the first signs of decaying nature in the tall, noble, sturdy trees that cast off their leaves to the drooping flowers, all present before humanity the general dissolution of beautiful nature, which God had created for His distinct benefit.

His Hand Can Also Destroy

As a Christian, life becomes a lot easier once we take God at his word. Nevertheless, many find it difficult to do so. One area of great difficulty concerns calamity. The word of God has said, **"If there is calamity in a city, will not the Lord have done *it*"** (Amos 3:6, NKJV)? Christians find it difficult to believe that a God of love can allow evil befall His children. However, one fact we need to understand is that nothing good or bad happens outside the will of God. The Bible states, **"Who can speak and have it happen if the Lord has not decreed it? Is it not from the mouth of the Most High that both calamities and good things come"** (Lam. 3:37, 38, NIV)?

Thus, Job asked his wife, **"Shall we indeed accept good from God, and shall we not accept adversity"** (Job 2:10, NKJV)? Indeed, God takes issue with those who are inclined to limit Him to one dimension. The Bible says, **"it shall come to pass at that time *That* I will search Jerusalem with lamps, And punish the men Who are settled in complacency, Who say in their heart, The Lord will not do good, Nor will he do evil"** (Zeph. 1:12, NKJV).

"I am instructed that when the Lord's time comes, should no change have taken place in the hearts of proud, ambitious human beings, men will find that the hand that has been strong to save will be strong to destroy. No earthly power can stay the hand of God" (White 1909, p.13). God is emphatic. **"My purpose will stand"; "Surely, as I have planned, so it will be, and as have purposed, so it will happen"** (Isaiah 46:10; 14:24, NIV). **"But the plans of the Lord stand firm forever"** (Ps. 33:11, NIV).

The First Global Disaster

Within the space of 2,000 years from the fall of Adam, the good earth and its inhabitants deteriorated rapidly, and the human race was faced with total annihilation.

> **And God saw that the wickedness of man *was* great in the earth, and *that* every imagination of the thoughts of his heart *was* only evil continually. And it repented the LORD that he had made man on the earth, and it grieved him at his heart. And the LORD said, I will destroy man whom I have created from the face of the earth; both man, and beast, and the creeping thing, and the fowls of the air; for it repenteth me that I have made them. (Genesis 6:5–7)**

This global destruction caused by the flood was God's judgment on the corrupt and sinful inhabitants of the earth. The Bible indicates that the waters of the flood came from two sources:

1. **All the fountains of the great deep broken up**
2. **The windows of heaven were opened**

The breaking up of the fountains of the great deep implies a shifting and clashing of tectonic plates with its violent rupture beneath the ocean bedrock, which causes disasters like tsunamis. Therefore, friends, when the rain poured nonstop for forty days and earthquakes shook the earth, and tectonic plates shifted, spurning multiple tsunamis in the flood of Noah's day. Havoc reigned in God's creation, permanently altering the face and formation of the earth.

While we live in this sinful world, we will inevitably face these kinds of natural disasters because they are the consequences of sin. Disasters serve to remind us that "the whole creation groaneth and travaileth in pain together until now…. waiting for the… redemption of our body" (Rom. 8:22, 23).

Sodom and Gomorrah

History confirms that in the time of Abraham, the city-states of Sodom and Gomorrah had tried God's patience with their grievous sins, and He destroyed them. He used a natural disaster as punishment for Sodom and Gomorrah. The flames that consumed the cities of the plain shed their warning light down even to our time.

We are taught the fearful and solemn lesson that while God's mercy bears long with the transgressor, there is a limit beyond which one may not go on in sin. When that limit is reached, then the offers of mercy are withdrawn, and the ministration of judgment begins. The fact that God sometimes uses natural disasters to punish human wickedness does not justify jumping to the conclusion that every natural disaster is a direct, divine judgment upon the wicked from above. Some are purely the handiwork of satanic manipulation.

Human Manipulation

"And the nations were angry, and thy wrath is come, and the time of the dead, that they should be judged…and shouldest destroy them which destroy the earth" (Rev 11:18). Here the Bible describes a condition that will exist shortly before Christ's second coming. People will be found in this closing moment of earth's history destroying the planet. Inspiration reveals that:

> **Satan...has studied the secrets of the laboratories of nature, and he uses all his power to control the elements as far as God allows...[he] has control of all whom God does not especially guard...he will bring trouble...and lead men to believe that it is God who is afflicting them....**
>
> **...In accidents and calamities by sea and by land, in great conflagrations, in fierce tornadoes and terrific hail-storms, in tempests, floods, cyclones, tidal waves, and earthquakes, in every place and in a thousand forms, Satan is exercising his power. He sweeps away the ripening harvest, and famine and distress follow. He imparts to the air a deadly taint, and thousands perish by the pestilence. These visitations are to become more and more frequent and disastrous. (White,** *The Great Controversy,* **pp. 589, 590)**

You've heard of environmental warfare today. Although denied by many, some respected researchers allege that secret electromagnetic warfare capabilities, which can create earthquakes and storms, have been developed. For instance, some declassified records show that from 1949 to 1955, the Royal Air Force (RAF) released various substances, including dry ice, silver iodide, and salt into the atmosphere at high altitudes in order to induce rain. "The clouds would then precipitate, pulled down below freezing point by the extra weight of dense particles, thus making it rain sooner and heavier than it might have done" (The Guardian, http://1ref.us/ox, accessed 9/5/2018).

"The first public description of weather modification techniques as a weapon of war was made on 20th, March, 1974. At that time the Pentagon revealed a seven year cloud seeding effort in Vietnam and Cambodia, costing $ 21.6 million. The objective was to increase rainfall in target areas, thereby causing landslides along roadways and making unpaved roads muddy, softening road surfaces hindering the movement of supplies (Science, "Weather Warfare: Pentagon Concedes 7-Year Vietnam Effort," Deborah Shapley, June 7, 1974. http://1ref.us/oz, accessed 9/5/2018).

However, interest in the exploitation of the environment for military purposes did not end there. Air University, located at Maxwell Air Force Base in Alabama, describes itself as a "center for advanced education" that "plays a vital role in States Air Force" and whose service members must place the nation's defense above self. The Chief of Staff of the US Air Force tasked Air University to "look 30 years into the future to identify the concepts, capabilities and technologies the United States will require to remain the dominant air and space force in the 21st century" (http://1ref.us/oz, accessed 10/24/2018).

The study, completed in 1996, was titled "Air Force 2025." It is a chilling document. It is evident that the authors regard our environment as nothing more than a resource to be exploited for military purposes. They claim that by 2025, US forces can "own the weather" by "capitalizing on emerging technologies and focusing development of those technologies to war fighting applications." The authors describe weather modification as having "tremendous military capabilities which can provide battle space dominance to a degree never before imagined," claiming the project would be "not unlike the splitting of the atom" (ibid.).

The paper goes on to discuss how "ionospheric research (The Ionosphere region of the earth's atmosphere ranging from about 30–1200 miles above the surface of the earth) is necessary to achieve goals in both enhancing US communication capabilities and as a method of disabling enemy communications. By 2025, it may be possible to modify the ionosphere and near space, creating a variety of potential applications" (ibid.).

High-Frequency Active Aurora Research Program

Since the early 1990s, the US Air Force has been sponsoring the world's largest ionospheric modification project called HAARP (High-Frequency Active Auroral Research Program). HAARP, located in the remote bush country of Gakona, Alaska, is a small version of the antenna discussed in the Eastland patents (Corporate Watch, http://1ref.us/oz, accessed 9/5/2018).

The HAARP program was scheduled for completion in 2002, and full-scale testing had started by early 2003. While there is currently no conclusive proof that HAARP has ever been used for weather manipulation, there have been numerous reports describing very unusual weather and environmental conditions throughout the world in recent years. In January 2003, Yuru Solomatin, secretary of the Ukrainian Committee for Economic Policy, writing in Pravda, reported the following:

> A lot of specialists and scientists believe that unpredictable natural disasters and several man-caused catastrophes that struck Europe and Asia in the summer of the year 2002 say that there might be certain global reason that caused them all. He posits, "it is an open secret that the USA (probably, not the USA alone) has already constructed high-frequency transmitter facilities. Those devices can heat the earth environment up to the state of plasma by means of pumping ions.
>
> The owners of this weapon are able to program floods, twisters and storms, even earthquakes in any region of the planet. it is also

possiblle to paralyze civil and military electric surveillance systems, and even to affect the mentality of whole nations." A lot of specialists and scientists believe that a special American program HAARP is one of those developments. (Pravda, http://1ref.us/p0, accessed 9/5/2018)

There is doubt that men have acquired the capability to intentionally modify or manipulate the natural ecology, "such as the climate and weather, the earth systems such as the ionosphere, magnetosphere, tectonic plate system, thus triggering a seismic events such as earthquakes to cause intentional physical, economic, and psycho-social, and physical destruction of an intended target of a geophysical or population location, as part of strategic or tactical war. (Eco News, quoted in Michel Chossudovsky, "the Ultimate Weapon of Mass Destruction: 'Owning the Weather for Military Use,'" September 27, 2004)

But interest in the exploitation of the environment for military purposes did not end there. More recently, Dennis M. Bushnell gave a talk to NASA in which he outlined plans for dispersing airborne viruses, such as Ebola and new, specially engineered viruses. (Dennis M. Bushnell, 'Future Strategic Issues/Future Warfare [Circa 2025]', NASA Langley Research Center, undated, at http://1ref.us/p1, accessed 9/6/2018)

Does this sound familiar? This is what we are witnessing across the world, mostly in Third World nations.

Creating Clouds to Stop Global Warming

The United States government has recommended spraying sulfur dioxide in the atmosphere to form clouds and artificially cool the earth. This would be done in combination with a reduction in greenhouse gases. However, whenever mankind intervenes in nature, there are unintended consequences that create more problems.

> **However, suddenly stopping that spraying would have a "devastating" global impact on animals and plants, potentially even leading to extinction,** according to the first study on the potential biological impacts of climate intervention.
>
> **"Rapid warming after stopping geoengineering would be a huge threat to the natural environment and biodiversity,"** said study co-author Alan Robock of Rutgers University. **"If geoengineering ever stopped abruptly, it would be devastating, so you would have to be sure that it could be stopped gradually, and it is easy to think of scenarios that would prevent that....**

...Starting geoengineering then suddenly stopping it isn't necessarily far-fetched.

"**Imagine large droughts or floods around the world that cloud be blamed on geoengineering, and demands that it stop. Can we ever risk that?**" Robock asked. (USA Today, http://1ref.us/ot, accessed 9/5/-5/2018)

The mere talk of it by the government suggests that it may already be happening.

Job's Experience

The book of Job draws back the curtain into the invisible realm, revealing how God and Satan relate in a case of great human adversity that includes two natural disasters. In the Bible, we are told that Job went through four primary crises. As he goes through these four crises, a fifth one unfolds. Job's crises come in the context of the great controversy between Christ and the devil.

The Scriptures declare that on one occasion, when the angels of God came to present themselves before Him, Satan also came among them **(see Job 1:6)**, not to bow before the Eternal King, but to further his own malicious designs against the righteous. "**And the LORD said unto Satan, Whence comest thou? Then Satan answered the LORD, and said, From going to and fro in the earth, and from walking up and down in it** (v. 7).

Of Job, the patriarch of Uz, the Searcher of hearts testified, "**Hast thou considered my servant Job, that** *there is* **none like him in the earth, a perfect and an upright man, one that feareth God, and escheweth evil**" (v. 8)?

Against this man, Satan brought a scornful charge. Describing his response, the Bible says:

> **Then Satan answered the LORD, and said, Doth Job fear God for nought? Hast not thou made an hedge about him, and about his house, and about all that he hath on every side? thou hast blessed the work of his hands, and his substance is increased in the land. But put forth thine hand now, and touch all that he hath, and he will curse thee to thy face.** (Job 1:9–11)

Satan said to Christ, in paraphrase, "Job is serving you only because you're blessing him, but if you remove the blessing from him—if he can no longer find food, transportation, housing, or the basic things of life, and loses all that makes life dear—he will curse you to your face." And what did God now say to Satan? "**And the LORD said unto Satan, Behold, all that he** hath *is* in thy power; only upon himself put not forth thine hand. So Satan went forth from the presence of the LORD" (v. 12).

The Bible says God told Satan, "Alright, you may remove the temporal blessing that Job has, but you must not touch his body." Satan then went forth from the presence of God to afflict Job.

Crisis 1: "And there came a messenger unto Job, and said, The oxen were plowing, and the asses feeding beside them: And the Sabeans fell *upon them*, and took them away; yea, they have slain the servants with the edge of the sword; and I only am escaped alone to tell thee" (vs. 14, 15).

In this passage we see that the first crisis Job experienced was that the Sabeans brought destruction and bloodshed. This was an act of terrorism against Job. What was the next news item delivered to him? Please underscore the recurring phrases:

Crisis 2: "While he *was* yet speaking, there came also another, and said, The fire of God is fallen from heaven, and hath burned up the sheep, and the servants, and consumed them; and I only am escaped alone to tell thee" (v. 16).

The second crisis is fire. What did Job's servant say was destroyed by the fire? Sheep and servants. That means both people and wealth were annihilated by this calamity of nature. Job's first two crises depict terrorism and natural catastrophe. What was his third crisis?

Crisis 3: "While he *was* yet speaking, there came also another, and said, The Chaldeans made out three bands, and fell upon the camels, and have carried them away, yea, and slain the servants with the edge of the sword; and I only am escaped alone to tell thee" (v. 17).

The third crisis was executed by the Chaldeans. They came forth looting and shedding blood. Please note that in the third crisis, the Chaldeans came in three groups and brought destruction. Who do the Chaldeans represent in the Holy Scriptures? **"And Babylon, the glory of kingdoms, the beauty of the Chaldees' excellency, shall be as when God overthrew Sodom and Gomorrah"** (Isa. 13:19).

"And Gedaliah sware to them, and to their men, and said unto them, Fear not to be the servants of the Chaldees: dwell in the land, and serve the king of Babylon; and it shall be well with you" (2 Kings 25:24). The Chaldeans are the Babylonians. In Job's third crisis, they came in three groups to attack him. This is terrorism from another perceptive. What was the fourth crisis?

Crisis 4: "While he *was* yet speaking, there came also another, and said, Thy sons and thy daughters *were* eating and drinking wine in their eldest

brother's house: And, behold, there came a great wind from the wilderness, and smote the four corners of the house, and it fell upon the young men, and they are dead; and I only am escaped alone to tell thee"** (vs. 18, 19).

In the fourth crisis, not only did the winds destroy the homes of Job's children, but the children themselves died in the calamity. Friends, do you see rapidity here? While the first man was telling Job his experience, the second, third, and fourth followed in quick succession. As he experienced these terrible, massive crises, the Bible says Job did not question or curse God. Instead, he worshiped God.

What was the fifth crisis? In the fifth crisis, Satan returned to God and said, "You know what? Job is still worshiping you because he is still healthy. Affect his health, and he will curse you to your face." Satan was permitted by God to afflict Job's body:

Crisis 5: "So went Satan forth from the presence of the LORD, and smote Job with sore boils from the sole of his foot unto his crown" (2:7).

The enemy had stripped Job of all he possessed; his family ties were broken; his children were taken from him. Now he was afflicted with boils and loathsome sores all over his body and suffered immensely. In his crises, what did his wife say? **"Then said his wife unto him, Dost thou still retain thine integrity? curse God, and die"** (v. 9).

Still another element of bitterness was added to his cup. His wife told him to curse God and die. Despite his challenging circumstances, Job maintained his integrity and commitment to God. **"But he said unto her, Thou speakest as one of the foolish women speaketh. What? shall we receive good at the hand of God, and shall we not receive evil? In all this did not Job sin with his lips"** (v. 10).

As his friends came to comfort him, they also tried to make him see that he was responsible, by his sinful course, for his afflictions, but he defended himself and denied the charge, declaring, "Miserable comforters are you all." The question that we must ask ourselves is, 'How does this Bible account relate to our present, global crises?

God wants us to focus on the end of Job's experience. Just as with Job, so with God's people in the last days. Just as the hour of trial may seem dark to our understanding now, it will soon be made plain. When we should see the "end of the Lord," then we would know that notwithstanding the trials resulting from our errors, His purposes of love toward us had been steadily fulfilling.

Therefore, Satan may stir up a natural disaster, but the book of Job makes it clear that God continues to reign, even while selectively allowing

Satan to do evil things. Satan knew he didn't have the authority to incite humans to do evil, bring down lightning, cause fires, or send the wind to blow down a building and take lives without God's explicit permission.

Signs of The Times

Jesus has predicted that these calamites will occur before His return. In fact, He said, "**And there shall be signs in the sun, and in the moon, and in the stars**" (Luke 21:25). The devastating heat of the sun today is igniting bushfires, destroying an enormous expanse of land vegetation. These unexpected outbreaks of fire are beyond what any human effort can quench. People beheld as they burned down their palaces and swept away their homes in the fury of the flames.

A series of studies over the past few years point not only to some warming of the world's atmosphere and oceans but to fundamental changes in the operation of the earth's natural systems. For example, a study on climate change, led by Rutgers University scientist Dr. Jennifer Francis, reported that large northward bulges in the upper atmospheric jet stream are linked **"to extreme weather events, such as the severe cold spells in the northern hemisphere in the winter** (2015), **the enduring drought in the west, and major storms like Hurricane Sandy in 2012"** (http://1ref.us/p3, accessed 9/6/2018).

A Washington Post article published in March 2015 reported that **"according to a new study just out in Nature Climate Change…we're now seeing a slowdown of the great ocean circulation that, among other planetary roles, helps to partly drive the Gulf Stream off the US Coast. The consequence could be dire-including significant extra sea level rise for coastal cities like New York and Boston"** (http://1ref.us/p2, accessed 9/6/2018).

There's also an astonishing loss of sea ice in the Arctic. This drives a whole series of changes such as extended heat waves and droughts in the Northern Hemisphere and decreasing rain around the middle latitudes, which is where much of the farmland is located. All these changes are accelerating. The results are striking: increased drying and subsequent fires and significantly decreased food security, especially in the underdeveloped parts of the world.

The temperatures today are seen rising around the world, creating deadly heatwaves, causing the rivers and lakes to dry up, and leaving the lands shattered and broken like the potters' clay, and this experience is causing a global water scarcity.

Global Water Scarcity

God said, "**I will waste the mountains and hills, and dry up all their herbs; and I will make the rivers islands, and I will dry up the pools**" (Isa. 42:15). Current reports indicate that this is happening already. Fears of dwindling global water supply are already being realized in many countries. In Joel, we have further confirmation that rivers shall dry up at the end, and as a result, livestock would suffer. "**The beasts of the field cry also unto thee: for the rivers of waters are dried up, and the fire hath devoured the pastures of the wilderness**" (Joel 1:20).

Global water scarcity is becoming a reality already. It has commenced and is spreading fast. If you are not feeling it yet, for sure, it is coming. It is God's curse upon the whole earth because of mankind's pride and rebellion.

Asteroid Inversion

There is another kind of strange happening in outer space that is shocking the world—the asteroid inversion. These are instruments of God' divine destruction preserved for the day of restitution. The Bible confirmed there would be, at the coming of Christ, an asteroid inversion upon the earth. "**And there fell upon men a great hail out of heaven, *every stone* about the weight of a talent: and men blasphemed God because of the plague of the hail; for the plague thereof was exceeding great**" (Rev. 16:21).

On July 30, 2013, mysterious lights were spotted in the sky across the United States of America. They were like fireballs in the sky above Alabama, Tennessee, Mississippi, Arizona, and Missouri. Our planet today is already entering a spectacular moment in history. We are now seeing the terrible effects of the shaking of the heavens and earth.

Volcanoes

"**For thus saith the LORD of hosts; Yet once, it *is* a little while, and I will shake the heavens, and the earth, and the sea, and the dry *land*"** (Hag. 2:6). We saw how God is shaking the heavens, and the earth is next. Fire beneath the surface causes the mountains to burn like a furnace and pour out their flood of lava over villages and cities. Molten masses of rocks thrown into the waters by the upheaval of things hidden in the earth cause the water to boil and send forth debris.

Earthquakes

"**[A]nd there shall be earthquakes in divers places**" (Mark 13:8). The Bible also speaks of increasing earthquakes in these last days. We see an increased acceleration in the number of earthquakes occurring. Each year we have 6,000 major earthquakes in the world. In the past ninety years alone, we have had 1,500,000 fatalities. In the last little while, we saw earthquakes taking 20,000 to 30,000 lives in one great rumble. Many of you will remember recent earthquakes that various countries have experienced.

Flooding

We saw how God is shaking the heavens and the earth. Next is the shaking of the seas. The book of Luke expresses the consequences of this shaking: **"The sea and the waves roaring…"** (21:25). Prophecy tells of a time when, as a result of the melting of the polar ice caps, the oceans and rivers will be overflooded, thus increasing the water levels to the point of flooding over their banks.

Also, great movements beneath the ocean bedrock shall send the water level tumbling with rage over large metropolises, submerging many coastal cities throughout the world. In these awful calamities by sea, vessels are hurled into eternity without a moment of warning. As the oceans rage, the coastal cities are washed away.

> A world addled by climate change **has seen a four-fold increase in major flooding events since 1980, and a doubling of significant storms, droughts and heat waves,** Europe's national science academies jointly reported Wednesday.
>
> In Europe, where precise data reaches back decades, the number of severe floods has jumped five fold since 1995, according to the report, which updates a 2013 assessment.
>
> "There has been, and continues to be, a significant increase in the frequency of extreme weather events," said Michael Norton…
>
> …Recent research has linked severe winters in North America and Europe, as well as some extreme summer weather, to Jet Stream fluctuations possibly driven by global warming in the Arctic, where temperatures have risen twice as fast as for the planet as a whole. (Phys.org, http://1ref.us/pu, accessed 9/6/2018)

Typhoons

Typhoons ignite their most deadly assault, with attending tidal waves and cyclones striking and sweeping the costliest structures of the earth. Hurricanes also make direct hits, while tornadoes level homes.

Climate and weather disasters have hit nearly every continent in 2017— flooding and monsoons in South Asia, hurricanes and major earthquakes in North America and Europe, landslides and drought in Africa, and a tsunami threat to Central America. Commentaries from experts seem to indicate that our planet is in danger and life on earth is itself severely threatened.

The great struggles of all ages have just entered their final state. The Spirit of God is gradually withdrawing. Calamities follow in quick succession. The Bible says, **"The land shall be utterly emptied, and utterly spoiled: for the LORD hath spoken this word"** (Isa. 24:3).

Pestilences

"[A]nd there shall be…pestilences…in divers places" (Matt. 24:7). Pestilence is defined as a fatal, epidemic disease that spreads quickly through large numbers of people. Did you see how fast Lassa fever, monkey pox, Ebola infections, and other viral diseases spread?

There are also organizations that focus on the effects that climate change is having on the health of our human society. They tell us to expect the global incidence of disease to increase significantly. An article in *Scientific American* lists twelve maladies that climate change may worsen. Among these are cholera, Ebola, Lyme disease, sleeping sickness, tuberculosis, and yellow fever.

"Bill Gates [recently stated that]: Terrorists could wipe out 30 million people by weaponizing a disease such as smallpox…A bioterrorist attack which could wipe out 30 million people is becoming increasingly likely because it is easier than ever to create and spread deadly pathogens, Bill Gates has warned" (The Telegraph, http://1ref.us/oj, accessed 9/5/2018).

> *Climate and weather disasters have hit nearly every continent in 2017—flooding and monsoons in South Asia, hurricanes and major earthquakes in North America and Europe, landslides and drought in Africa, and a tsunami threat to Central America. Commentaries from experts seem to indicate that our planet is in danger and life on earth is itself severely threatened*

Famine

"[A]nd there shall be famines...in divers places" (Matt. 24:7). Today the world is running out of food to feed its growing population. Ten thousand people a day, more than 3.5 million people per year, die of starvation (out of the 156,000/57 million who experience starvation). The Lord said there would be famines in these last days.

A great deal of highly credible analysis of the effect of climate change on the society has been conducted by some think tank entities that belong to one of the organizations that usually do all their work for various agencies of the United States government.

Thus far this board has released two non-classified reports on the emerging, accelerating threat of climate change. These reports warn of a significant increase in global instability and conflict because of threats to food and water supplies for a rather sizable portion of the world's population. In fact:

> The CNA Corporation Military Advisory Board **found that climate-induce drought in the Middle East and Africa is leading to conflicts over food and water and escalating longstanding regional and ethnic tensions into violent clashes. The report also found that rising sea levels are putting people and food supplies in vulnerable coastal regions like eastern India, Bangladesh and the Mekong Delta in Vietnam at risk and could lead to a new wave of refugees.** (*The New York Times*, http://1ref.us/of, accessed 9/5/2018)

Therefore, friends, the present intensification of natural and manmade disasters must be seen as clear signs of God's final warning to mankind of the impending divine judgment, to call us to repentance before Christ's coming.

Chapter 2

GLOBAL CONSCIOUSNESS

Is climate change creating a consciousness towards a worldwide rule? Yes, it is! Are we not seeing the urge for globalism in the world's attempt to resolve climate change? Are we not witnessing how the top world leaders, notable scientists, and environmentalists around the world are also giving their credibility to the climate change agenda?

When Pope Francis reached beyond the world's 1.2 billion Catholics to call for action on climate change, his message was endorsed by other religious leaders and organizations, including the Dalai Lama, the Islamic Society of North American, an influential group of Jewish rabbis, and the Church of England.

Are you also seeing how the two largest coalitions of cities in the world—the EU-based Covenant of Mayors and the UN-backed Compact of Mayors—are allying to link more than 600 million city dwellers in the fight against climate change? A partnership called "The Global Covenant of Mayors for Climate & Energy" is now providing unprecedented support for city efforts and accelerated progress against climate change in several ways. They stated that:

> The Global Covenant will link more than 7,100 cities, representing more than 600 million people, in one unified effort to address the causes and impacts of climate change. Cities will speak with one clear, coordinated voice, sending a strong signal to national governments that they are committed to this fight and to assisting one another....
>
> In the fight against climate change, cities are where the action is. (*The Guardian*, http://1ref.us/oc, accessed 9/5/2018).

California Gov. Jerry Brown predicted that if carbon emissions aren't reduced, billions of people will die from "heat events," and one billion will be subjected to vector diseases....

"We're going to have widespread disruption, more conflicts, more terrorism, more insecurity because of climate disruption. The prospect is 3 billion people on this planet will be subject to fatal lethal heat events – 3 billion – and 1 billion will be subjected to vector diseases that they're not now subject to now," he said. "This is a horror." (CNSNews, http://1ref.us/p4, accessed 9/6/2018)

Just as news reports show the most recent devastating calamities around the world, the leaders of the various nations are blaming these on climate change and global warming. One of their primary solutions to combat climate change is to persuade the leading nations to accept the policies laid out in the Climate Change Agreement, which was officially signed on April 22, 2016 (Earth Day) by leaders from at least 175 countries. Never have so many countries signed an agreement on the first available day. **"The Paris climate deal just became law. Now countries must figure out how to make good on their pledges."** States that did not sign that day had a year to do so (*Los Angeles Times*, http://1ref.us/p5, accessed 9/6/2018).

UN And Climate Change

Despite a vast body of scientific knowledge, the issue of deliberate climate manipulations has never been explicitly part of the UN agenda on climate change. Neither the official delegations nor the environmental action groups participating in any climate change conference raised the broad issue of "weather warfare" or ecological modification as relevant to an understanding of climate change. The clash between the official negotiators of the 2015 Paris Climate Change Accord and US President Donald Trump's outright refusal to abide by this accord have nothing to do with climate, but the economy.

Why are weather modifications not an object of discussion or concern? Instead, they narrowly confined the debate to greenhouse gases. Though there are definitely many parts to this unfolding story, the principal piece of the puzzle by far still goes completely unacknowledged by most of the scientific community and the entire mainstream media/corporate/military/industrial complex. Why this conspiracy of silence? Well, the scenario suggests a hidden agenda.

The Global Agenda

The ability to generate precipitation, fog, and storms on earth or modify space weather to produce artificial manifestations has become one of the tools that wicked people are using to achieve a global awareness towards the establishment of a one world government and religion. For almost a century, this small group of conspirators has been waging a quiet, non-declared war of attrition against the people of the world. For instance, on January 10, 1920, the League of Nations was formed as a result of the Paris Peace Conference that ended World War I. Their primary objective was to have a one world government as a means to ensure that war never broke out again.

After the United Nations was founded, it was built on the League of Nations' concept. The UN was created primarily to end war by ending national divisions. The logic was that if there are no nations, then there can be no wars between nations. This was clearly stated in the United Nations World Constitution with these words: **"The age of nations must end. The governments of the nations have decided to order their separate sovereignties into one government to which they will surrender their arms"** (Biblioteca Pleyades, http://1ref.us/oh, accessed 9/5/2018).

In 1976, thirty-two US Senators and ninety-two members of the House of Representatives signed the Declaration of Interdependence, which reads, in part, **"Two centuries ago our forefathers brought forth a new nation; now we must join with others to bring forth a new world order"** (Amerikan Exposé, http://1ref.us/oy, accessed 9/5/2018).

The primary objective of the world political elites is to have a global government, but to achieve their goal, they must first create disorder so the people can demand order. The price of order always entails a handing over of control and freedom on the part of the citizenry.

> *The primary objective of the world political elites is to have a global government, but to achieve their goal, they must first create disorder so the people can demand order. The price of order always entails a handing over of control and freedom on the part of the citizenry*

The trick of creating chaos and then seizing power under the pretense of putting things back in order is a tried and true method of deception and manipulation that is as old as politics itself. This method is called "management by crisis."

Management by Crisis

"Management by crisis is a technique as old as politics itself. However, its widespread use on an international scale is much more recent".

These evil elites have not been content to see their goals achieved in the normal course of time. **"Therefore they have utilized a method known as 'management by crises to help move their agenda forward. The objective of a managed crisis is to have people accept something as a solution to a particular crisis that they never would have accepted if that crisis had not been brought to their attention"** (Lalonde, p. 125).

"A managed crisis has three stages.

1. First, those who desire a change in a specific direction, and who have sufficient resources, present a crisis to the public. The crisis can be created or invented, or an existing crisis can be adopted.
2. Second, the crisis is widely publicized.
3. Finally, when there is sufficient public alarm the managers propose their academically hailed solution to the crisis" (Ibid.).

The present global climate change movement looks very much like one of those invented crises, and available scientific evidence, as well as observed weather events and jet stream anomalies, confirm this. This is the same as the Hegelian Dialectic Technique, also used today to guide the thoughts and actions of the inhabitants of earth into conflicts that lead to a predetermined solution.

All these techniques are designed to manipulate us into patterns of thought and action. Each time we fight for or defend against an action or ideology, we are all playing a necessary role in a grand design which prepares us to accept a Hegelian solution to that very conflict. There can't be a Hegelian solution to a conflict unless we all take sides that will advance the agenda. First, thesis versus antithesis equates to synthesis. In the Hegelian Dialectic, two false premises do not make a sound conclusion, even if the argument follows the formula. You must have at least one sound premise to reach a sound conclusion.

Three-Way Global Competition

One prominent author, Malachi Martin, a Jesuit and Vatican insider, in his book *The Keys of This Blood*, announced a series of events destined to change the world forever. It points out the chief players in these events and their ultimate goal. He takes a pro-papal view of this battle for the control of the world. The book makes particular prophecies about the future of the world and defines much of the Vatican's strategy to take control of it.

One of the prophecies delineates the pope's strategy to eliminate the USSR. The fulfillment of that prophecy is now well-documented history.

The presses of the world have correctly identified the pope's active role in the disintegration of Communism as symbolized by the downfall of the Berlin Wall on November 9, 1989.

Now that the former Soviet Union is just a part of history, the players who remain in this battle to influence and even control the future of mankind are the United States of America, the United Nation, and the Vatican. Martin, describing the ongoing competition among these three powers, wrote:

> **Willing or not ready or not, we are all involved in an all-out, no-holds-barred, three-way global competition. Most of us are not competitors, however. We are the stakes. For the competition is about who will establish the first one world system of government that has ever existed in the society of Nations… The competition is all-out because, now that it has started, there is no way it can be reversed or called off….**
>
> **Those of us who are under seventy will see at least the basic structure of the new-world government installed. Those of us under forty will surely live under its legislative, executive, and judicial authority and control. Indeed, the three rivals themselves –and many more besides as time goes on-speaks about this New World Order not as something around a distant corner of time, but something that is imminent.** (Martin, *Keys of This Blood*, pp. 15, 16)

Having identified the three major powers that are contending for world control, he quoted the late Pope John Paul II's statement in which he **"insists that men have no reliable hope of creating a viable geopolitical system, unless it is on the basis of Roman Catholic Christianity"** (Ibid., p. 492). By this quote, Martin affirmed that the Roman Catholic Church is indeed the only institution that is in a better position to establish the new world order. How valid can this assertion be?

Catholic and World Control

Pope Francis concurred with Martin's sentiment when he said, **"Read Robert Hugh Benson's *Lord of the World* to understand me"** (The Australian, http://1ref.us/qj, accessed on 9/12/2018—Subscribers only). What is one of the principal themes of Benson's book? "Moynihan also provides a link to Fr Robert Barron's blog about Benson's famous book. Barron writes that it is the story '**of the cataclysmic struggle between a radically secularist society and the one credible alternative to it, namely the Catholic Church**'" (Catholic Herald, http://1ref.us/p6, accessed 9/6/2018).

The book points to the Roman Catholic Church as not only the world's ruler but its only credible alternative. A Catholic priest once quoted the Holy Father, saying, **"The Pope is the ruler of the world. All the emperors, all the kings, all the princes, all the presidents of the world are as altar boys of mine"** (Priest D.S. Phelan, Western Watchman, June 27, 1912). Barron shows that the ultimate goal of the Roman Church is to rule the world. The Catholic Church believed that by virtue of her calling, the pope had an inalienable right to a temporal sovereignty. Only then could he conduct fully and freely his duties as head of the universal church.

The Papal tiara is to Catholics a sign that the pope is "the ruler of the world." Pope Pius XI wrote, "the hand of God, who guides the course of history, has set down the Chair of His Vicar on earth, in this city of Rome which, from being the capital of the wonderful Roman Empire, was made by Him the capital of the whole world, because He made it the seat of a sovereignty which, since it extends beyond the confines of nations and states, embraces within itself all the peoples of the whole world" [In Pope Pius XI, encyclical letter UBI ARCANO DEI CONSILIO (On the Peace of Christ in the Kingdom of Christ), December 23, 1922, p. 67].

> *Thus, the world today faces multiple challenges, and the major world powers and their leaders struggle in frustration to place things in order, while notable scientists, environmentalists, and religious leaders around the world express grave concern over what is coming upon the earth*

Thus, the world today faces multiple challenges, and the major world powers and their leaders struggle in frustration to place things in order, while notable scientists, environmentalists, and religious leaders around the world express grave concern over what is coming upon the earth.

Into this frustrating struggle to bring some form of unity and hope to the earth strode a personage, a man, the most powerful man in our modern history, standing with offers of a solution to the felt needs of mankind for peace and stability. Elected as Pope in March 2013, this obscure, Latin-American, Argentina-born archbishop of Italian origin, Mario Bergoglio, stepped upon the throne as both religious head of the Catholic Church and civil head of Vatican City. Taking the name Francis, after Saint Francis of Assisi, Pope Francis has become the highest authority in the west.

Today many consider Pope Francis to be the first modern-day pope to possess the potential for accomplishing the goal of the church by visibly sitting on the world throne. Pope Francis is apparently utilizing his dual role of leadership in an effort to implement his conviction that he is the pope who will return to the throne as earth's monarch. There's no doubt that today he is the most powerful man on earth. He is considered the absolute, complete, and veritable king of the world. Former Catholic Bishop of Guatemala, Bishop Gerard Bouffard, in his testimony, confessed that the Vatican is indeed the real spiritual controller of the Illuminati and New World Order (see http://1ref.us/oq, accessed 9/5/2018).

US/Catholic Cooperation

The United States has carried out many intelligence activities since the days of George Washington, but only since World War II have they been coordinated on a government-wide basis. President Franklin D. Roosevelt appointed New York lawyer and war hero, William J. Donovan, a devout Catholic born into a poor, Irish Catholic family in upstate New York, to become first the Coordinator of Information, and in 1942 he founded the Office of Strategic Service (OSS) that was responsible for espionage and sabotage operations during World War II.

The OSS—the forerunner to the CIA—was mandated to collect and analyze strategic information, and the office used its Foreign Nationalities branch, based in New York, to recruit from American ethnic groups. Though it did not exclusively recruit Catholics, many Catholics ended up in the OSS.

In 1944, the year before the OSS was officially constituted, Donovan forged a close alliance with Father Felix Morlion, founder of a European Catholic intelligence service known as Pro Deo.

> **Donovan earned his knighthood by virtue of the services he rendered to the Catholic hierarchy in World War II…in July 1944, as the Second World War raged throughout Europe, General William "Wild Bill" Donovan was ushered into an ornate chamber in Vatican City for an audience with Pope Pius XII. Donovan bowed his head reverently as the pontiff intoned a ceremonial prayer in Latin and decorated him with the Grand Cross of the Order of Saint Sylvester, the oldest and most prestigious of papal knighthoods.** (Church and State, http://1ref.us/ok, accessed 9/5/2018).

Pope Pius' decoration of William Donovan marked the beginning of a longstanding, intimate relationship between the Vatican and US intelligence that continues to the present day. After World War II, however, the OSS was abolished, along with many other war agencies, and its functions were transferred to the State and War Departments.

It did not take long before President Truman recognized the need for a postwar, centralized intelligence organization. To make a fully functional intelligence office, Truman signed the National Security Act of 1947, establishing the Central Intelligence Agency (CIA).

Today the CIA has been dubbed Catholics in Action because of how its faithful have occupied so many senior positions. Having infiltrated the highest levels in departments of the US government, they are today custodians of the intelligence behind the present global environmental warfare.

> **The CIA is the best known of the 17 agencies that comprise the American intelligence community. It has earned itself nicknames like "Catholic Intelligence Agency" and "Catholics In Action".** It's worth exploring why....
>
> **...one interesting clue is the relatively high number of Catholics who have served as director of the agency....**
>
> ...three out of the last five CIA directors have been Catholic: Michael Hayden, Leon Panetta, **and the current director, John Brennan.** (http://1ref.us/p7, accessed 9/6/2018)

There is no doubt that the Vatican intelligence agency is very much aware of current global weather modifications, and the Pope has not said anything publicly about this deadly style of warfare. However, the attention is diverted to other causes rather than the real cause. It, therefore, suggests that the present crisis is intentionally created for a purpose. Our question is, Why are the United Nations, world leaders, and the pope obsessed with climate change?

CHAPTER 3

THE GREEN SABBATH

World leaders from various nations blame the devastating calamities on climate change. Science claims that due to climate change, our planet is today facing a dramatic and lasting alteration. Unless we take significant actions to reverse greenhouse gas emission trends and enhance climate resilience, we risk irreversible damage to our planet. Various world leaders express their opinions about the imminent danger.

"**'We are losing the battle,'** [French President Emmanuel Macron] said, **urging new phase in the fight against global warming**" (Reuters, http://1ref.us/ol, accessed 9/6/2018).

Francois Hollande, the former President of the French Republic, on climate change. "We have a single mission to protect and hand on the planet to the next generation. The time is past when humankind thought it could selfishly draw on exhaustible resources. We know now the world is not a commodity" (Jose Santiago, Digital Content Specialist, Public Engagement, World Economic Forum. 27, Nov. 2015).

Angela Merkel, Chancellor of Germany, on climate change: "We must now agree on a binding review mechanism under international law, so that this century can credibly be called a century of decarbonisation" (Ibid.).

Barack Obama, former President of the United States of America, on climate change: "There's one issue that will define the contours of this century more dramatically than any other, and that is the urgent threat of a changing climate. Climate change is no longer some far-off problem; it is happening here, it is happening now" (Ibid.).

**Ban KI-Mor, Former Secretary General of the United Nations: "We are the first generation to be able to end poverty, and the last generation that can take steps to avoid the worst impacts of climate change. Future generations will judge us harshly if we fail to uphold our moral and historical responsibilities" (Ibid.).

Pope Francis, Bishop of Rome, on climate change: "Pope Francis Says World Nearing Climate-Change 'Suicide'…Pope Francis, who pushed for Catholics to pay attention to climate change last year, **pointed to rising sea levels and Greenland's melting glaciers** as evidence of a need for nations to act during a conference with reporters on a flight back to Rome after his six-day visit to Africa" (http://1ref.us/og, accessed 9/5/2018).

Francis and Climate Change

Pope Francis has made the fight against climate change one of the cornerstones of his papacy. In 2015 he wrote, "'LAUDATO SI', ON CARE FOR OUR COMMON HOME." This is an official document that carries binding force for every Catholic and is designed as a road map to worldwide cooperation. It touches on many issues, as well as doctrines. There is Mariology, sacrament advancement, and the promotion of Sunday worship as a replacement of the Bible Sabbath. Francis uses this document as a soapbox to preach the Catholic version of religion.

During one of his remarks, he echoed many of the points in his recent environmental encyclical, *Laudato Si'*. **He lamented global exclusion and injustice; the farmer with no land; the family with no home; the worker with no rights.** He warned that **unfettered greed** is the driving force behind these injustices. "Behind all this pain, death and destruction there is the stench of what Basil of Caesarea called 'the dung of the devil,'" he said. **"An unfettered pursuit of money rules.** The service of the common good is left behind" (Catholic News Agency, http://1ref.us/p8, accessed 9/6/2018).

Pope Francis' solution to fix the "unfettered greed," climate change, and care for the poor is that all nations must enforce the Sunday Law.

> **Sunday, like the Jewish Sabbath, is meant to be a day which heals our relationships with God, with ourselves, with others and with the world.…It protects human action from becoming empty activism; it also prevents that unfettered greed and sense of isolation which make us seek personal gain to the detriment of all else. The law of weekly rest forbade work on the seventh day…**(*Ex* 23:12). **Rest opens our eyes to the larger picture and gives us renewed sensitivity to the rights of others. And so the day of rest, centered on the Eucharist, sheds its [sic] light on the whole week, and motivates us to greater concern for nature and the poor.** (The Holy See, http://1ref.us/lc, accessed 9/6/2018)

Pope Francis has been issuing statements that greatly rock the world. Here is one example:

> **A global consensus is essential for confronting the deeper problems, which cannot be resolved by unilateral actions on the part of individual countries...International negotiations cannot make significant progress due to positions taken by countries which place their national interest above the global common good... Global regulatory norms are needed to impose obligations and prevent unacceptable actions... what is needed, in effect, is an agreement on systems of governance for the whole range of so-called "global commons...there is urgent need of true world political authority.** (http://1ref.us/p9, accessed 9/6/2018)

This indeed is a subtle bid for much greater Catholic control over the global economy, politics, and even the whole world in general. Pope Francis doesn't hide his intention for a one world government.

Earth Day

Earth Day has been an annual event celebrated on April 22 worldwide. Various events are held on this day to demonstrate support for environmental protection. It was founded by United States Senator Gaylord Nelson in 1970. After Nelson saw the damage done by a 1969 massive oil spill in Santa Barbara, California, he was inspired to organize an environmental protection awareness day. "Earth Day had reached into its current status as the largest secular observance in the world, celebrated by more than a billion people every year, and a day of action that changes human behavior and provokes policy changes" (Earth Day Network, http://1ref.us/pa, accessed 9/6/2018).

Although it is not a celebration that traces its origin to ancient times, it is very significant to nature-based religion. Despite its secular roots, Earth Day has come to be viewed as sacred. Just as in ancient times, each day in the planetary week is named after a different planet in the universe according to pagan deities. It has played a vital role in their ancient worship.

"The English names of the days of the week are derived from the Saxons. The ancient Saxons had borrowed the week from some Eastern nation, and substituted the names of their own divinities for the gods of Greece. In legislative and judiciary acts, the Latin names are still retained" (*Encyclopedia Britannica*, 11th ed., vol. 4, "Calendar," p. 988).

NAMES GOD GAVE	LATIN PAGAN NAMES
First day—Genesis 1:5	Dies Solis
Second Day—Genesis 1:8	Dies Lunae
Third Day—Genesis 1:13	Dies Martis
Fourth Day—Genesis 1:19	Dies Mercurii
Fifth Day—Genesis 1:23	Dies Jovis
Six Day—Genesis 1:31	Dies Veneris
Seventh Day (Sabbath)—Genesis 2:1–3	Dies Saturni

SAXON NAMES	ENGLISH NAMES
1. Sun's Day	Sunday
2. Moon's Day	Monday
3. Tiw's Day	Tuesday
4. Woden's Day	Wednesday
5. Thor's Day	Thursday
6. Frigg's Day	Friday
7. Saturn Day	Saturday

"The week is a period of seven days, having no reference to celestial motions, a circumstance to which it owes its unalterable uniformity... It has been employed from time immemorial in almost all eastern countries" (*The Catholic Encyclopedia*, vol. III, "Chronology," p. 740).

"According to a Religious Studies scholar, Michael York, a nature religion is one that has 'a this-worldly focus and deep reverence for the earth as something sacred and something to be cherished. Not surprisingly then, Earth Day (April 22) is a holy day for many Pagans" (HuffPost, http://1ref.us/pb, accessed 9/6/2018).

The chief god for the pagans is the sun. Bear in mind that the Bible and history teach that sun worship originated from paganism. **"And he put down the idolatrous priests, whom the kings of Judah had ordained to burn incense in the high places in the cities of Judah, and in the places round about Jerusalem; them also that burned incense unto Baal, to the sun, and to the moon, and to the planets, and to all the host of heaven"** (2 Kings 23:5).

Why was the Climate Change Agreement signed by the nations on Earth Day, April 22, 2016? As you can see, ancient paganism is centered on nature and the worship of the planets. Because nature-based faith or earth-centered spirituality is something sacred and cherished by many religions, and because it is one common point that unifies politicians, religions, pantheists, and pagans, the agreement was signed on this day.

This same action also led to the recent global call for sun worship in India. In a conference organized by the International Solar Alliance in India, Prime Minister Narendra Modi addressed the attendees:

> "For millions of years, the sun has been giving light and life to the world. From Japan to Peru, France to Rome, Egypt and the eastern civilization –the sun has been given utmost importance," he said.
>
> "But in Indian viewpoint, for thousands of years, the sun has been the unparalleled centre. In India, the Vedas for thousands of years have considered the sun the soul of the world. In India, the sun is considered the nourisher. Now that we are looking for a way to deal with the challenge of climate change, we have to look back at ancient view of balance and perspective," he added.

Because nature-based faith or earth-centered spirituality is something sacred and cherished by many religions, and because it is one common point that unifies politicians, religions, pantheists, and pagans, the agreement was signed on this day

Swaraj used five Sanskrit names for the **"Sun God"** while speaking of India's push for solar energy. She said the following with folded hands:

> **I would like to bow before the Sun God and address him by five different names in Sanskrit, 'Om Suriyaya namaha, om Adityaya Namaha, om Dinkaraya namaha, om Divakaraya namaha, om Bhaskarya namaha'… this means 'Oh Sun God, we bow before you, you illuminate the external and the internal world and you are the best to be adored and worshipped. May you bless us.** (http://1ref.us/qd, accessed on 10/24/2018)

What's happening here? To combat climate change, you have to worship the sun. Where is this world heading?

Thousands deify nature while they deny the God of nature. Though in a different form, idolatry exists in the Christian world today as verily as it existed among ancient Israel in the days of Elijah. The god of many professedly wise men, of philosophers, poets, politicians, journalists—the god of polished fashionable circles, of many colleges and universities, even of some theological institutions—is little better than Baal, the sun-god of Phoenicia. (White, *The Great Controversy*, p. 583)

Green Sabbath

Today, what common denominator links Earth Day, the climate change movement, and modern Christianity? It's the weekly Sunday rest. Because Earth Day is viewed as sacred by those with an earth-centered spirituality or nature-based religion, it has become one mutual point that unifies politicians, religions, pantheists, and pagans.

"It's a solution that will have a profound impact on climate change for little to no capital investment! Once A Week can result in over 15% annual emission reductions per country" ("Green Sabbath," http://1ref.us/pd, accessed 9/6/2018).

Can you see the reason it is now proposed by climate movement managers that Earth Day should now be observed once a week and that we should give our beautiful planet a day of rest— a "green" sabbath? **"The approach of World Environment Day also signals the return of another unique UN-conceived event – the Earth Sabbath – a day of worship that transcends denominations and welcomes all faiths to participate in a day of global reverence for the Earth"** (Forcing Change, http://1ref.us/pe, accessed 9/6/2018).

This decision to dedicate one day of the week as a green sabbath day is fully in line with Pope Francis's global policy. In the encyclical *Laudato Si'*, he is pushing for enforcement of a worldwide Sunday Law. He said:

> On Sunday, our participation in the Eucharist has special importance. Sunday, like the Jewish Sabbath, is meant to be a day which heals our relationships with God, with ourselves, with others and with the world….The law of weekly rest forbade work on the seventh day… (*Ex* 23:12). Rest opens our eyes to the larger picture and gives us renewed sensitivity to the rights of others. And so the day of rest [Sunday], centered on the Eucharist, sheds it light on the whole week, and motivates us to greater concern for nature and the poor. (The Holy See, http://1ref.us/lc, accessed 9/6/2018)

Therefore, the one common denominator linking Earth Day, the climate change movement, and Catholic Christianity is the global enactment of Sunday as the new Earth Day. Pope Francis, in his encyclical *Laudato Si'* and other speeches, has called climate change a manmade, moral problem, thus necessitating a moral solution—a mandatory Sunday observance for all people. Not only does he allege that government-enforced Sunday observance would be the primary component to solving the issue of climate change, but he also asserts that it would greatly benefit the poor and improve family relations.

The idea of observing an environmental "Sabbath-Sunday" and having the same enforced is not only being urged to deal with the issue of preserving the environment, but it is also associated with assisting the poor and less fortunate. In a piece written on the official website of the Salvation Army, a Christian organization dubbed **"A Call for Climate Justice"** made the following assertions:

> **The call to climate justice is deeply rooted in biblically based Christian convictions. The scriptures provide a wealth of reasons why Christ followers simply cannot ignore this crisis....**
>
> **...Keep the [Sunday] Sabbath: It could be the most radical thing a church can do for environmental stewardship—to commit to keeping the [Sunday] Sabbath. The scriptures make constant reference to rest and care for the land as well as for people on the Sabbath. Spending time with family and friends and enjoying the free outdoors is an act of resistance to the pressures of materialism and consumerism.** ("A Call for Climate Justice - Release 7," http://1ref.us/pf, accessed 9/6/2018)

Polish Sunday Law

"The good existing bilateral relations between the Holy See and Poland were emphasized, **as well as the fruitful collaboration between the Church and the State in their respective spheres of action**," it read.

> **The Pope and the Polish Prime Minister also talked about family policy and the protection of creation**, "with a view to the United Nations Conference on climate change to be held in Katowice in December 2018." ("Pope Francis meets with Polish PM Morawiecki," http://1ref.us/pg, accessed 9/6/2018)
>
> Poland lawmakers voted last week to reclaim Sunday as a day of rest by phasing out Sunday shopping by 2020....
>
> ... **The country's Catholic bishops have praised the move, but say it doesn't go far enough**....

> ...The bishops underscore the need to restore Sunday to society as a day of rest and time of building family ties as well as strengthening social relationships," he said, adding: "They point out also that Sunday rest cannot be a luxury for a chosen few but is an integral part of equal treatment for all employees. Therefore, there is an urgent need to make all Sundays free from work, just as is already the case in many European Union countries....
>
> ...In 2012, Pope Benedict said that in defending Sunday as a day of rest, one **"defends human freedom....**
>
> ...Sunday is the day of the Lord and of men and women, a day in which everyone must be able to be free, free for the family and free for God. In defending Sunday we defend human freedom!"** he said. ("Poland to reclaim 'day of rest' by phasing out Sunday shopping," http://1ref.us/ph, accessed 9/6/2018)

The above sentiments are in tune with the agenda of Pope Francis. Just as Earth Day has unified politicians, religions, pantheists, and pagans to combat climate change, so Sunday worship by law, under the guise of battling climate change, is believed to unite the world as well.

Pope Francis, who is pushing for Catholics to pay attention to climate change, is pointing to the rising sea levels and Greenland's melting glaciers as evidence of a need for nations to act during a conference with reporters on a flight back to Rome after his six-day visit to Africa (http://1ref.us/og, accessed 9/6/2018).

Looking back to American history when the first "Sunday blue laws" were passed, in no state did this conflict play out more dramatically than in Arkansas:

> **In 1885, the Arkansas Legislature outlawed Sunday baseball, along with a host of other activities. Seventh Day Adventists, who do not recognize Sunday as the Sabbath, were especially unwelcome in Arkansas during the 1880s, when more than 200 were prosecuted....**
>
> ...Moreover, the conservative forces unleashed a torrent of bills to bolster the defense of the Sabbath: outlawing golf, tennis, and fishing on Sundays; forbidding the sale of gasoline on Sundays; prohibiting men and women swimming together; and prohibiting women's "bathing suits which strike above the knee." (Pressreader, http://1ref.us/pi, accessed 9/6/2018)
>
> **Arkansas was not alone in this, however, though it was worse there than anywhere else. I myself, with other brethren in California, had to send hundreds of dollars into Tennessee, to support the families**

of the brethren of our own faith there, while the husbands and fathers who made the money for their support were in jail because they chose to work for their families on Sunday, and make bread for them after having kept the Sabbath according to their conscience. That has been done, Mr. Chairman, in these United States. That is the care these people have for the laboring man. [(1889 ATJ, NSLS18 126.2), Arguments of Alonzo T. Jones Before the Senate Committee, Washington D.C.]

Today, Pope Francis has stated that the nations must accept and implement the instructions given in *Laudato Si'* (his encyclical on climate change) to preserve the world from destruction. Will the present measures taken by the world leaders solve the crises? What about the deliberate, secret manipulation of the weather system? Well, speaking of the wicked activities of evil men in these last days, John wrote, **"And the nations were angry, and thy wrath is come, and the time of the dead, that they should be judged… and shouldest destroy them which destroy the earth"** (Rev. 11:18).

God's Word reveals that the Supreme Ruler will judge all who are currently destroying the earth. Not long hence will they receive their reward. Already God's judgment has begun:

The land shall be utterly emptied, and utterly spoiled: for the LORD hath spoken this word. The earth mourneth *and* fadeth away, the world languisheth *and* fadeth away, the haughty people of the earth do languish. The earth also is defiled under the inhabitants thereof; because they have transgressed the laws, changed the ordinance, broken the everlasting covenant. Therefore hath the curse devoured the earth, and they that dwell therein are desolate: therefore the inhabitants of the earth are burned, and few men left. (Isaiah 24:3–6)

People do not understand that it is the violation of God's constitution and laws, the transgression of His commandments, the breaking of the everlasting covenant, that is today causing the prospering hand of God to be removed from the earth. This brings us to the following question: What is God's everlasting covenant? We shall look at this subject in our next chapter.

CHAPTER 4

GOD'S COVENANT WITH MANKIND

To solve the current global crises facing mankind today, we must first understand God's original purpose in the creation of the earth. The Bible says, **"For thus saith the LORD that created the heavens; God himself that formed the earth and made it; he hath established it, he created it not in vain, he formed it to be inhabited: I** *am* **the LORD; and** *there is* **none else"** (Isa. 45:18).

God's purpose in creating the heavens and forming the earth was so that it would be inhabited. Our next question is, Who did He have in mind to populate the earth? **"The heaven,** *even* **the heavens,** *are* **the LORD's: but the earth hath he given to the children of men"** (Ps. 115:16).

Mankind is the very object of God's divine benevolence. It is us for whom the earth was created as an inheritance. Since we cannot deny this, we need to understand what kind of people He desires to inhabit the earth. **"The righteous shall inherit the land, and dwell therein for ever"** (Ps. 37:29).

God's original plan was to establish a world of holy people; a peculiar treasure; a chosen generation; a holy nation; a kingdom and royal priesthood. It was His design that they lift up the praises of their Creator. That was why ample provisions were made to sincerely, earnestly, and thoughtfully set humanity on a path to perfecting holiness in the fear of the Lord. Power, strength, grace, and glory were provided for us, God's cherished nobility.

"As man came forth from the hand of his Creator, he was of lofty stature and perfect symmetry. His countenance bore the ruddy tint of health, and glowed with the light of life and joy. Adam's height was much greater than that of men who now inhabit the earth. Eve was somewhat less in stature; yet her form was noble, and full of beauty" (White 1958, p. 29).

The Covenant of Love

Please note that each covenant God made with mankind was designed to bring us into an intimate relationship with Him. When He made the first couple, He bonded them to Himself with a tie that cannot be broken. He demonstrated his love for them through the command He gave them to be fruitful and multiply. **"For this cause shall a man leave his father and mother, and shall be joined unto his wife, and they two shall be one flesh. This is a great mystery: but I speak concerning Christ and the church"** (Eph. 5:31, 32). God was talking about the human family here. His magnificent design was to enter into a marriage-like relationship with mankind so it can reflect the image of the Father, Son, and Holy Spirit, the Divine Family.

It is interesting to note that **a covenant is an agreement or contract built on well-defined terms between two unequal parties.** In fact, our modern word "covenant" is of Latin origin (*con venire*), meaning "a coming together." It presupposes two or more parties who come together to make a contract, agreeing on promises, stipulations, privileges, and responsibilities.

In God's covenant with humanity, Adam was required to obey the terms in order not to suffer the consequences of breaking the covenant. **"And the LORD God commanded the man, saying, Of every tree of the garden thou mayest freely eat: But of the tree of the knowledge of good and evil, thou shalt not eat of it: for in the day that thou eatest thereof thou shalt surely die"** (Gen. 2:16, 17). In this covenant the term is well spelled out: the condition is obedience, and the consequence is death. It was voluntarily accepted by both participants. Please note that a covenant has at least two sides: the *covenantor* side (God) and the *covenantee* side (mankind).

In His relationship with humanity, God used marriage to illustrate His divine plan. His design was that the male and female should become one in the covenant of marriage, and the union should communicate life. In other words, the one flesh they become shall be so real that nine months later they have to give it a name, and the child shall embody their covenant oneness, thus reflecting how God wants His union with our race to give birth to His own life. Unfortunately, humanity **"sinned, and come short of the glory of God"** (Rom. 3:23).

The Covenant of Grace

With the fall of mankind, a covenant of grace was made with Adam and Eve in Eden. They were given a divine promise of restoration, and this restoration was to be accomplished through the seed of the woman who would bruise the serpent's head. **"And I will put enmity between thee and the woman, and between thy seed and her seed; it shall bruise thy head, and thou shalt bruise his heel"** (Gen. 3:15).

The plan of redemption in the Garden of Eden was an assurance to God's people that He has renewed His covenant with them. In this plan, a system of sacrificial offerings was instituted. This was to serve as an object lesson pointing to the part God would play in the salvation of mankind. Therefore, to cover Adam and Eve's nakedness, the Bible says, **"Unto Adam also and to his wife did the LORD God make coats of skins, and clothed them"** (v. 21).

For God to cover the nakedness of sin, the life of an innocent lamb was required. The shed blood typified Christ's great sacrifice. This is the incredibly good news of the gospel of salvation by grace. This is the unmerited favor that God through Christ Jesus granted mankind.

The Abrahamic Covenant

"And I will establish my covenant between me and thee and thy seed after thee in their generations for an everlasting covenant" (17:7). If you carefully observe what God said, you will notice that the covenant is not just regarding Abraham and a Seed, though it applies to that, but within a secondary context, it also encompasses all of Abraham's descendants throughout all their generations. Speaking of Abraham's faithfulness in influencing his family unto obedience, the Bible says:

> **Seeing that Abraham shall surely become a great and mighty nation, and all the nations of the earth shall be blessed in him? For I know him, that he will command his children and his household after him, and they shall keep the way of the LORD, to do justice and judgment; that the LORD may bring upon Abraham that which he hath spoken of him.** (Geneses 18:18, 19)

Here we see God's commendation of faithfulness. His covenant with Abraham was not only for the entire family throughout all their generations, but also for the great nation which He envisioned in His divine plan. What promise did God make to Abraham in response to his faithfulness, and why? **"And I will make thy seed to multiply as the stars of heaven, and will give unto thy seed all these countries; and in thy seed shall all the nations of the earth be blessed;"** Why? **"Because that Abraham obeyed my voice, and kept my charge, my commandments, my statutes, and my laws"** (26:4, 5).

This is God's promise to Abraham and the reason why such a promise is made. Inasmuch as the content of the commandments, statutes, and laws were not yet revealed, by comparing spiritual things with spiritual things we come to believe that this refers to what we know now as the Ten Commandments. If not, then what were the commandments that Abraham obeyed? Does God change? This confirms that they existed even at that time, and Abraham was obedient to them. What was the sign of God's covenant with Abraham?

"**And ye shall circumcise the flesh of your foreskin; and it shall be a token of the covenant betwixt me and you**" (17:11). Circumcision was the sign of the Abrahamic covenant. By it, men became members of the covenant family. Our next question is this: In the formation of the commonwealth of the household of God, who are the principal figures with whom God confirmed the covenant, and how did He do so?

"**Be ye mindful always of his covenant; the word *which* he commanded to a thousand generations; *Even of the covenant* which he made with Abraham, and of his oath unto Isaac; And hath confirmed the same to Jacob for a law, *and* to Israel *for* an everlasting covenant**" (1 Chron. 16:15–17). The principal figures in the Abrahamic covenant between his time and the appearance of the Seed are:

1. Isaac
2. Jacob
3. Children of Israel

Each of Abraham's descendants changes in their phases of development as God reaffirms His divine plan.

Delivered from Captivity

Upon which covenant was the children delivered from Egypt? "**And God heard their groaning, and God remembered his cove-**

> *The children of Israel were delivered under the Abrahamic covenant. God remembered His covenant with Abraham, Isaac, and Jacob and had respect unto them. Therefore, a proper understanding of the Abrahamic covenant is the key to understanding God's purpose for Israel and the nations, as well as His way of dealing with humankind in general*

nant with Abraham, with Isaac, and with Jacob. And God looked upon the children of Israel, and God had respect unto *them*" (Ex. 2:24, 25). The children of Israel were delivered under the Abrahamic covenant. God remembered His covenant with Abraham, Isaac, and Jacob and had respect unto them. Therefore, a proper understanding of the **Abrahamic covenant** is the key to understanding God's purpose for **Israel** and the nations, as well as His way of dealing with humankind in general.

Genesis 26:5 says that Abraham kept God's laws, statutes, and commandments, and though it does not declare which laws, statutes, and commandments they were, in no reasonable way can we say that they don't refer to the Ten Commandments. The first point to realize is that laws, statutes, and commandments existed in Genesis. The second point is that Exodus 16 reveals that those laws, statutes, and commandments Abraham observed included the Sabbath.

Why do I say that? The covenant with which God was working when dealing with the children of Israel in Exodus 16 was still the Abrahamic covenant, not the Sinaitic, because it had not been made. The story in Exodus 16 began exactly one month after the exodus and forty days before the Ten Commandments were given.

In delivering Israel, the Bible says God remembered His covenant with Abraham. Therefore, Israel was liberated under the Abrahamic covenant, and with that covenant, He related with them. Under that same covenant, He commanded them to keep the Sabbath. In other words, Sabbath observance occurred before Mount Sinai. "**And he said unto them, This *is* that which the LORD hath said, To morrow *is* the rest of the holy sabbath unto the LORD: bake *that* which ye will bake *to day*, and seethe that ye will seethe; and that which remaineth over lay up for you to be kept until the morning**" (Ex. 16:23).

The evidence in Exodus 16 reveals that God withheld manna on the seventh day of each week, approximately 2,500 years after Creation. What does that suggest? The order of the seventh-day Sabbath in the weekly cycle has not been lost. What did some of the people do on the seventh day? "**And it came to pass, *that* there went out *some* of the people on the seventh day for to gather, and they found none**" (v. 27).

How did God reprove Israel's disobedience? "**And the LORD said unto Moses, How long refuse ye to keep my commandments and my laws**" (v. 28). This is the same terminology used for Abraham in Genesis 26, now referring to those who broke the Sabbath as having refused to keep His commandments and laws, long before Moses was given the tablets of stone on Mount Sinai. Therefore, this shows that the commandments to which God made referred when He addressed Abraham also contain the command to keep the Sabbath.

Confirming the Covenant

God promised to Abraham, **"Sarah thy wife shall bear thee a son indeed; and thou shalt call his name Isaac: and I will establish my covenant with him for an everlasting covenant,** *and* **with his seed after him"** (Gen. 17:19). We later see that the same promise made to Abraham was also repeated to Isaac, and the assurance was given that it would also continue with the seed after him.

Did God also repeat the same assurance to Jacob? **"Then will I remember my covenant with Jacob, and also my covenant with Isaac, and also my covenant with Abraham will I remember; and I will remember the land"** (Lev. 26:42). Here we see God confirming His covenant with Abraham, Isaac, and Jacob in their respective generations. Now concerning Jacob, what was the basis of that covenant? **"He hath remembered his covenant forever, the word** *which* **he commanded to a thousand generations.... And confirmed the same unto Jacob for a law,** *and* **to Israel** *for* **an everlasting covenant"** (Ps. 105:8, 10).

The primary Hebrew root word for "confirmed" in this passage is *amad*, which denotes "to stand, establish, endure, continue, or remain" concerning law. The Hebrew word for "law" used in this verse is *Choq*, which also denotes "commandment, law, statute, task, even ordinance." This clearly shows that the laws, statutes, and commandments were still the basis of that covenant that was reaffirmed with Jacob. Therefore, we learn in Exodus 16 that the Israelites knew of the laws and commandments, even the Sabbath, before the Ten Commandments were given to Moses on Mount Sinai.

The Sinaitic Covenant

In confirming the covenant with the children of Israel as promised to Abraham, what covenant obligation was imposed upon them? **"Now therefore, if ye will obey my voice indeed, and keep my covenant..."** (Ex. 19:5). It's interesting to note that the word "covenant" means "a coming together." It presupposes two or more parties who come together to make a contract, agreeing on promises, stipulations, privileges, and responsibilities. The obligation for Israel was obedience. What were God's promise and responsibility? **"...then ye shall be a peculiar treasure** unto me above all people: for all the earth *is* mine: And ye shall be unto me a kingdom of priests, and an holy nation..." (vs. 5, 6).

What was the covenant stipulation for Israel? "**...And he wrote upon the tables the words of the covenant, the ten commandments**" (Ex. 34:28). "**And he declared unto you his covenant, which he commanded you to perform,** *even* **Ten Commandments; and he wrote them upon two tables of stone**" (Deut. 4:13). The stipulation for Israel is based upon the Ten Commandments, as recorded in Exodus 20:3–17.

Ten Commandments

1. Thou shall have no other gods before me.
2. Thou shall not make unto thee any graven image, or any likeness *of anything* that *is* in heaven above, or that *is* in the earth beneath, or that *is* in the water under the earth: Thou shall not bow down thyself to them, nor serve them.
3. Thou shall not take the name of the LORD thy God in vain; for the LORD will not hold him guiltless that takes his name in vain.
4. Remember the sabbath day, to keep it holy. Six days shall thou labour, and do all thy work: But the seventh day *is* the Sabbath of the LORD thy God.
5. Honor thy father and thy mother:
6. Thou shall not kill.
7. Thou shall not commit adultery.
8. Thou shall not steal.3
9. Thou shall not bear false witness against thy neighbor.
10. Thou shall not covet

Obedience to these commandments was the condition under which God made certain promises to the people. What did Moses say about the covenant God made with Israel? "**The LORD our God made a covenant with us in Horeb. The LORD made not this covenant with our fathers, but with us,** *even* **us, who** *are* **all of us here alive this day**" (Deut. 5:2, 3). Moses told the children of Israel that the covenant God made with them is not the same one He made with their fathers, for when He made the covenant with Abraham, he and Sara were just a couple with no kids yet.

While we may note that with Isaac the covenant was confirmed in a family context, with Jacob it was confirmed in a community context, and with Israel it was confirmed in a national context. In God's ultimate divine plan, His draft is for a nation. The promise to Abraham was to make him a great nation. That was why the inheritance of the saved is called a nation.

"And the nations of them which are saved shall walk in the light of it: and the kings of the earth do bring their glory and honour into it" (Rev. 21:24).

How was Israel's covenant so different? The Bible says, **"Wherefore the children of Israel shall keep the sabbath, to observe the sabbath throughout their generations,** *for* **a perpetual covenant. It** *is* **a sign between me and the children of Israel for ever"** (Ex. 31:16, 17). The covenant made with Abraham had circumcision as its sign or token, but for Israel, it was the Sabbath.

What else makes it different? **"The LORD talked with you (them) face to face in the mount out of the midst of the fire"** (Deut. 5:4). Moses continued, **"I stood between the LORD and you at that time, to show you the word of the LORD: for ye were afraid by reason of the fire, and went not up into the mount"** (v. 5). Here we see God talked with the people face to face, openly and clearly, not in dark visions, and all the thousands of Israel heard and understood Him. God also set a pattern whereby Moses stood between Him and the Israelites at the foot of the mount, and by that was made a type of Christ, who shall stand between God and mankind.

What response did the people speak to God after His proposition? **"And all the people answered together, and said, All that the LORD hath spoken we will do. And Moses returned the words of the people unto the LORD"** (Ex. 19:8). The people told Moses that all that the Lord said, they would do. What did Moses do to prevent a misunderstanding on the part of the people? **"And Moses wrote all the words of the LORD...And he took the book of the covenant, and read in the audience of the people..."** (24:4–7).

What did the people once again promise to do? **"...and they said, All that the LORD hath said will we do, and be obedient"** (v. 7). How was this covenant then confirmed and dedicated? **"And Moses took the blood, and sprinkled** *it* **on the people, and said, Behold the blood of the covenant, which the LORD hath made with you concerning all these words"** (v. 8; see also Heb. 9:19, 20).

Here we have the account of God making the covenant with Israel. He promised to make Israel His peculiar people on condition that they would keep His Ten Commandments. Again, they promised to obey. The agreement was then ratified and sealed with blood. Less than forty days after making this covenant, while Moses tarried on the mount, what did Israel say to Aaron? **"And when the people saw that Moses delayed to come down out of the mount, the people gathered themselves together unto Aaron, and said unto him, Up, make us gods, which shall go before** us; for *as for* this Moses, the man that brought us up out of the land of Egypt, we wot not what is become of him" (Ex. 32:1).

Aaron made a molten calf in imitation of the gods of Egypt, built an altar before it, and proclaimed that tomorrow would be a feast to the Lord. The next day he offered burnt offerings and brought peace offerings, and the people sat down to eat and drink, then rose up to play (a euphemism for engaging in fornication). Here lies the secret of Israel's failure. When Moses came down from Sinai, what did he see? "...he saw the calf, and the dancing: and Moses' anger waxed hot, and he cast the tables out of his hands, and break them beneath the mount" (v. 19).

> *The people did not realize the weakness and sinfulness of their own hearts or their need for divine grace and help to keep the law, so in their ignorance, they readily pledged obedience*

The people did not realize the weakness and sinfulness of their own hearts or their need for divine grace and help to keep the law, so in their ignorance, they readily pledged obedience. However, almost immediately they began to commit idolatry, thus breaking the law of God, the very conditions laid down as their part in the covenant. In and of themselves the conditions were good, but in their own strength, the people were unable to fulfill them.

The Reign of Death

Another interesting question is, How did the children of Israel survive during those long years they lived under the shadow of a broken covenant? The Bible says:

> And the LORD spake unto Moses, saying, Speak unto the children of Israel, saying, If a soul shall sin through ignorance against any of the commandments of the LORD *concerning things* which ought not to be done, and shall do against any of them… the priest that is anointed shall take of the bullock's blood, and bring it to the tabernacle of the congregation. (Leviticus 4:1, 2, 5)

Here we see the ordinances of divine service and the sanctuary service. These stood as an interruption in the reign of death. Thus, we read, **"Then verily the first *covenant* had also ordinances of divine service, and a worldly sanctuary"** (Heb. 9:1). What key ordinance was part of this system? **"These *are* the feasts of the LORD, *even* holy convocations, which ye shall proclaim in their seasons. In the fourteenth *day* of the first month at even *is* the LORD's passover"** (Lev. 23:4, 5).

When was Passover initially observed?

> **Now the sojourning of the children of Israel, who dwelt in Egypt, *was* four hundred and thirty years. And it came to pass at the end of the four hundred and thirty years, even the selfsame day it came to pass, that all the hosts of the LORD went out from the land of Egypt. It *is* a night to be much observed unto the LORD for bringing them out from the land of Egypt: this *is* that night of the LORD to be observed of all the children of Israel in their generations. And the LORD said unto Moses and Aaron, This *is* the ordinance of the passover: There shall no stranger eat thereof.** (Exodus 12:40–43)

Please note this ordinance was observed for the first time right at the end of the 430 years of Israel's sojourn. Of what did the Bible say this ceremony is a part? **"And when a stranger shall sojourn with thee, and will keep the passover to the LORD, let all his males be circumcised, and then let him come near and keep it…One law shall be to him that is homeborn, and unto the stranger that sojourneth among you"** (vs. 48, 49). The Lord describes the Passover as an ordinance, and also a law. It was the first ordinance given to the children of Israel, and it marks the end of the 430 years of the people's time in Egypt.

Besides the Passover, there were other ordinances of divine services listed in Leviticus 23. The following are the major feasts or religious festivals: 1) Passover, 2) Unleavened Bread, 3) First Fruits, 4) Pentecost, 5) Trumpets, 6) Day of Atonement, 7) Feast of Tabernacles. These are all classified as ordinances.

In confirming the covenant with Israel, the ceremonial laws and worldly sanctuary were also added. Please note God had to call this covenant the first covenant.

> **Why was the covenant made with Israel called the first covenant when it was by no means the first covenant that God made with humanity? It is because this covenant made with Israel contained all the object lessons and was ratified by the blood of an animal sacrifice. It was a system designed as a schoolmaster to teach us through symbol the import of Christ's redeeming sacrifice.** (Obasi, *The Final Atonement*, p. 14)

Why was this law of ordinance added? **"Wherefore then *serveth* the law? It was added because of transgressions"** (Gal. 3:19). The lamb, priest, and sacrificial system were shadows pointing to Christ; they were designated as a schoolmaster to teach us through symbol Christ's redeeming sacrifice and mediation.

Why would God specially choose Israel? What was the purpose? The Bible says, **"I the LORD have called thee in righteousness, and will hold thine hand, and will keep thee, and give thee for a covenant of the people, for a light of the Gentiles"** (Isa. 42:6). God, in order to fulfill His promise to Abraham that he would be a blessing to all the nations, chose Israel to further His divine plan and purpose, so that by them all mankind would be blessed.

The New Covenant

As we noted earlier, a covenant is an agreement and cannot take place without involving two parties or more. Covenant makers must present some stipulation to those with whom they are making the covenant. Agreement to observe the stipulation, keep the promises, and grant privileges and responsibilities constitute covenant. In the new covenant, who is the maker and with whom was the covenant made? **"Behold, the days come, saith the LORD, that I will make a new covenant with the house of Israel, and with the house of Judah"** (Jer. 31:31; see also Heb. 8).

The prophecy in Jeremiah reveals who made the covenant. We are told that the principal figure is **God,** while those with whom the covenant was made are the houses of **Israel and Judah.** What did God promise He would do under the new covenant, and how did He fulfill the promise? **"But this *shall be* the covenant that I will make with the house of Israel; After those days, saith the LORD, I will put my law in their inward parts, and write it in their hearts; and will be their God, and they shall be my people"** (v. 33).

Why would God make a second covenant with Israel when there's already one that exists? The Bible says, **"For if that first *covenant* had been faultless, then should no place have been sought for the second"** (Heb. 8:7). Here we are told why a second covenant was needed. It was because the first one had a fault. However, the big question is, Where was the fault found? In the stipulation or with the promises made by the covenant maker? **"For finding fault with them… because they continued not in my covenant"** (vs. 8, 9).

The fault was neither in the covenant stipulation, nor with God's promises, but rather with the people. They broke their own part of the agreement; they did not continue to keep what they agreed to keep, even when God **"took them by the hand to lead them out of the land of Egypt;**

because they continued not in [His] covenant, and [He] regarded them not" (v. 9).

They did not continue as they promised they would. What did Moses say was the cause of their disobedience? **"For I know thy rebellion, and thy stiff neck: behold, while I am yet alive with you this day, ye have been rebellious against the LORD; and how much more after my death"** (Deut. 31:27)? The children of Israel were rebellious and stiff-necked towards God. The psalmist further added, **"a stubborn and rebellious generation; a generation *that* set not their heart aright, and whose spirit was not stedfast with God"** (Ps. 78:8).

Here we are told that they had a heart problem and their spirit was not right with God. Nevertheless, thank God all hope was not lost! In His divine plan a solution was formulated, and in that solution, God said, **"A new heart also will I give you, and a new spirit will I put within you: and I will take away the stony heart out of your flesh, and I will give you an heart of flesh. And I will put my spirit within you, and cause you to walk in my statutes, and ye shall keep my judgments, and do *them*"** (Ezek. 36:26, 27).

Here God promised to resolve the stony heart problem by removing it, replacing it with a heart of flesh, and putting His spirit in them. What else did He promise to do? **"I will put my laws into their hearts, and in their minds will I write them; And their sins and iniquities will I remember no more"** (Heb. 10:16, 17).

At what time and where was this new covenant made?

> And he took bread, and gave thanks, and brake *it*, and gave unto them, saying, This is my body which is given for you: this do in remembrance of me. Likewise also the cup after supper, saying, This cup *is* the new testament [new covenant] in my blood, which is shed for you. (Luke 22:19, 20)
>
> And when he had given thanks, he brake *it*, and said, Take, eat: this is my body, which is broken for you: this do in remembrance of me. After the same manner also *he took* the cup, when he had supped, saying, This cup is the new testament [new covenant] in my blood: this do ye, as oft as ye drink *it*, in remembrance of me. (1 Corinthians 11:24, 25)

The new covenant was made the night Jesus was betrayed among the Jewish brethren. By whom and with what was it rectified? The Scripture says, **"whereupon neither the first *testament* was dedicated** [rectified] **without blood"** (Heb. 9:18). **"Neither by the blood of goats and calves, but by his own blood... the blood of Christ, who through the eternal Spirit offered himself without spot to God"** (v. 12, 14).

The new covenant was rectified on the cross when Christ shed His blood. In the old covenant, Moses was the mediator; who was the new covenant's mediator? **"And for this cause he is the mediator of the new testament, that by means of death, for the redemption of the transgressions** *that were* **under the first testament, they which are called might receive the promise of eternal inheritance"** (v. 15).

Christ became the Mediator of the new covenant through His shed blood, redeeming those who were called (the Israelites, among whom were the twelve apostles) from the transgression of the old covenant. Thereby He opened the door by which mankind can now receive the promise of an eternal inheritance that was made to Abraham.

Chapter 5

THE LAW OF THE NEW COVENANT

In this age of suspicion, fear, panic, despair, terror, and war, hearts long for peace. Beyond question, we all need peace, courage, hope, guidance, and direction. With the gathering storm today, we need a light that will not go out. Amid the increasing darkness and confusion, we need a voice to say with certainty "This is the way."

For years now, calamities have been ravaging the earth. Terrorism, climate change, droughts, floods, cyclones, volcanoes, and earthquakes have followed one after another in steady succession. Thousands have lost their lives in accidents by land, sea, and air. Crashes of large jetliners have become the norm. In Africa, millions are dying from starvation. Most Third World countries have become bankrupt and are unable to repay their loans. All over the world, we see an increase in crime, violence, riots, and civil wars. Could all this be the result of the worldwide disregard for the Law of God?

In the Bible, we find significant predictions regarding our time. **"The people have defiled the earth by breaking God's laws and by violating the covenant he made to last forever. So God has pronounced a curse on the earth. Its people are paying for what they have done"** (Isa. 24:5, 6, GNT).

In this chapter, we are going to look closely at the subject that deals with the law of the new covenant. Please note that the Koine Greek word for "law" in the New Testament is *nomos* (Strong's Concordance #3551). The term "law" is defined differently from the term "commandment." What is the Koine Greek term for "commandments"? It is *entole* (#1785).

Entole

The word *entole* is used in the New Testament in reference to all of God's commandments. For instance, **"And they returned, and prepared spices** and ointments; and rested the sabbath day according to the commandment [*entole*]" (Luke 23:56). It is also used in the book of Revelation and John's three epistles. Jesus answered the man who addressed Him as "good master," saying, **"Why callest thou me good?** *there is* **none good but one,** *that is,* **God. Thou knowest the commandments** [*entole*], **Do not commit adultery, Do not kill, Do not steal, Do not bear false witness, Defraud not, Honour thy father and mother"** (Mark 10:18, 19).

The word *entole* is used sixty-nine times in the New Testament and applies to the Ten Commandments, thus proving beyond a reasonable doubt that the commandment of the new covenant is the same Ten Commandments.

Nomos

The Greek word for "law" (*nomos*) which applies to the Old Testament law was the same word used in Hebrews and 1 John. **"For this *is* the covenant that I will make with the house of Israel after those days, saith the Lord; I will put my laws into their mind, and write them in their hearts: and I will be to them a God, and they shall be to me a people"** (Heb. 8:10). **"This *is* the covenant that I will make with them after those days, saith the Lord, I will put my laws into their hearts, and in their minds will I write them"** (10:16). **"Whosoever committeth sin transgresseth also the law: for sin is the transgression of the law"** (1 John 3:4). The verbal links show that the law or commandment of the old covenant was the same stipulation of the new covenant. How was the law written in the heart?

The Law of the New Testament

The Bible demonstrates that the Ten Commandments continued during the New Testament era. Now let's compare the instructions written by the New Testament apostles regarding how Christians should conduct themselves:

> *The Bible demonstrates that the Ten Commandments continued during the New Testament era*

1. **"Then saith Jesus unto him, Get thee hence, Satan: for it is written, Thou shalt worship the Lord thy God, and him only shalt thou serve"** (Matt. 4:10—Have no other gods)

2. **"Little children, keep yourselves from idols. Amen"** (1 John 5:21—Do not make idols or images)

3. "**Let as many servants as are under the yoke count their own masters worthy of all honour, that the name of God and *his* doctrine be not blasphemed**" (1 Tim. 6:1—Do not take the name of God in vain)

4. "**There remaineth therefore a [Sabbath] rest to the people of God. For he that is entered into his rest, he also hath ceased from his own works, as God *did* from his**" (Heb. 4:9, 10—Remember the Sabbath)

5. "**Children, obey your parents in the Lord: for this is right. Honour thy father and mother; (which is the first commandment with promise;) That it may be well with thee, and thou mayest live long on the earth**" (Eph. 6:1–3—Respect your parents)

6. "**For this… Thou shalt not kill**" (Rom. 13:9—Do not kill)

7. "**Now the works of the flesh are manifest, which are *these*; Adultery, fornication, uncleanness, lasciviousness**" (Gal. 5:19—Do not commit adultery)

8. "**Let him that stole steal no more: but rather let him labour, working with *his* hands the thing which is good, that he may have to give to him that needeth**" (Eph. 4:28—Do not steal)

9. "**Thou shalt not bear false witness**" (Rom. 13:9—Do not bear false witness)

10. "**Mortify therefore your members which are upon the earth; fornication, uncleanness, inordinate affection, evil concupiscence, and covetousness, which is idolatry: For which things' sake the wrath of God cometh on the children of disobedience**" (Col. 3:5, 6—Do not covet)

Tables of the Heart

God's Word reveals that **"*Forasmuch as ye* are manifestly declared to be the epistle of Christ ministered by us, written not with ink, but with the Spirit of the living God; not in tables of stone, but in fleshly tables of the heart"** (2 Cor. 3:3). Here we are told that the believers' hearts are the very epistle of Christ. The fact that the Bible employs familiar terminology such as "tables of stone" in conjunction with the "tables of the heart" and uses the phrase "written not with ink, but with the Spirit of the living God" shows that God was talking about the transcription of the contents from the two tables of stones to the heart.

Why was the Holy Spirit given? **"A new heart also will I give you, and a new spirit will I put within you: and I will take away the stony heart out of your flesh, and I will give you an heart of flesh. And I will put my spirit within you, and cause you to walk in my statutes, and ye shall keep my judgments, and do *them*"** (Ezek. 36:26, 27). Pentecost was specially bestowed, just like when Moses received the law on Mount Sinai and Israel became "married" to God. The Day of Pentecost was when the Holy Spirit came and wrote the laws of the new covenant on the hearts of believers, and the church was born.

1. **Type:** Exodus 19–24—God spoke to seventy elders in a language they all could hear
2. **Antitype:** Acts 2—They spoke in tongues to sixteen nations
3. **Type:** God's voice issued as a flame of fire
4. **Antitype:** Tongue of fire descended upon them
5. **Type:** God gave Moses the Ten Commandments written on two tables of stone
6. **Antitype:** God writes His law on the hearts of new covenant believers
7. **Type:** Three thousand were slain for worshiping idols
8. **Antitype:** Three thousand died to sin and were converted to Christ

Gentiles and the Covenant

The new covenant was made with Israel, not the Gentiles. How do Gentiles attain salvation? Speaking about Gentiles, Paul wrote:

> **Wherefore remember, that ye *being* in time past Gentiles in the flesh, who are called Uncircumcision by that which is called the Circumcision in the flesh made by hands; That at that time ye were without Christ, being aliens from the commonwealth of Israel, and strangers from the covenants of promise, having no hope, and without God in the world: But now in Christ Jesus ye who sometimes were far off are made nigh by the blood of Christ.** (Ephesians 2:11–13)

Through the death of Christ, the Gentiles, who were afar off, were brought close to the divine plan of salvation. How did they come into the new covenant? The Bible says, **"For when the Gentiles, which have not the law, do by nature the things contained in the law, these, having not the law, are a law unto themselves: Which shew the work of the law written in their hearts, their conscience also bearing witness"** (Rom. 2:14, 15).

> **For thus saith the LORD unto the eunuchs that keep my sabbaths, and choose *the things* that please me, and take hold of my covenant; Even unto them will I give in mine house and within my walls a place and a name better than of sons and of daughters: I will give them an everlasting name, that shall not be cut off. Also the sons of the stranger, that join themselves to the LORD, to serve him, and to love**

the name of the LORD, to be his servants, every one that keepeth the sabbath from polluting it, and taketh hold of my covenant; Even them will I bring to my holy mountain, and make them joyful in my house of prayer: their burnt offerings and their sacrifices *shall be* **accepted upon mine altar.** (Isaiah 56:4–7)

From the testimonies of Paul to the Romans, we confirmed that through nature, God writes things contained in the law upon human hearts. **"Hearken unto me, ye that know righteousness, the people in whose heart** *is* **my law; fear ye not the reproach of men, neither be ye afraid of their revilings"** (Isa. 51:7).

Law of Sin and Death

"For I delight in the law of God after the inward man: But I see another law in my members, warring against the law of my mind, and bringing me into captivity to the law of sin which is in my members" (Rom. 7:22, 23). Paul stated that he delighted in the law of God inwardly, but then noticed that there was another law within him fighting the law of God, in whom he delights. About which law was he talking? **"Know ye not, that to whom ye yield yourselves servants to obey, his servants ye are to whom ye obey; whether of sin unto death, or of obedience unto righteousness"** (6:16)?

Sin and death have a law and righteousness and life also have a law. The one to which you yield yourself becomes your master, and you its servant. Paul stated, **"For the good that I would I do not: but the evil which I would not, that I do"** (7:19). For instance, he desired not to commit adultery or fornication, but there was another desire in his flesh urging him to commit that which the law of God has commanded him not to do. He then added, **"Now if I do that I would not, it is no more I that do it, but sin that dwelleth in me"** (v. 20).

Finding himself doing what he wished not to do confirmed to him that another power has overtaken him. James defined this power: **"Then when lust hath conceived, it bringeth forth sin: and sin, when it is finished, bringeth forth death"** (James 1:15). He clearly stated that what inflames sin in us is lust, and the finishing point is death. Paul added, **"I find then a law, that, when I would do good, evil is present with me. For I delight in the law of God after the inward man: But I see another law in my members, warring against the law of my mind, and bringing me into captivity to the law of sin which is in my members"** (Rom. 7:21–23).

There was another law in him opposing the law of God. This law is called the law of sin, and it dwelt in his body. James identified this law as lust; the law of disobedient; the law that counters God's law and prompts you to do that which He commanded you not to do. Paul's question and answer were, **"O wretched man that I am! who shall deliver me from the body of this death? I thank God through Jesus Christ our Lord. So then with the mind I myself serve the law of God; but with the flesh the law of sin"** (vs. 24, 25).

His rhetorical question was who would deliver him from the body of death, the body in which dwells the law of sin and death. He then gave glory to God for Christ Jesus, who is able to destroy the sinful nature in him. **"The sting of death *is* sin; and the strength of sin *is* the law. But thanks *be* to God, which giveth us the victory through our Lord Jesus Christ"** (1 Cor. 15:56, 57).

Under the Law

As you consider the phrase "under the law," it is essential to understand that the word "law" in Scripture does not always refer to the Ten Commandments. The law consists of all the dos and don'ts of the moral and civil codes that are revealed in the first five books of the Old Testament (**Genesis, Exodus, Leviticus, Numbers, and Deuteronomy**).

What is the meaning of the phrase "under the law" as used by Paul in some of his epistles? Well, to answer that question, to be under the law means to be saved by the law. It also means to live under its jurisdiction and authority. That is why Paul wrote, **"But before faith came, we were kept under the law, shut up unto the faith which should afterwards be revealed. Wherefore the law was our schoolmaster *to bring us* unto Christ, that we might be justified by faith. But after that faith is come, we are no longer under a schoolmaster"** (Gal. 3:23–25).

The law we are actually under is the law that serves as our schoolmaster to bring us to Christ. Then our question is, Which law is this schoolmaster? To give us a clue, Paul wrote, **"Wherefore then *serveth* the law? It was added because of transgressions, till the seed should come to whom the promise was made; *and it was* ordained by angels in the hand of a mediator"** (v. 19). From the previous chapter, we learned that this law was that which was added because of the broken covenant. This is the ceremonial law, the law of the sacrificial system. This law was given four hundred thirty years after Israel's captivity.

This law points to Christ. Paul later wrote, **"when the fulness of the time was come, God sent forth his Son, made of a woman, made under the law, to redeem them that were under the law, that we might receive the adoption of sons"** (4:4, 5). This reference shows that Christ was made under the law and came to redeem those who were under the law, that they might be adopted as sons and daughters of God. Writing to the redeemed, Paul said, **"For sin shall not have dominion over you: for ye are not under the law, but under grace"** (Rom. 6:14).

God's purpose for our lives is not just to lead us out of bondage to rules and regulations, but more so lead us by grace through which our lives are comprehensively governed by the Holy Spirit, His Word, and love. The Scripture says, **"But if ye be led of the Spirit, ye are not under the law"** (Gal. 5:18). What really counts is being led by the Spirit. Describing His personal experience, Paul wrote, **"To those who are without the law I become like a person who is without the law.... (But really, I am not without God's law—I am ruled by Christ's law)"** (1 Cor. 9:21, NCV). In other to reach out to those not under the law, he became like a person who is not under the law, even when he was under the law of God, which he affirmed to be the same as the law of Christ, thus differentiating the moral law from the schoolmaster.

> *God's purpose for our lives is not just to lead us out of bondage to rules and regulations, but more so lead us by grace through which our lives are comprehensively governed by the Holy Spirit, His Word, and love*

The Law of the Spirit

"For the law of the Spirit of life in Christ Jesus hath made me free from the law of sin and death" (Rom. 8:2). Which law is the law of the Spirit of life in Christ Jesus? In this phrase, three things are composed together:

1. Law
2. Spirit
3. Life

To unravel this mystery, we must begin by asking some important questions to identify the Spirit and life in this picture. Whose Spirit and life are we talking about here? Of course, it's none other than that of Christ, who also confirmed by saying, **"the words that I speak unto you, *they* are spirit, and *they* are life"** (John 6:63). This passage contains a similar composition:

1. Word
2. Spirit
3. Life

What we can deduce from the above-inspired statement is the significance of the words or commands that proceed out of the mount of Jehovah. In what way does the law of the Spirit set us free from the law of sin and death? "**For we know that the law is spiritual**" (Rom. 7:14). If something is spiritual, it means it's relating to or affecting the spiritual dimension of human life, as opposed to the material or physical dimension.

Why is the spiritual dimension of the law necessary? It's so "**That the righteousness of the law might be fulfilled in us, who walk not after the flesh, but after the Spirit**" (8:4). "**Wherefore, the law *is* holy, and the commandment holy, and just, and good**" (7:12). "**But ye are not in the flesh, but in the Spirit, if so be that the Spirit of God dwell in you. Now if any man has not the Spirit of Christ, he is none of his**" (8:9).

The Law of Christ

Many Christians today talk about the law of Christ, and our question is, What is the law of Christ? The Bible says, "**A new commandment I give unto you, That ye love one another; as I have loved you, that ye also love one another. By this shall all *men* know that ye are my disciples, if ye have love one to another**" (John 13:34, 35).

"**And this commandment have we from him, That he who loveth God love his brother also**" (1 John 4:21). Here we notice that the command to love our neighbors and God is the law of Christ. Paul gave the following working definition of the law of Christ: "**Bear ye one another's burdens, and so fulfil the law of Christ**" (Gal. 6:2).

To bear one another's burden in love is to love our neighbors just as we love God. Is this law a new commandment? The Bible says, "**Brethren, I write no new commandment unto you, but an old commandment which ye had from the beginning. The old commandment is the word which ye have heard from the beginning.... He that loveth his brother abideth in the light, and there is none occasion of stumbling in him**" (1 John 2:7, 10).

We are told that the law of Christ is not a new law, but an old commandment we've heard. What old commandment are we talking about here?

> **And, behold, a certain lawyer stood up, and tempted him, saying, Master, what shall I do to inherit eternal life? He said unto him, What is written in the law? how readest thou? And he answering said, Thou shalt love the Lord thy God with all thy heart, and with all thy soul, and with all thy strength, and with all thy mind; and thy neighbour as thyself.** (Luke 10:25–27)

> Jesus said unto him, Thou shalt love the Lord thy God with all thy heart, and with all thy soul, and with all thy mind. This is the first and great commandment. And the second *is* like unto it, Thou shalt love thy neighbour as thyself. On these two commandments hang all the law and the prophets. (Matthew 22:37–40)

Speaking about love, Paul wrote to the Romans defining Jesus' second set of commandments. He said:

> Owe no man any thing, but to love one another: for he that loveth another hath fulfilled the law. For this, Thou shalt not commit adultery, Thou shalt not kill, Thou shalt not steal, Thou shalt not bear false witness, Thou shalt not covet; and if *there be* any other commandment, it is briefly comprehended in this saying, namely, Thou shalt love thy neighbour as thyself. Love worketh no ill to his neighbour: therefore love *is* the fulfilling of the law. (Romans 13:8–10)

Loving our neighbors encompasses the second six commandments, thus showing that the greatest commandment Jesus first mentioned deals with the first four commandments, of which the Sabbath is a part. Dear reader, can you see that the express requirements of the Old Testament are in perfect agreement with the teaching of the New Testament?

The Ministration of Death

"But if the ministration of death, written *and* engraven in stones, was glorious, so that the children of Israel could not stedfastly behold the face of Moses for the glory of his countenance; which *glory* was to be done away" (2 Cor. 3:7). What is the meaning of the word "engraved"? To engrave is to cut or curve a text or design an image on a hard surface of a stone or metal plate. What is it that was engraved in stone? Here is the clue the Bible gave: **"And he declared unto you his covenant, which he commanded you to perform, *even* ten commandments; and he wrote them upon two tables of stone"** (Deut. 4:13).

It was the Ten Commandments that were engraved in stone. What makes the Ten Commandments the ministration of death? The Bible says, **"for by the law *is* the knowledge of sin"** (Rom. 3:20). From this text, we clearly understand the purpose for which God's law was given, for by the law comes the knowledge of sin. However, is that what makes it the ministration of death? **"For I was alive without the law once: but when the commandment came, sin revived, and I died. And the commandment, which *was ordained* to life, I found *to be* unto death"** (Rom. 7: 9, 10).

Paul said he was alive without the law. Everything was fine; he was living the way that pleased him, and there was no prick in his mind until he came to the knowledge of all the righteous requirements of the law; then he realized how sinful he was and that the wage of sin is death.

Glorious Ministration

After Moses' encounter with God on the mount, what happened to him physically?

> **And it came to pass, when Moses came down from mount Sinai with the two tables of testimony in Moses' hand, when he came down from the mount, that Moses wist not that the skin of his face shone while he talked with [Aaron]… he put a vail on his face. But when Moses went in before the LORD to speak with him, he took the vail off, until he came out… And the children of Israel saw the face of Moses, that the skin of Moses' face shone: and Moses put the veil upon his face again…** (Exodus 34:29, 33–35)

Moses' encounter with God changed his physical appearance to the point that the children of Israel could not look at his face. Now our question is, Was the glorious countenance permanent throughout Moses' lifetime on earth, or was it temporary (see 2 Cor. 3:7)?

Yes, the ministration of death was glorious at the time it was engraved on the stones, as well as when they were held by Moses, who also had the same glory. Please note that the Scripture did not anywhere state that the ministration of death was done away. Instead it says, "**so that the children of Israel could not stedfastly behold the face of Moses for the glory of his countenance; which** *glory* **was to be done away.**"

Moses' glorious countenance went away. The glorious countenance was not permanent, but temporal. It spiritually represents the righteousness of God. "**And he [Moses] said, I beseech thee, shew me thy glory**" (Ex. 33:18). What was God's response? "**And it shall come to pass, while my glory passeth by, that I will put thee in a clift of the rock, and will cover thee with my hand while I pass by**" (v. 22).

> **And the LORD descended in the cloud, and stood with him there, and proclaimed the name of the LORD. And the LORD passed by before him, and proclaimed, The LORD, The LORD God, merciful and gracious, longsuffering, and abundant in goodness and truth, Keeping mercy for thousands, forgiving iniquity and transgression and sin, and that will by no means clear** *the guilty***; visiting the iniquity**

of the fathers upon the children, and upon the children's children, unto the third and to the fourth *generation.* (Exodus 34:5–7)

The Lord passed by Moses and showed him His glory. As you can see above, this wasn't just a glorious personage that God was revealing; He was also revealing His character—merciful, gracious, longsuffering, forgiving, and just. These attributes of character are also referred to as the glory of the Lord. It represents the righteousness of God as revealed by the law. The bible says, **"For even that which was made glorious had no glory in this respect, by reason of the glory that excelleth"** (2 Cor. 3:10).

The glory emanating from the Ten Commandments is God's glory. The law has none in itself; it is a reflection or mirror of God's glory or righteousness. Did the children of Israel attain to God's righteousness through the law? The Bible says, **"But Israel, which followed after the law of righteousness, hath not attained to the law of righteousness"** (Rom. 9:31).

Why is it that they could not attain to God's righteousness through their works of the law? The Bible says, **"Because [they sought it] not by faith, but as it were by the works of the law. For they stumbled at that stumblingstone"** (v. 32).

How did the lack of faith affect the carnal-minded Jews as they read the Old Testament? The Bible says, **"But their minds were blinded: for until this day remaineth the same vail untaken away in the reading of the old testament; which** *vail* **is done away in Christ. But even unto this day, when Moses is read, the vail is upon their heart"** (2 Cor. 3:14, 15).

Which two spiritual aspects of the Old Testament were done away at the cross? The glory from the work of the law and the veil; the glory is righteousness, which is of the law; what is the veil? Here is the clue the Bible gives: **"Having therefore, brethren, boldness to enter into the holiest by the blood of Jesus, By a new and living way, which he hath consecrated for us, through the veil, that is to say, his flesh"** (Heb. 10:19, 20).

The newly consecrated veil is the flesh of Christ that was crucified on the cross an antitype to the sacrificial offering. The veil represents the partitioning wall between the Holy Place and Most Holy place, which provides a covering for the Shekinah glory. It also represents the middle wall of partition between the Jews and Gentiles. For those who may not be too familiar with the fence within the outer courtyard of the temple, please take note of this: there was a low fence called the *soreg* built by the Pharisees in the outer court of the temple. Beyond this *soreg*, the Gentiles could not pass.

There were signs posted all around the *soreg* stating that any Gentile found within it would be responsible for the loss of life. At the same time, within the temple, there was also a veil between the Holy and Most Holy Places, which none could enter through except the high priest. With that said, what did the death of Christ accomplish? The Bible says, **"But now in Christ Jesus ye who sometimes were far off are made nigh by the blood of Christ. For he is our peace, who hath made both one, and hath broken down the middle wall of partition** *between us*" (Eph. 2:13, 14).

By breaking down the middle wall of partition, the way into the Holiest is laid open. The veil is now torn apart; a new and living way is now prepared for all by Christ's death. Also, the spirit of racial distinction in the minds of the Jews against the Gentiles is now abolished by Christ's death, thus establishing a religion in which there is no caste; a religion by which Jews and Gentiles, free and bond, are linked in a common brotherhood, equal before God. This is the gospel truth many Jews have failed to understand, even to this day.

Not One Jot or Tittle

Jesus explained His view of the law quickly after giving the beatitudes. He said, **"Think not that I am come to destroy the law, or the prophets: I am not come to destroy, but to fulfil"** (Matt. 5:17). The "law and prophets" was a term commonly used for the Old Testament. The "law" referred to the first five books of the Bible—the books of Moses in which God's law was written. The "prophets" referred not only to the writings of the biblical prophets but also the historical books of what came to be known as the Old Testament.

What does it mean to abolish and fulfill? According to *American Heritage Dictionary*, to **"abolish"** means **"to do away with; put an end to,"** while **"fulfill"** means "to achieve or realize (something desired, promised, or predicted); (**fulfill oneself**) gain happiness or satisfaction by fully achieving one's potential. Satisfy or meet (a requirement or condition)."

The Greek word for "fulfill" is *pleroo*, the same word used in Matthew 3:15: **"And Jesus answering said unto him, Suffer** *it to be so* **now: for thus it becometh us to fulfil all righteousness. Then he suffered him."** The word "fulfill" in the original context means to "fill it up full." Speaking of Christ, the Bible says, **"For in him dwelleth all the fulness of the Godhead bodily"; "For it pleased** *the Father* **that in him should all fulness dwell"** (Col. 2:9; 1:19).

Jesus, by explaining, expanding, and exemplifying God's law, fulfilled a prophecy of the Messiah found in Isaiah: **"The LORD is well pleased for** his righteousness' sake; he will magnify the law, and make *it* honourable" (42:21). The Hebrew word *gadal*, translated "exalt" or "magnify" (KJV) literally means "to be or become great" (William Wilson, *Wilson's Old Testament Word Studies*, "Magnify"). Jesus Christ did exactly that, showing the holy and spiritual intent, purpose, and scope of God's law. He met the law's requirements by obeying it perfectly in thought and deed, both in the letter and intent of the heart.

The second key statement given by Jesus in the same context makes it even clearer that He did not come to destroy, rescind, nullify or abolish the law. **"For verily I say unto you, Till heaven and earth pass, one jot or one tittle shall in no wise pass from the law, till all be fulfilled"** (Matt. 5:18). With these words, Jesus likened the continuance of the law to the permanence of heaven and earth. He is saying that the law is immutable, inviolable, and unchangeable, and can only be fulfilled, never abrogated.

We should note that in this verse, a different Greek word is used for "fulfilled"—*ginomai* (Strong's #1096), meaning "to become," "to come into existence," or "to come to pass." Until the ultimate completion of God's plan to glorify humanity in His Kingdom comes to pass—that is, as long as there are still fleshly human beings—the physical codification of God's law in Scripture is necessary. This, Jesus explained, is as certain as the continued existence of the universe.

The third statement of Jesus pronounces that our fate rests in our attitude toward and treatment of God's holy law. **"Whosoever therefore shall break one of these least commandments, and shall teach men so, he shall be called the least** [by those] **in the kingdom of heaven: but whosoever shall do and teach *them*, the same shall be called great in the kingdom of heaven"** (v. 19). The "by those" is added for clarification, since, as explained in other passages, those who persist in lawbreaking and teach others to break God's law will not be in the kingdom at all.

Jesus makes it very clear that those who follow Him and aspire to His kingdom have a perpetual obligation to obey and uphold God's law. He is saying that we cannot diminish the law of God by even a jot or tittle (the equivalent of the crossing of a "T" or dotting of an "I"). The value He places on the commandments of God is also unmistakable, as well as the high esteem toward the law that He requires from all those who teach in His name. His disapproval falls on those who slight the least of the law's commands, and His honor will be bestowed on those who impart and obey the commandments.

Chapter 6

THE REAL EARTH DAY

World leaders from various nations are today blaming the devastating calamities on climate change—global warming. One of their primary solutions to combat climate change is to persuade the leading nations to accept an international day of rest. They are demanding a green sabbath day to be enforced globally. Soon international law will require the observation of SUN-day, the pagan day of sun worship, as a day of rest and worship for everybody. The United States of America will be foremost in enacting and later enforcing a national Sunday law in defiance of God's commandments. However, the question remains, why must it be Sunday? Why not the Sabbath, the day on which God commanded His people to rest?

Holy Day

In God's Word we are commanded:

> **Remember the sabbath day, to keep it holy. Six days shalt thou labour, and do all thy work: But the seventh day *is* the sabbath of the LORD thy God: *in it* thou shalt not do any work, thou, nor thy son, nor thy daughter, thy manservant, nor thy maidservant, nor thy cattle, nor thy stranger that *is* within thy gates: For *in* six days the LORD made heaven and earth, the sea, and all that in them *is*, and rested the seventh day: wherefore the LORD blessed the sabbath day, and hallowed it.** (Exodus 20:8–11)

In blessing the Sabbath day, God endowed it with a special relationship to Him who alone is intrinsically holy. Although you may ask, How can a day be holy? A day is a unit of time, which is not a material object, so it cannot be made holy by application of a sanctifying substance, such as anointing oil. It must be consecrated in relation to those who are affected by it. The only way for intelligent beings to make or treat times as holy is by altering their behavior.

Roman 14

In Roman 14, Paul was addressing Gentile Christians in Rome who were faced with formidable challenges of maintaining their Christian faith in the midst of paganism and senseless tradition. For instance, most of the meat sold in the Gentile markets were offered to idols. Some Christians bought those meats and ate them, believing it had no power over them, while the weak and baby Christians were offended by what others were doing. Therefore, Paul came to address the issue. He said, **"For one believeth that he may eat all things: another, who is weak, eateth herbs. Let not him that eateth despise him that eateth not; and let not him which eateth not judge him that eateth: for God hath received him"** (Rom. 14:2, 3).

This was similar to an experience encountered in Corinth, where he also addressed the same issue:

> **Now as touching things offered unto idols…As concerning therefore the eating of those things that are offered in sacrifice unto idols, we know that an idol *is* nothing in the world…For if any man see thee which hast knowledge sit at meat in the idol's temple, shall not the conscience of him which is weak be emboldened to eat those things which are offered to idols.** (1 Corinthians 8:1, 4, 10)

After addressing the food matter, he also addressed another issue related to pagan holidays. He said, **"One man esteemeth one day above another: another esteemeth every day [alike]. Let every man be fully persuaded in his own mind. He that regardeth the day, regardeth *it* unto the Lord; and he that regardeth not the day, to the Lord he doth not regard *it*"** (Rom. 14:5, 6).

If you look carefully, the word "Sabbath" was not mentioned. Why not? Because it's not the focus of Paul's letter. He was rather addressing the pagan holidays, and nothing more. That was why he went further to add **"He that eateth, eateth to the Lord, for he giveth God thanks; and he that eateth not, to the Lord he eateth not, and giveth God thanks."** The person of strong faith that chooses to eat does so to God, but the one who feels like abstaining also does so to God. **"But if any man says unto you, This is offered in sacrifice unto idols, eat not for his sake that shewed it"** (1 Cor. 10:28).

Rested and Refreshed

Thus, God altered His behavior on the seventh day of creation, the archetype of the weekly Sabbath, and proclaimed the day holy. The Bible says, **"for in six days the LORD made heaven and earth, and on the seventh day he rested, and was refreshed"** (Ex. 31:17). What does it mean that God rested and was refreshed? We are also told in the Bible that **"the Creator of the ends of the earth, fainteth not, neither is weary"** (Isa. 40:28).

With that said, what is the idea that God rested and was refreshed or revived? Why would a God who cannot be weary or tired be resting? Of course, He did not rest because He was tired or fatigued, just as Isaiah said. The concept of God resting and refreshing speaks very strongly of something important. The only answer we can have for this is that God was modeling a lifestyle for the human family.

This was not a rest God needed for Himself, but to teach mankind the importance of rest. That is why Jesus said, **"The sabbath was made for man, and not man for the sabbath"** (Mark 2:27). The statement made by Jesus, if you go back to the Greek text, really reads, "the Sabbath was made for the man." All the scholars that have examined the text have concluded that the reference "the man" is no other than Adam himself.

Delighting in the Lord

The Sabbath is not an institution that exists or ceases with its observance by mankind; the divine rest is a fact as much as is the divine work, so the sanctity of the day exists whether a person assimilates the benefit or not. What sense would it make to say that God blessed the day if He intended this unit of holy time to benefit only Himself? **"Blessed *is* the man *that* doeth this, and the son of man *that* layeth hold on it; that keepeth the sabbath from polluting it, and keepeth his hand from doing any evil"** (Isa. 56:2).

God blessing the day should not be interpreted as meaning that He blessed the day for Himself. It was for His creation—mankind in particular—that God blessed the Sabbath day. The blessing of the Sabbath is for the created beings living in the world where time operates. To receive the blessing, these beings would consecrate the day as God did, by altering their behavior. Isaiah wrote:

> **If thou turn away thy foot from the sabbath, *from* doing thy pleasure on my holy day; and call the sabbath a delight, the holy of the LORD, honourable; and shalt honour him, not doing thine own ways, nor finding thine own pleasure, nor speaking *thine own* words: Then shalt thou delight thyself in the LORD; and I will cause thee to ride upon the high places of the earth, and feed thee with the heritage of Jacob thy father: for the mouth of the LORD hath spoken *it*.** (Isaiah 58:13, 14)

From the above text, we can see that the blessing of this day had a significant effect on humanity. The reference to God making His children ride on the high places of the earth is indeed striking. The blessing results from the activity that acknowledges the consecration. The Sabbath is a constant source of wellbeing to the person who recognizes its true nature and purpose.

It was a gift for mankind. God knows that as our energy level goes down and wastes accumulate, as a result of our daily physical labor, we experience fatigue and a desire for rest. During rest, energy is restored, and waste buildup is diminished. Looking at this verse from the context of creation, humanity was created from the beginning; and the Sabbath was also created from the beginning. Both the creation of humanity and the Sabbath were right at the beginning when the man and woman existed. It clearly shows that the Sabbath was made for their race.

Sabbath and Marriage

"And the LORD God caused a deep sleep to fall upon Adam, and he slept: and he took one of his ribs, and closed up the flesh instead thereof; And the rib, which the LORD God had taken from man, made he a woman, and brought her unto the man" (Gen. 2:21, 22). On the sixth day the heavens, the earth, and the host of them were finished. On the same day, He caused Adam to fall into a deep sleep, took one of his ribs, and formed a woman who became his helpmeet. As Adam awoke from his sleep, he saw her standing by his side.

Adam's joy knew no bounds when the Lord God of hosts greeted him with a special gift. "Behold thy wife!" Adam, in joyful expression, exclaimed, **"This *is* now bone of my bones, and flesh of my flesh: she shall be called Woman, because she was taken out of Man. Therefore shall a man leave his father and his mother, and shall cleave unto his wife: and they shall be one flesh"** (vs. 23, 24).

The morning stars sang together as the young couple, in elation and gladness, partook in the joy of the Lord. The Scripture says, **"When the morning stars sang together, and all the sons of God shouted for joy"** (Job 38:7)? It was a unique moment and memorable day for both mankind and God as this event marked the end of creation. Thus, the Bible says, **"And on the seventh day God ended his work which he had made; and he rested on the seventh day from all his work which he had made. And God blessed the seventh day, and sanctified it: because that in it he had rested from all his work which God created and made"** (Gen. 2:2, 3).

The significance of this is that God first labored for six days and then rested on the seventh day from His perfect and finished work of creation. Adam and Eve did not work first, but rather they began their lives by resting with God on the seventh day. This was designed to show the young couple that their first priority was communion with their Maker and depending completely on Him for all their needs. Without Him, they could do nothing.

Jesus and the Sabbath

It was Jesus who formed Adam from the dust of the ground:

> **In the beginning was the Word, and the Word was with God, and the Word was God. The same was in the beginning with God. All things were made by him; and without him was not anything made that was made....And the Word was made flesh, and dwelt among us, (and we beheld his glory, the glory as of the only begotten of the Father,) full of grace and truth.** (John 1:1–3, 14)

It was Jesus who also gave Adam a helpmeet. The Bible says, **"And the LORD God said, *It is* not good that the man should be alone; I will make him an help meet for him"** (Gen. 2:18). It was Christ who made all things; it was He who created the Sabbath. Throughout His ministry on earth, He observed the Sabbath. **"And he came to Nazareth, where he had been brought up: and, as his custom was, he went into the synagogue on the sabbath day, and stood up for to read"** (Luke 4:16).

Does the following verse suggest that Christ broke the Sabbath? **"Therefore the Jews sought the more to kill him, because he not only had broken the sabbath, but said also that God was his Father, making himself equal with God"** (John 5:18). Did Jesus break the Sabbath? Let's hear what He had to say: **"Think not that I am come to destroy the law, or the prophets: I am not come to destroy, but to fulfil.... Whosoever therefore shall break one of these least commandments, and shall teach men so, he shall be called the least in the kingdom of heaven: but whosoever shall do** and teach *them*, the same shall be called great in the kingdom of heaven" (Matt. 5:17, 19). "I have kept my Father's commandments, and abide in his love" (John 15:10). Jesus never broke any of God's commandments; it was mere Jewish supposition, which was false.

Why He Is Worshipped

Christ's real purpose for instituting the Sabbath is to keep afresh in the minds of people God's creative ability, which distinguishes Him as the only true God to whom alone worship is due. John wrote, **"Fear God, and give glory to him; for the hour of his judgment is come: and worship him that made heaven, and earth, and the sea, and the fountains of waters"** (Rev. 14:7).

This was the same reason given for Sabbath observance. **"For *in* six days the LORD made heaven and earth, the sea, and all that in them *is*, and rested the seventh day: wherefore the LORD blessed the sabbath day, and hallowed it"** (Ex. 20:11). Therefore, the Sabbath was designed to serve as a sign that points to God as the creator of all things, who alone deserves our worship. It is the great memorial of the creative power of the only true living God.

Sanctifier and Redeemer

Why else does God say He gave the Sabbath? **"Moreover also I gave them my sabbaths, to be a sign between me and them, that they might know that I *am* the LORD that sanctify them"** (Ezek. 20:12). God gave the Sabbath to be a sign that he is our God who sanctifies us. Sanctification is an act of setting one apart in holiness. Therefore, the Sabbath was designed to remind people not only of their origin but also that they were set apart to reflect the perfect image of their Maker. The Scripture says, **"And hallow my sabbaths; and they shall be a sign between me and you, that ye may know that I *am* the LORD your God"** (v. 20).

As the Sabbath was the sign that distinguished Israel when they came out of Egypt to enter the earthly Canaan, so it is the sign that now distinguishes God's people as they come out from the world to enter the heavenly Canaan. The Sabbath is a sign of a relationship existing between God and His people; a sign that they honor His law.

Key of Hell and Death

After His death on the cross, as He was laid in the tomb, Christ rested. The Scripture says, **"And that day was the preparation, and the sabbath drew on. And the women also, which came with him from Galilee, followed after, and beheld the sepulchre, and how his body was laid. And they** returned, and prepared spices and ointments; and rested the sabbath day according to the commandment"** (Luke 23:54–56).

When Christ gave up the ghost on Friday (the preparation day; the sixth day), He rested on the seventh day. When Jesus, as He hung upon the cross, cried out 'It is finished," the price for our redemption was paid in full. His voice echoed through the realm of the wicked and wrestled the key of the grave and death from him who for centuries had held people in captivity. He then rested on the Sabbath day.

Now having obtained the key of hell and death, He exclaimed at His resurrection: **"I *am* he that liveth, and was dead; and, behold, I am alive for evermore, Amen; and have the keys of hell and of death"** (Rev. 1:18). **"O death, where *is* thy sting? O grave, where *is* thy victory? The sting of death *is* sin; and the strength of sin *is* the law. But thanks *be* to God, which giveth us the victory through our Lord Jesus Christ"** (1 Cor. 15:55–57).

In a prophetic utterance, Isaiah spoke of this day:

> **Shall the prey be taken from the mighty, or the lawful captive delivered? But thus saith the LORD, Even the captives of the mighty shall be taken away, and the prey of the terrible shall be delivered: for I will contend with him that contendeth with thee, and I will save thy children. And I will feed them that oppress thee with their own flesh; and they shall be drunken with their own blood, as with sweet wine: and all flesh shall know that I the LORD *am* thy Saviour and thy Redeemer, the mighty One of Jacob.** (Isaiah 49:24–26)

This is God's promise and assurance to all who believe in Christ's saving grace. Today Christ declares to every soul: **"I am the resurrection, and the life: he that believeth in me, though he were dead, yet shall he live"** (John 11:25). The key to hell and the grave has been obtained by Christ. **"*And* Having spoiled principalities and powers, [Christ] made a show of them openly, triumphing over them in it"** (Col. 2:15). Therefore, by this, He made the Sabbath a sign and symbol of victory. Christ is the one through whom we obtain victory via sanctification. The Sabbath is a sign or memorial that we are united with Him.

It is interesting to note that on the cross Christ proclaimed that the redemption price was paid in full when He said, "It is finished!" And just as God's original creation was perfect and finished at the end of the six days, so the price of mankind's redemption was paid in full, settled, and finalized at the end of the sixth day, the very day Jesus died on the cross.

No person can add anything to this finished work. All that remains is for the children of Adam to accept the spiritual rest in Christ and reflect on

His righteousness. The Sabbath, therefore, becomes a constant reminder that our redemption price was paid in full in Christ at the cross. We can add nothing to it. This is the gospel truth that the Jews completely failed to realize.

Due to their unbelief, they did not truly experience this rest that the Bible taught. However, the good news of the gospel today is that the Sabbath rest, on which Adam turned his back, and the Jews rejected through unbelief, has been restored by Christ's earthly mission, life, and death.

There Remains a Sabbath Rest

Today Scripture is teaching that the Sabbath is to be observed by Christians. Paul wrote, **"there remains a Sabbath rest for the people of God"** (Heb. 4:9, ESV). If something remains, it means it existed before. If it remains for the people of God, it must be observed by the people of God. The Greek word translated "rest" in every other verse throughout Hebrews 3 and 4 is *katapausis*. However, the word translated "rest" in Hebrew 4:9 is *sabbatismos*. This is the only New Testament occurrence of this word, and its meaning is fundamental to understanding this pivotal verse.

The *Anchor Bible Dictionary* states this regarding the meaning of *sabbatismos*: **"The words 'Sabbath rest' translate the [Greek] noun sabbatismos, a unique word in the NT. This term appears also in Plutarch… for Sabbath observance and in four post-canonical Christian writings… for seventh day 'sabbath celebration'"** (p. 855, emphasis added). It decisively and correctly concludes that *sabbatismos* means keeping the seventh-day Sabbath. Therefore, Hebrew 4:9 stresses the need to continue to keep the Sabbath in a new covenant context, even though the day also embodies all it meant under the old covenant. Paul continues, **"for whoever** [not just Jews] **has entered God's rest has also** [in addition] **rested from his works** [literal work] **as God did from his"** (v. 10, ESV).

If Christ and God rested from their work, and this verse states that if we enter into God's rest, which implies we came to Christ and found rest in Him, we too will rest from our work, just as God did. Then the question is, How did God rest after His work? **"And God rested on the seventh day from all his works"** (v. 4, ESV). Therefore, those who come to Christ must also rest from their work, just as God did from His work on the seventh day. **"Let us therefore strive to enter that rest, so that no one may fall by the same sort of** [Israel's] **disobedience"** (v. 11, ESV).

What's the question that comes to your mind? After going through the above verse, what was Israel's example of disobedience? Well, to unravel that, we must search the Scripture to find the answer. Let's begin with the clue given in verse 3. **"As I swore in my wrath, 'they shall not enter into my rest.'"** At the time God was warning them about their disobedience, the Bible says He swore. With that clue we need to go to the Scriptures to find when and where that happened:

> Yet the people of Israel rebelled against me in the wilderness. They did not follow my decrees but rejected my laws… and they utterly desecrated my Sabbaths. Also with uplifted hands I *swore* to them in the wilderness that I would not bring them into the land I had given them… because they rejected my laws and did not follow my decrees and desecrated my Sabbaths. (Ezekiel 20:13, 15, 16, NIV, emphasis mine)

That is why Israel did not enter into the Promised Land, because they desecrated the Sabbath, and many of them perished in the wilderness. For Christians today to enter God's eternal rest and the heavenly Promised Land, they must keep the Sabbath and not follow Israel's example of disobedience. Therefore, God designed that through the Sabbath we should be closely linked together with Christ. Glorious to the eyes of the heavenly beings, now the victory is gained. A restored creation, a redeemed race, and the Sabbath upon which Christ and God rested is now forever linked. On this sacred day shall all flesh in heaven and on earth be united and bow in worship and praise.

Let No-one Judge You

Another chapter that many quote to prove that Paul was admitting the abrogation of the Sabbath and the holy days is Colossians 2:16–17: **"Let no man therefore judge you in meat, or in drink, or in respect of an holyday, or of the new moon, or of the sabbath** *days*: **Which are a shadow of things to come; but the body** *is* **of Christ."** To understand what Paul meant, we need to go back to verses 8 and 22: **"Beware lest any man spoil you through philosophy and vain deceit, after the tradition of men, after the rudiments of the world, and not after Christ….Which all are to perish with the using;) after the commandments and doctrines of men?"**

Paul was admonishing the Christians to beware of those who came with enticing words of deception to enforce human traditions and doctrines on them. These are the same people about whom Jesus spoke when He said, **"Howbeit in vain do they worship me, teaching** *for* **doctrines the commandments of men. For laying aside the commandment of God, ye hold the tradition of men,** *as* **the washing of pots and cups: and many** other such like things ye do" (Mark 7:7, 8).

Those who preach or call the attention of the Christians to their manmade traditions were the ones about whom Paul was warning the Colossian Christians. At the time the above statement was made to the Colossians, Jesus had already died, was buried, and rose and went back to heaven. Paul was presenting the spiritual import of the Sabbath, holy days, and new moons to the Colossians. He pointed to the future and not the past.

He said the holy days, new moons, and sabbath days were all "**shadows of things to come,**" not things already fulfilled, thus proving that the Sabbath was not done away with on the cross, but continues to the end. Other things mentioned alongside the Sabbath in this chapter were also shadows of things to come, although the text is wrongly interpreted. Paul said that these things point to the future. How does God's word confirm this?

Meat and Drink

"**For my flesh is meat indeed, and my blood is drink indeed. He that eateth my flesh, and drinketh my blood, dwelleth in me, and I in him**" (John 6:55, 56).

"**And as they were eating, Jesus took bread, and blessed** *it*, **and brake** *it*, **and gave** *it* **to the disciples, and said, Take, eat; this is my body. And he took the cup, and gave thanks, and gave** *it* **to them, saying, Drink ye all of it; For this is my blood of the new testament, which is shed for many for the remission of sins**" (Matt. 26:26–28).

Therefore, the meat and drink spoken of in the book of Colossians are referring to the body and blood of Christ, as represented in the holy Communion. Jesus commission this to His disciples: "**And when he had given thanks, he brake** *it*, **and said, Take, eat: this is my body, which is broken for you: this do in remembrance of me. After the same manner also** *he took* **the cup, when he had supped, saying, This cup is the new testament in my blood: this do ye, as oft as ye drink** *it*, **in remembrance of me**" (1 Cor. 11:24, 25).

This meat-and-drink ceremony was to be continued as a shadow; that was the instruction of Jesus. How long was it designed to last? The Bible says, "**And he said unto them, With desire I have desired to eat this passover with you before I suffer: For I say unto you, I will not any more eat thereof, until it be fulfilled in the kingdom of God**" (Luke 22:15, 16). Here we see Jesus present the institution of Communion as something that continues and consummates in the kingdom of God. Paul admonished the

Colossians not to be judged by anyone regarding this holy ritual, whose substance is Christ.

God's Divine Purpose

Dear friends, can you see the that Sabbath teaches eternal truths about salvation? God's rest is threefold. **First,** God's rest is the seventh day of the week. **Second,** God's rest is a mental and spiritual rest. God is a spirit (see John 4:24); therefore, God's rest must be spiritual (see Matt. 11:28–30). **Third,** God's rest is eternal because God is eternal (see Isa. 66:22, 23). The Sabbath rest has a threefold application for all believers:

1. **It points to a perfect and finished creation, which fallen humanity has ruined.**
2. **It points to a perfect and finished redemption; a price paid in full, in which believers rejoice, being reminded weekly by their Sabbath keeping.**
3. **It points believers to the blessed hope, a perfect and finished restoration, which the Bible described as follows:** "For as the new heavens and the new earth, which I will make, shall remain before me, saith the LORD, so shall your seed and your name remain. And it shall come to pass, *that* from one new moon to another, and from one sabbath to another, shall all flesh come to worship before me, saith the LORD" (Isa. 66:22, 23).

Even in the new heaven and new earth, the new moon cycle is still relevant, and that was why Paul said, **"let no one judge you about the new moon"** because of its relevance in God's coming new kingdom.

It is interesting to note that on each of the first six days of creation, God did something that had ongoing results for our world. Thus, we expect that what He did on the seventh day would also have continuing consequences. God set up cyclical time even before humankind was created. According to Genesis 1:14, He made heavenly bodies, chiefly the sun and moon, to mark earthly time as "signs," "seasons," appointed times, day, and years.

Therefore, when the Bible says that God blessed and hallowed the seventh day, this blessing and consecration could be ongoing in a cyclical sense, applying to each subsequent seventh day. From our study so far, we've been able to prove that climate change is not only God's judgment against godless and rebellious mankind, but also a sign of the imminent return of Jesus.

The Global Agenda

The false attribute of the cause of the present climate change and their solution are designed to lead mankind astray and destroy hope and faith, not only in the second coming of our Lord and Savior Jesus Christ, but also His commandments, particularly the Sabbath. One of their primary solutions to combat climate change, Pope Francis said in *Laudato Si'*, is that all nations must unite to enforce Sunday rest.

Pope Francis talks about **"'ecological sins' made individually and collectively by humans who destroy Mother Earth"**... Cardinal Bo, in his appeal, calls on mankind to **"Repent to save the planet... Today we are faced with an environmental holocaust. It is a very delicate moment"** (Vatican News, http://1ref.us/qf, accessed 10/24/2018).

Cardinal Bo, in his appeal, calls on mankind to repent and save the planet. Concurring with Pope Francis, who talked about the **"'ecological sin' made individually and collectively by humans who destroy Mother Earth,"** Cardinal Bo said, **"Today we are faced with an environmental holocaust...It is a very serious moment"** (Lifesite, http://1ref.us/qe, accessed 10/24/2018).

However, the solution they proffer is contrary to God's Word. Inspiration reveals, **"The time will come when men will not only forbid Sunday work, but they will try to force men to labor on the Sabbath. And men will be asked to renounce the Sabbath and to subscribe to Sunday observance or forfeit their freedom and their lives. But the time for this has not yet come, for the truth must be presented more fully before the people as a witness"** (White 1966, p. 69).

In the last great conflict of the controversy with Satan, those who are loyal to God will see every earthly support cut off. Because they refuse to break His law in obedience to worldly powers, they will be forbidden to buy or sell. It will finally be decreed that they shall be put to death. Life today is already made difficult for Sabbath observers:

> **Seventh-day Adventists are sometimes finding it difficult to get and keep work because of their observance of the Sabbath from sunset on Friday to sunset on Saturday.**
>
> That's according to the latest International Religious Freedom Report published by the State Department of the United States....
>
> **...some businesses remained reluctant to hire employees who could not work Saturdays,** the report has further stated.
>
> **One Spanish Town-based worshipper...**

"That is true. It is something we talk about all the time, and nobody seems to be paying it any attention. **If you cannot work on Saturdays, they do not want to hire you,**" the woman, who has had three job changes because of clashes with the requirements of her faith, told **The Gleaner** yesterday.

"'Can you work on Saturdays?' It's such a haunting question," she added.

"**The biggest problem for us is that some bosses are paying extra to work on Saturday, so it is as if they are using money to entice us to work on the Sabbath, which is not right,**" she continued.

But just how much extra is being paid to work on weekends?

Gleaner sources say that as much as $2,000 is on offer in some areas for those willing to give up their weekend, and for Adventists - church, for work.

"**When we hear that, all we have to do is pray because we know we are being discriminated against. But God is not sleeping,**" another Seventh-day Adventist worshipper said."

Reacting to the US State Department disclosure, Nigel Coke, public affairs and religious liberty director for the Seventh-day Adventist Church in Jamaica, described the situation as unfortunate.

"**It is unfortunate, whichever country or whichever organisation, that they don't [recognise] the religious right of individuals according to their God-given conscience. It is a fundamental right to every single man at creation,**" Coke said....

...Coke noted that the discrimination also transcends the workplace into tertiary institutions, where coursework and exams are set during hours Seventh-day Adventists reserve for their Sabbath.

"**And they fail them when they do not turn up,**" he said.

"**The situation is getting more and more intense as we go along, but we, as a Church, are doing the best we can to alleviate the stress of our members,**" the religious liberty advocate stated. (http://1ref.us/os, accessed 9/5/2018)

Those who take Christ at His word, and surrender their souls to His keeping, their lives to His ordering, will find peace and quietude. Nothing of the world can make them sad when Jesus makes them glad by His presence. In perfect acquiescence there is perfect rest. The Lord says, "Thou wilt keep him in perfect peace, whose mind is stayed on Thee: because he trusteth in Thee." Isaiah 26:3. Our lives may seem a tangle; but as we commit ourselves to the wise Master Worker, He will bring out the pattern of life and character that will be to His own glory....

...As through Jesus we enter into rest, heaven begins here. We respond to His invitation, Come, learn of Me, and in thus coming we begin the life eternal. Heaven is a ceaseless approaching to God through Christ. The longer we are in the heaven of bliss, the more and still more of glory will be opened to us; and the more we know of God, the more intense will be our happiness. As we walk with Jesus in this life, we may be filled with His love, satisfied with His presence. All that human nature can bear, we may receive here. But what is this compared with the hereafter? (White, *The Desire of Ages*, pp. 331, 332)

Chapter 7

THE APOSTOLIC TRADITION

After the death, resurrection, and ascension of Christ into heaven, the community of predominantly Jewish Christians was centered in Jerusalem. However, after the death of Stephen, there arose against the believers in Jerusalem a persecution so relentless that they were all scattered abroad throughout the regions of Judea and Samaria and in the regions beyond.

At that time, it was brought to view that Rome was the metropolis of the world, and the church in Rome was predominantly composed of Gentile converts. After the first Jewish revolt against Rome in AD 66–70, which was militarily crushed by Vespasian and Titus, the Jews were subject to discriminatory taxation (*fiscus judaicus*), which was introduced by Vespasian and increased first by Domitian (AD 81–96) and later by Hadrian (S. Krauss, "Barkokba," Jewish Encyclopedia, 1907, vol. 11, p. 509).

This means the Jews had to pay a penalty tax simply for being Jews. Vespasian abolished the Sanhedrin and the office of the high priest between AD 69–79. The second Jewish revolt, known as the Barkokba Revolt, was staged against the Romans in AD 132–135, and in this revolt, many Roman regions suffered casualties.

However, when Jerusalem was finally captured by Emperor Hadrian, he decided to deal with the Jewish problem in a radical way (Ibid.). He slaughtered thousands of the Jews and took thousands of them as slaves to Rome. He made Jerusalem into a Roman colony, calling it *Aelia Capitolina*. He forbade Jews and Jewish Christians from entering the city (Ibid.). He outlawed the practice of the Jewish religion in general and Sabbath-keeping in particular throughout the empire (Ibid.).

A Mark of Differentiation

At this critical time, for the sake of expedience, many Christians followed the lead of the Bishop of Rome in changing the time and manner of the observance of the two institutions associated with Judaism, namely the Sabbath and Passover. The Sabbath was changed to Sunday and Passover to Easter Sunday in order to avoid even the semblance of Judaism. History confirms that Christians in Constantinople and almost everywhere assembled together on the Sabbath, as well as on the first day of the week. Such custom was never observed in Rome or Alexandria (Socrates, "Ecclesiastical History," book 7, ch. 19).

Please note that anti-Judaism influenced the abandonment of the observance of the Sabbath by Christians at a time when the Jewish religion in general and Sabbath-keeping in particular were outlawed in the Roman Empire. Sun worship influenced the adoption of Sunday observance to show differentiation from the Jews and identification with the customs and cycles of the Roman Empire.

Battle of the Milvian Bridge

When Constantine first became emperor of the west, he faced many problems with other claimants of the throne. One of his great threats was Maxentius, who reigned in Rome. As Constantine was preparing for war against Maxentius in the Battle of the Milvian Bridge, one day, at noon, he saw a cross of light imposed over the sun. Attached to it, in Greek characters Τούτῳ Νίκα, was the saying *in hoc vinci*.

Constantine did not know what the vision meant, and he consulted with many of his men about the meaning of the dream. Each gave him one interpretation or the other, but after meditation, he concluded that since the cross is the symbol of Christianity and the sun the symbol of paganism, a union of the two religions could give him success.

He quickly sought the Christians to ask for their support and pledged to make Christianity a lawful religion. After the war and his victory, Constantine decided to keep his promise by providing full freedom and civil rights to Christians by enacting the Edict of Milan in AD 313.

Compromise and Conformity

After the edict, Constantine began pondering the misfortunes that befell commanders that invoked the help of many different gods and decided to unite all the religions in the empire. However, each religion must first make a compromise. Paganism must sacrifice her identity by submerging it under Christianity, while Christianity had to accommodate certain pagan doctrines, ceremonies, and superstitions. This compromise between paganism and Christianity gave birth to the Roman universal religion, Catholicism.

Among all the pagan festivities that have been foisted upon Christianity by Constantine, there is none that is so clearly marked, so definitely outlined in its origin and enforcement, as the festival of the sun, which is cerebrated on the first day of the week. This is well expressed. It was, indeed, a new phase of paganism, for though the venerable day of the sun had very long been venerated by them and their heathen ancestors, the idea of rest from worldly labor on Sunday and it identification with Christianity was entirely new.

Having reached this compromised with Christians, Constantine, on March 7, 321, passed the first national Sunday law in history. This was the first blue law to be issued by a civil government. Here is the text of Constantine's Sunday Law Decree:

> Let all judges and townspeople and occupations of all trades rest upon the venerable day of the Sun; but let those who are situated in the country, freely and at full liberty, attend to the business of agriculture; because it often happens that no other day is so fit for sowing corn and planting vines; lets the critical moment being let slip, men should lose the commodities granted by Heaven (*The Code of Justinian*, book 111, title 12, law 3)

The fact that Constantine gave it the title **"Venerable Day of the Sun,"** by which it was known in pagan worship, shows that it was never connected with Christian institution, but as a pagan festival. How and when did the church recognized this day as a holy day? It wasn't until several years later, at the Council of Laodicea, that there was a universal acceptance of this compromise by the church leaders. They decided to go along with it, and the Council of Laodicea stated, **"Christians shall not Judaize (keep Sabbath) and be idle on Saturday (Sabbath original), but shall work on that day, but the Lord's Day they shall especially honor."**

The most popular argument used to defend the apostolic origin of Sunday is Christ's resurrection and appearances on the first day of the week. In view of its popularity and importance, careful consideration must be given to this argument. The first question is, What is the meaning of the phrase "first day of the week"?

In the New Testament, the expression "first day of the week" is from the Greek *mai ton sabbaton*. The literal translation is broken down as follows: ***mai*** means **"one,"** ***ton*** means **"of the,"** and ***sabbaton*** means **"sabbaths."** Please note that the Greek word ***sabbaton*** is a plural word, while the Greek singular word is ***sabbatou***. Therefore, when it is expressed according to the original Greek, it is rendered **"one of the sabbaths,"** or **"one of the weeks,"** an expression used in connection with the annual, biblical, Jewish festival called the **Feast of Weeks,** or ***shavout*** (Pentecost).

There are eight texts in the New Testament that mention the first day of the week:

1. **Matthew 28:1**
2. **Mark 16:2**
3. **Mark 16:9**
4. **Luke 24:1**
5. **John 20:1**
6. **John 20:19**
7. **Acts 20:7**
8. **1 Corinthians 16:2**

The Hebrews' Feast

To understand why this rendition was used, there are certain biblical feasts or ceremonies we need to understand. For instance, the feast of **First Fruits** takes place on the sixteenth day of Nisan, two days after **Passover** begins on the twilight of Nisan 14. The Feast of **Unleavened Bread** begins on Nisan 15 and ends on Nisan 21, seven days later. Therefore, on the Nisan 16, both **First Fruits** and **Unleavened Bread** are celebrated.

For clarification purposes, I wish to say that Leviticus does not tell us when the First Fruits was to be celebrated. The Bible only states, **"And he shall wave the sheaf before the LORD, to be accepted for you: on the morrow after the sabbath the priest shall wave it"** (Lev. 23:11). The Sabbath did not only occur on "Saturday" (the seventh day); a sabbath also occurred on Nisan 15, the first day of the **Feast of Unleavened Bread,** when Israel was to do no work but hold a holy convocation or sacred assembly (see v. 7).

Josephus, the Jewish historian, who lived in the first century, wrote, "But on the second day of Unleavened bread, which is the sixteen day of the month, they first partake of the fruits of the earth, for before that day they do not touch them" (*Antiquities of the Jews*, 3.10.15). **First Fruits** marked the start of Israel's grain harvest and the beginning of the count toward the **Feast of Weeks** (Pentecost), Israel's fourth holiday. The Feast of Weeks took place forty-nine days after First Fruits, on the fiftieth day.

"And ye shall count unto you from the morrow after the sabbath, from the day that ye brought the sheaf of the wave offering; seven sabbaths shall be complete: Even unto the morrow after the seventh sabbath shall ye number fifty days; and ye shall offer a new meat offering unto the LORD" (vs. 15, 16).

All the ceremonies of the feast were types of the work of Christ. Christ, the antitypical Lamb of the Passover, was crucified at the time of the morning sacrifice on Nisan 14 (9:00 a.m.) and died right at the time of the evening sacrifice (3:00 p.m.). This day was the sixth day of the week, identified by the Jews as "preparation day." "**And that day was the preparation, and the sabbath drew on**" (Luke 23:54).

On Nisan 15, Christ rested in the tomb through the Sabbath, because it was the first day of the feast of Unleavened Bread, and that Sabbath was a high day (the overlap of the weekly Sabbath and a ceremonial sabbath). Christ the sinless sacrifice (without leaven) was in the tomb unleavened. "**The Jews therefore, because it was the preparation, that the bodies should not remain upon the cross on the sabbath day, (for that sabbath day was an high day,)**" (John 19:31).

Christ resurrected on Nisan 16, the day of First Fruits. Therefore, the Bible says, "**But now is Christ risen from the dead,** *and* **become the firstfruits of them that slept**" (1 Cor. 15:20). "Like the wave sheaf, which was the first ripe grain gathered before the harvest, Christ is the first fruits of that immortal harvest of redeemed ones that at the future resurrection shall be gathered into the garner of God" (White 1911, p. 399).

Speaking about the resurrection of Christ, the Holy Scripture says, "**Now** **upon the first** *day* **of the week…**" (Luke 24:1). According to the original Greek expression, the phrase **"first** *day* **of the week"** is to be rendered as follows "**one of the sabbaths,**" or "**one of the weeks.**"

Therefore, it originally reads "Now upon **one of the sabbaths (or weeks).**" The word "day" was actually added by the Bible translators; it was not originally there, and that was why in all the pertinent Bible references, the word **"day"** is in italics, thus showing that the six references made to the phrase **"first day of the week"** in the gospels were actually referring to the first weeks of Pentecost, not the **first day of the week.**

1 Corinthians 16

It is interesting to note that many Christians refer to 1 Corinthians 16. However, the big question is, Are there any biblical quotations, or a single instance, where a reference to the first day of the week was made besides the Feast of Unleavened Bread or Pentecost? The answer is no! Does the Bible in any way suggest we are to worship on Sunday? Of course, the answer is no, though many Christians commonly cite 1 Corinthians 16 to prove that believers came together for worship on Sunday during apostolic times.

That's why we want to critically look at this chapter and unravel the truth. It's interesting to note that on the second day of the Feast of Unleavened Bread, the first fruits of the year's harvest, a sheaf of barley, was presented before the Lord. What the priest normally did with every Jewish family was step into their field before planting season and set aside a portion of the barley field to be used for the harvest on Nisan 16. This portion of the barley field would be cultivated solely to be used for the first-fruits harvest.

Every Jewish family always prepared to celebrate three festival days in Jerusalem: Passover, Unleavened Bread, and First Fruits, since they were celebrated within one week. Each family always set aside a portion of crops to be marked for first fruits by tying a cord around the area to be harvested for the annual pilgrimage to Jerusalem. Therefore, when the crop was harvested, the family would take it along, with their lambs, to Jerusalem to celebrate the feasts.

At what time or season did Paul instruct the Christians to lay in store as the Lord prospered them? The Bible says:

> **Now concerning the collection for the saints, as I have given order to the churches of Galatia, even so do ye. Upon the first *day* of the week let every one of you lay by him in store, as *God* hath prospered him, that there be no gatherings when I come. And when I come, whomsoever ye shall approve by *your* letters, them will I send to bring your liberality unto Jerusalem.** (1 Corinthians 16:1–3)

Paul was actually making reference to "**one of the weeks**" of **Pentecost** or *Shavout*. How do we prove that Paul was actually referring to Pentecost and not Sunday? The Bible says, **"For I will not see you now by the way; but I trust to tarry a while with you, if the Lord permit. But I will tarry at Ephesus until Pentecost"** (vs. 7, 8).

The above comments are a follow up to the previous ones he made in verses 1 through 3, thus confirming that he was talking about the annual feast of Pentecost and not Sunday. Also, the gathering to which he referred was the first fruits donation that he required every Christian to give according to how the Lord had blessed them. This brings us to the following question: Did the early apostles continue to keep the feast even after the death of Christ?

And Paul *after this* tarried *there* yet a good while, and then took his leave of the brethren, and sailed thence into Syria...And he came to Ephesus...When they desired *him* to tarry longer time with them, he consented not; But bade them farewell, saying, I must by all means keep this feast that cometh in Jerusalem: but I will return again unto you, if God will. And he sailed from Ephesus. (Acts 18:18–21)

The early Christians kept the feast, although in a different way from how it was observed by the Jews in the past. Writing to the Corinthian Christians, Paul admonished, "**Purge out therefore the old leaven, that ye may be a new lump, as ye are unleavened. For even Christ our passover is sacrificed for us: Therefore let us keep the feast, not with old leaven, neither with the leaven of malice and wickedness; but with the unleavened *bread* of sincerity and truth**" (1 Cor. 5:7, 8).

The Christians may not go to their field on the day of First Fruits to harvest barley, but they could in a liberal way engage in the work of charity according to how the Lord had blessed them. Paul used this season to solicit donations for the Christians in Jerusalem who were suffering because of their persecution in the hands of Jews. If the believers were worshiping on Sunday, Paul wouldn't have recommended laying aside one's gift at home, because that is what the original Greek translation said. Why should Christians deposit their offering at home on Sunday if on this day they were gathering for worship? Should not the money have been brought to the Sunday service?

Acts 20:7

"**At Philippi Paul tarried to keep the Passover. Only Luke remained with him, the other members of the company passing on to Troas to await him there. The Philippians were the most loving and truehearted of the apostle's converts, and during the eight days of the feast he enjoyed peaceful and happy communion with them**" (White 1911, pp. 390, 391).

"**And upon the first *day* of the week, when the disciples came together to break bread, Paul preached unto them, ready to depart on the morrow; and continued his speech until midnight. And there were many lights in the upper chamber, where they were gathered together**" (Acts 20:7, 8).

The Greek expression *mai ton sabbaton*, which we saw before, was used here in verse 7. How do we prove that Paul was referring to Pentecost and not Sunday? Please take note of this: "**And we sailed away from Philippi after the days of unleavened bread, and came unto them to Troas in five days; where we abode seven days**" (v. 6).

Paul wrote that they left Philippi after the days of Unleavened Bread. In other words, they were already numbering the seven weeks to the Feast of Weeks (Pentecost). That's why Luke wrote that on **"one of the Sabbaths (or weeks),"** when they came together to break bread, Paul preached unto them, ready to depart the next day. It's interesting to note that **"Sailing from Philippi, Paul and Luke reached their companions at Troas five days later, and remained for seven days with the believers in that place. Upon the last evening of his stay the brethren 'came together to break bread.' The fact that their beloved teacher was about to depart, had called together a larger company than usual"** (White 1911, pp. 390, 391).

The Bible says he continued his speech until midnight. It was a night meeting and was taking place within the weeks of Pentecost. There were many lights in the upper room where they were gathering until midnight. It then suggests that the meeting was not a Sunday morning worship, but an evening meeting which extended to midnight. One would say it is not their custom to break bread every first day of the week. The Bible says, **"And they, continuing daily with one accord in the temple, and breaking bread from house to house, did eat their meat with gladness and singleness of heart"** (Acts 2:46).

The term "breaking bread" is used both for Communion and eating ordinary meals. It was the daily custom of the apostles to break bread in temples and their various homes. In fact, Jesus, who first gave us this institution, celebrated the breaking of bread on Thursday and not Sunday. In the entire Scriptures, there was no express command to break bread on Sunday.

> **And there sat in a window a certain young man named Eutychus, being fallen into a deep sleep: and as Paul was long preaching, he sunk down with sleep, and fell down from the third loft, and was taken up dead. And Paul went down, and fell on him, and embracing *him* said, Trouble not yourselves; for his life is in him. When he therefore was come up again, and had broken bread, and eaten, and talked a long while, even till break of day, so he departed.** (Acts 20:9–11)

If you look at this text carefully, you will notice that the breaking of bread in Acts 20 is merely eating food to satisfy hunger, not Communion. With this understanding comes our next question: If the Bible does not use the phrase **"first day of the week"** to identify Sunday, how is day numbered? **"And it came to pass about an eight days after these sayings, he took Peter and John and James, and went up into a mountain to pray"** (Luke 9:28). **"And after eight days again his disciples were within, and Thomas with** them: ***then* came Jesus, the doors being shut, and stood in the midst, and said, Peace *be* unto you"** (John 20:26).

It's interesting to note that to the Jews, the word "week" means seven. In the Bible the days of the week were called the first day, second day, third day, and so forth. They do not name the weekdays; they numbered them from 1 to 30. The month was a unit of time closely tied to the moon. The only two days of the week that were named were the sixth day (the preparation) and seventh day (Sabbath). The day after the Sabbath in their ceremonial calendar is called the eighth day, and that was why John used eight days to identify the next Sunday, not "first day of the week," because that is not how they number their month.

Let's look at another crucial New Testament passage used to defend the apostolic origin of Sunday. **"I was in the Spirit on the Lord's day, and heard behind me a great voice, as of a trumpet"** (Rev. 1:10). It will be seen that this verse of Scripture, while mentioning the Lord's day, does not in any particular sense indicate which day of the week is the Lord's day. One may read the context of the biblical passage and find no elucidation of the term. Since the term "the Lord's Day" occurs nowhere else in Scripture, it will not help to seek another reference containing it to discover the biblical meaning. We must allow the Bible to interpret itself.

The New Testament specifies the day which is the Lord's Day in two passages of Scripture: **"For the Son of man is Lord even of the sabbath day"** (Matt. 12:8). **"And he said unto them, That the Son of man is Lord also of the sabbath"** (Luke 6:5). Plainly, the Sabbath is the Lord's Day. The Bible itself has cited this fact. God's promise is:

> **If thou turn away thy foot from the sabbath, *from* doing thy pleasure on my holy day; and call the sabbath a delight, the holy of the LORD, honourable; and shalt honour him, not doing thine own ways, nor finding thine own pleasure, nor speaking *thine own* words: Then shalt thou delight thyself in the LORD; and I will cause thee to ride upon the high places of the earth, and feed thee with the heritage of Jacob thy father: for the mouth of the LORD hath spoken *it*.** (Isaiah 58:13, 14)

The City of Antioch

Speaking about the early Christians' Sabbath-keeping practice, the Bible says:

> **Now when Paul and his company loosed from Paphos, they came to Perga in Pamphylia: and John departing from them returned to Jerusalem. But when they departed from Perga, they came to Antioch**

in Pisidia, and went into the synagogue on the sabbath day, and sat down. And after the reading of the law and the prophets the rulers of the synagogue sent unto them, saying, *Ye* men *and* brethren, if ye have any word of exhortation for the people, say on. Then Paul stood up, and beckoning with *his* hand said, Men of Israel, and ye that fear God, give audience. (Acts 13:13–16)

It was in AD 45, in the very city of Antioch, where the believers were first called Christians. That's where these God-fearing Jews and Gentiles appealed to Paul for his words of exhortation. The Bible states, **"And when the Jews were gone out of the synagogue, the Gentiles besought that these words might be preached to them the next sabbath. Now when the congregation was broken up, many of the Jews and religious proselytes followed Paul and Barnabas: who, speaking to them, persuaded them to continue in the grace of God"** (vs. 42, 43).

As you can see, the Bible clearly states that after Paul's message, many Jews and Gentiles who accepted it followed him as he encouraged them to continue in the grace of Christ. In response to Paul's persuasion, these faithful converts appealed to him to come back the next Sabbath. The Gentiles pleaded with Paul to repeat his message next Sabbath. What was the result of this request from the Gentiles? **"And the next sabbath day came almost the whole city together to hear the word of God"** (v. 44). Almost the whole city came to hear the word of God, and these followers were called Christians.

The City of Macedonia of Philippi

What happened in the city of Macedonia of Philippi, where there was no Jewish synagogue? The Bible says, **"And on the sabbath we went out of the city by a river side, where prayer was wont to be made; and we sat down, and spake unto the women which resorted** *thither"* (16:13). What shows that upon his arrival in the city, the apostles waited for the Sabbath before attempting to hold a meeting? **"And from thence to Philippi, which is the chief city of that part of Macedonia,** *and* **a colony: and we were in that city abiding certain days"** (v. 12).

Paul and Barabbas waited until it was Sabbath before they went out to the side of the river, a natural, quiet environment to have fellowship with God, and while they were doing this, a woman named Lydia, who dealt purple fabric, arrived. When Paul began to minister to her, she accepted his message, became his first convert in that city, and welcomed him and Barabbas into that city. The Word of God further reveals this about Paul:

"And Paul, as his manner was, went in unto them, and three sabbath days reasoned with them out of the scriptures" (17:2). "And he reasoned in the synagogue every sabbath, and persuaded the Jews and the Greeks" (18:4).

From our study so far, we've seen that the Creator of all things blessed the Sabbath by making the appointed time a blessing He hallowed/sanctified/set apart the Sabbath day for a distinctive purpose—to focus on what is holy, namely God Himself. Therefore, Christians today are also required to depend fully on God's perfect and finished work of redemption. They need not look unto themselves for their salvation; for it is received as a gift through faith in Jesus Christ, with whom we enter by faith into His rest, of which the Sabbath is a sign.

> *Both creation and redemption were accomplished by God through Christ. Both were finished by Christ on the sixth day. And in both cases, Christ rested on the seventh day*

Both creation and redemption were accomplished by God through Christ. Both were finished by Christ on the sixth day. And in both cases, Christ rested on the seventh day. Therefore, if we must choose a day as Earth Day, there's none better fitted than the Sabbath day of the Bible.

"This time is right upon us. The Spirit of God is being withdrawn from the earth. When the angel of mercy folds her wings and departs, Satan will do the evil deeds he has long wished to do" ("A Time of Trouble," The Review and Herald, September 17, 1901).

"The assertion that God's judgments are visited upon men for their violation of the Sunday-sabbath, will be repeated; already it is beginning to be urged. And a movement to enforce Sunday observance is fast gaining ground" (White 1911, pp. 579, 580).

Chapter 8

HISTORY IN OUTLINE

If all current trends point to an approaching end of our modern age, it is only reasonable to ask, "What kind of end?" How will it happen? How will history terminate? Dear friends, we are not left to mere guesswork regarding these vital questions. History and Bible prophecy combine have provided some startling and sobering insights into this imperative question. Perhaps the most dramatic of all the prophecies to be found in the Bible is the one recorded in Daniel 7.

Daniel 7

As we turn the pages of history backward, we find in the year **550 BC** that Daniel had a dream. He related his dream and gave the sum of the matter. What did Daniel say he saw in vision? **"Daniel spake and said, I saw in my vision by night, and, behold, the four winds of the heaven strove upon the great sea. And four great beasts came up from the sea, diverse one from another"** (vs. 2, 3).

Indeed, this was a strange vision to Daniel. Now we must discover just what these beasts represent. Again, let the Bible provide the answer. **"These great beasts, which are four, *are* four kings, *which* shall arise out of the earth....Thus he said, The fourth beast shall be the fourth kingdom upon earth, which shall be diverse from all kingdoms, and shall devour the whole earth, and shall tread it down, and break it in pieces"** (vs. 17, 23).

Note that **a beast in Bible prophecy represents a kingdom**. From the account of Daniel's testimony, we know that the beasts represent four kingdoms because the angel said so. Therefore, they are not to be taken as literal beasts, but rather kingdoms that acted like beasts.

Troubled Waters and Winds

What does it mean when a beast rises out from the sea in prophecy? Here is what the Bible says, **"And he saith unto me, The waters which thou sawest, where the whore sitteth, are peoples, and multitudes, and nations, and tongues"** (Rev. 17:15). However, did you notice the four winds of heaven were blowing on the sea when these four beasts came up from it? What does that represent? The Bible says, **"Thus saith the LORD; Behold, I will raise up against Babylon, and against them that dwell in the midst of them that rise up against me, a destroying wind"** (Jer. 51:1).

Whenever a beast is seen to be rising out of the sea, it denotes that the power arose in a thickly populated territory, and the winds represent destruction, political commotion, civil strife, or revolution. Therefore, when the winds were blowing on the sea, and the four beasts came up, it implies that the nations of the earth were in a state of war, commotion, and strife, and that was the condition when these four kingdoms came to power. Which kind of beast do we identify as the first beast in this prophetic vision?

The First Beast

"The first *was* like a lion, and had eagle's wings: I beheld till the wings thereof were plucked, and it was lifted up from the earth, and made stand upon the feet as a man, and a man's heart was given to it" (Dan. 7:4). In a prophetic vision, God through the prophet Jeremiah identified the kingdom that constituted the first beast. This is what He said: **"The king of Babylon hath heard the report of them, and his hands waxed feeble: anguish took hold of him, *and* pangs as of a woman in travail. Behold, he shall come up like a lion from the swelling of Jordan unto the habitation of the strong"** (Jer. 50:43, 44).

The first of the four kingdoms was Babylon, described as a lion. Daniel saw in his dream that the lion (Babylon) would get its wings plucked off. In other words, he would no longer be able to move rapidly in its conquest. The reign of Babylon began in 606 BC and terminated in 539 BC. Who do we identify as the second beast in this prophetic vision?

The Second Beast

"And behold another beast, a second, like to a bear, and it raised up itself on one side, and *it had* three ribs in the mouth of it between the teeth of it: and they said thus unto it, Arise, devour much flesh" (Dan. 7:5). We are told in Daniel 5:28 that it was Persia that succeeded Babylon. The second beast is described as a bear. This kingdom was composed of the Medes and Persians. You will notice that this bear is described as raising itself on one side. The Medes rose up first. The bear had three ribs in its mouth. This denotes that Medo-Persia would devour three Babylonian provinces, namely Babylon, Lydia, and Egypt. The reign of Medo-Persia began in 539 BC and terminated in 331 BC. Who do we identify as the third beast in this prophetic vision?

The Third Beast

"After this I beheld, and lo another, like a leopard, which had upon the back of it four wings of a fowl; the beast had also four heads; and dominion was given to it" (v. 6). The third kingdom is likened unto a leopard. This kingdom is Greece, under Alexander the Great. Notice also that this animal has four heads. Upon the death of Alexander, the kingdom was divided among his four generals. Syria and the East were under the head of General Seleucus. Bithynia and Thrace were under General Lysimachus. Egypt was under General Ptolemy. Sotor and Macedonia were under General Cassander. The reign of Greece began in 331 BC and terminated in 168 BC. Who do we identify as the fourth beast in this prophetic vision?

The Fourth Beast

"After this I saw in the night visions, and behold a fourth beast, dreadful and terrible, and strong exceedingly; and it had great iron teeth: it devoured and brake in pieces, and stamped the residue with the feet of it: and it *was* diverse from all the beasts that *were* before it; and it had ten horns" (v. 7). This fourth kingdom is Rome. For 600 years the whole world was under the iron hand of the Roman Empire. The reign began in 168 BC and terminated in AD 476. Rome, the nondescript beast, dominated Western Europe until the middle of the fourth century, when it was overthrown, not by another nation, but from within itself.

The Ten Horns

The Bible says, "And the ten horns out of this kingdom *are* ten kings *that* shall arise" (v. 24). The ten horns refer to the ten European governments that were within the Roman Empire. Instead of another world empire appearing on the scene of history at the fall of the fourth one, prophecy predicted that there would be a division of the Roman Empire, resulting in ten lesser kingdoms. History confirms this portion of Daniel's prophecy.

Dream of Multi-metal Image

It is interesting to note that a similar revelation was also given to a heathen king. It all began about 2,600 years ago. A king had a dream that seemed to answer most of our heart-rending questions. His dream also outlined the history of our world, just as Daniel's dream did.

The story of the dream is well documented. It was written and told by the man who experienced it. He had a dream about a strange image composed of several different metals.

However, as so often happens with all of us, when the king awoke the next morning, he could not remember anything; only the impression remained. He felt sure he saw something of very great importance, but his inability to recall the dream was another thing that troubled him so much. Finally, he resolved to consult with his counselors.

The Confused Magicians

"**Then the king commanded to call the magicians, and the astrologers, and the sorcerers, and the Chaldeans, for to shew the king his dreams. So they came and stood before the king. And the king said unto them, I have dreamed a dream, and my spirit was troubled to know the dream**" (Daniel 2:2, 3). The magicians asked the king to tell them the dream so they could give him the interpretation. "**The king answered and said to the Chaldeans, The thing is gone from me: if ye will not make known unto me the dream, with the interpretation thereof, ye shall be cut in pieces, and your houses shall be made a dunghill**" (v. 5).

Daniel the Prophet

Daniel, though just in his twenties, was already reckoned among the wise men of Babylon and therefore became involved. Hearing the news, he sent word to the palace that, given

> *Daniel, though just in his twenties, was already reckoned among the wise men of Babylon and therefore became involved. Hearing the news, he sent word to the palace that, given time, he would recall the dream and interpret it. The king accepted his offer. This led to one of the most remarkable conferences of all time*

time, he would recall the dream and interpret it. The king accepted his offer. This led to one of the most remarkable conferences of all time.

Daniel sought God in prayer, and the Lord revealed to him in a separate dream the king's dream and its interpretation. Then Daniel went to the king to tell him the dream and its interpretation:

> **Daniel answered in the presence of the king, and said, The secret which the king hath demanded cannot the wise *men*, the astrologers, the magicians, the soothsayers, shew unto the king; But there is a God in heaven that revealeth secrets, and maketh known to the king Nebuchadnezzar what shall be in the latter days. Thy dream, and the visions of thy head upon thy bed, is these.** (Daniel 2:27, 28)

Interpretation of the Dream

Daniel proceeded to recount the dream:

> **Thou, O king, sawest, and behold a great image. This great image, whose brightness was excellent, stood before thee; and the form thereof was terrible. This image's head was of fine gold, his breast and his arms of silver, his belly and his thighs of brass, his legs of iron, his feet part of iron and part of clay. Thou sawest till that a stone was cut out without hands, which smote the image upon his feet that were of iron and clay, and brake them to pieces. Then was the iron, the clay, the brass, the silver, and the gold, broken to pieces together, and became like the chaff of the summer threshing floors; and the wind carried them away, that no place was found for them: and the stone that smote the image became a great mountain, and filled the whole earth"** (Daniel 2:31–35)

By this time Nebuchadnezzar was on the edge of his throne. This was exactly what he saw in his dream. It was incredible. How could this captive Hebrew know what he had dreamed while alone in his bedchamber?

The Head of Gold

Then the king said to Daniel, "Go on, please. What does it mean? What does it have to do with the future?" Calmly and confidently, Daniel went on. The image made up of different metals represented a sequence of kingdoms, and the head of gold equaled Babylon. **"Thou *art* this head of gold"** (v. 38).

Arms of Silver

"And after thee shall arise another kingdom inferior to thee" (v. 39). The chest and arms of silver equaled the kingdom of the Medes and Persians that came to power as Babylon came to an inglorious end.

Belly of Bronze

"[A]nd another third kingdom of brass, which shall bear rule over all the earth" (v. 39). The bronze belly and thighs represented Greece, which defeated the Persian kingdom in the Battle of Arbela in 331 BC.

The Feet of Iron and Clay

"And the fourth kingdom shall be strong as iron: forasmuch as iron breaketh in pieces and subdueth all *things*: and as iron that breaketh all these, shall it break in pieces and bruise" (v. 40). In 168 BC, on June 22, at the Battle of Pydna, the iron legs, a representation of Rome, defeated Greece and became the fourth world empire. The fourth kingdom was not to be succeeded by another global empire. Daniel emphasized this in three different and increasingly significant expressions. First, he said, "The kingdom shall be divided"; second, "the kingdom shall be partly strong and partly weak"; and third, "they shall not cleave one to another, even as iron is not mixed with clay."

It is one of the most fascinating and momentous occurrences in history when the Roman Empire, weakened by internal corruption, was overrun by invading tribes from the north and east and divided into ten separate kingdoms: 1) Anglo Saxons (England), 2) Alemanni (Germany), 3) Visigoths (Spain), 4) Franks (France), 5) Lombards (Italy), 6) Burgundians (Swiss), 7) Suevi (Portugal), 8) Heruli, 9) Ostrogoths, and 10) Vandals. Historians tell us that the division of Rome was completed by AD 476. According to the English historian, Edward Elliott, in his book *Horae Apocalypticae*, the barbaric tribes overran the Roman Empire from AD 351–476.

The Little Horn

The last three kingdoms (Heruli, Ostrogoths, and Vandals) were destroyed, thus paving the way for the rise of the little horn. Describing what transpired, Daniel said, "**I considered the horns, and, behold, there came up among them another little horn, before whom there were three of the first horns plucked up by the roots: and, behold, in this horn *were* eyes like the eyes of man, and a mouth speaking great things**" (7:8).

I want you to carefully note that the little horn power or kingdom is said to have risen from among the other ten kingdoms. These were all a part of Rome, so likewise this last little kingdom also arose from Rome. Now to which power are we referring?

The Eyes of a Man

Here the Bible says the little horn has the eyes of a man. What it means is that it has a man acting and speaking for it. What other things did the Bible say it would do? **"And he shall speak *great* words against the most High, and shall wear out the saints of the most High, and think to change times and laws: and they shall be given into his hand until a time and times and the dividing of time"** (v. 25).

The man that speaks for this little kingdom will speak great words against God. The Bible says that he will kill God's saints and think to change times and laws. God's people shall be under his grip for a time, times, and half a time. Which power is the Bible identifying here?

Iron Dome of Rome

Historians tell us that the division of Rome was completed by AD 476 as it was broken up into ten independent kingdoms. Besides these kingdoms, the Bible says an eleventh kingdom shall emerge, but it will be different from the others. The Bible goes on to show the areas that make this little horn different from the others. It has a single man acting and speaking for it. He speaks words against God, kills His saints, changes times and laws, and rules for a specified set of time. That means this little kingdom is deeply involved in religious matters. Our question now is, Which kingdom arises from Rome and is deeply involved with religion? There is no other kingdom than the papal political kingdom.

The Papacy and the Fall of the Heruli

The Vatican is the only one power in history that fits every detail of the prophetic description. Now let's review the Roman Catholic Church: **"The Pope is the only spokesman for the entire Roman Church"** (*Encyclopedia Britannica*, 1990, vol. 26, p. 950). History records that the Roman papacy wiped out three of the original ten tribes or monarchies of divided Europe. In fact:

> Odovacar, the Heruli leader, had, only sixty-two years before 538, unseated the last emperor of the Western Roman Empire in 476. This led to the fall of that mighty empire. At this pinnacle of power Odovacar had extended his nation into a domain where Emperor Zeno of the Eastern Roman Empire would tolerate no more Usurpation of imperial power by the Heruli.
>
> Empire Zeno commissioned Theodoric, the king of the Ostrogoths, to deal with this Herulian affront to the Empire. Theodoric needed

no urging from Zeno for he, too, was envious of Odovacar's success. Zeno's command was motivated by a second consideration. The Ostrogoths then occupied territory close to Constantinople and the Emperor hoped that by this military distraction he could ease the pressure he received from the Powerful Ostrogoths. The conquest began in 487 and after fifty years the Heruli was quelled, never again to arise as a nation." *(Two Beast, Three Deadly Wound, & Fourteen Popes pg 29-30. Copyright 2001 by Russell and Colin Standish, Published by Hartland Publication, Rapidan, VA USA)*

In AD 487, the first of the three horns had been uprooted. "[By] mid 6th century they [Heruli] vanished from History" (*Encyclopedia Britannica*, 1990 edition, "Heruli").

The Papacy and the Fall of the Vandals

Justinian became emperor of the Eastern Roman Empire in AD 527. A man of religious inclinations, he instituted "holy" wars against the Vandals and Ostrogoths, the latter being under the control of Rome. Procopius, Justinian's campaign historian, revealed that Justinian's motivation was to "protect the Christians." By Christians he meant Catholics. He was protecting the Catholic faith against Arian invaders. The Arians taught that Christ was altogether human and not divine.

The Vandals were a Teutonic race related to the Burgundians and Goths. In AD 439, they captured Carthage, the third most significant city in the Roman Empire and held it until AD 533. In the fifth century, they became the leading maritime power in the Mediterranean.

In AD 455, their king, Gaiseric, conquered Rome and appropriated its wealth to himself. With the exception of one king, Hilderic, the Vandal rulers were Arians. When Hilderic's cousin, Gelimer, imprisoned him, Justinian found an excuse to attack. Under Justinian's general, Belisarius, the Vandals were overthrown in AD 536. After this, the Vandals disappeared from history (*Encyclopedia Britannica*, 1963 edition, vol. 22, p. 973).

The second horn had been uprooted just two years prior to Pope Vigilius exercising the title of Universal Bishop, which emperor Justinian had accorded with the words, **"head of all the holy churches."** Another historical work described the demise of all the Vandals in the following words: they **"disappeared as a mist"** (C.W. Previte Orton, *Shorter Cambridge Medieval History*, 4th ed., vol. 1, p. 189).

The Papacy and the Fall of the Ostrogoths

A third horn, the Ostrogoths, held a stranglehold on Italy, the conquest of which they had made at the behest of the Emperor Zeno in destruction of Heruli tribe. In AD 538, Justinian's force evicted the Ostrogoths from Rome. They were extinct before AD 554 (*Encyclopedia Britannica*, 1990 edition, "Goths").

Today there is not a single bloodline that can be trace back to any of these three kingdoms they were literally eradicated plucked out by the roots. Daniel said, "**And he shall speak [great] words against the most High**" (Dan. 7:25).

Great Words Against the Most High

Indeed, the Roman Church speaks great words against the Lord. For instance, the sovereign of this kingdom exalts himself to God's level. Here is one of the statements made by Pope Leo XIII: "**We hold upon this earth the place God Almighty**" (Encyclical Letter Dated June 20, 1894). Furthermore, the following statement is made in the Catholic National, July 1895: "**The pope is not representative of Jesus Christ, but he is Jesus Christ hidden under a veil of flesh.**"

"In 1335, Bishop Alvarez Pelayo laid down the doctrine that as Christ partook of the nature of God, **so the Pope… is not simply a man, but rather God on earth**" (H.C Lea reported, *Studies in Church History,* p. 389).

"Doctor F. Lucii Ferraris stated, The Pope is of so great dignity and so exalted that he is not a mere man, but as it were God, the vicar of God.... Hence the Pope is crowned with a triple crown, as king of heaven and of earth and of the lower regions" (*Prompta Bibliotheca Canonica Juridica Moralis Theologica,* vol. 4, p. 48).

Change of Times and Laws

"**[H]e shall… think to change times and laws.**" He also attempted to change God's time and laws. Describing what they did in their publication, they state, "**the pope is of so great authority and power that he can modify, explain, or interpret even divine law**" (Lucius Ferraris Prompta Bibliotheca, article PAPA, vol. 6, p. 29).

"**Sunday is a Catholic institution and its claim to observance can be defended only on Catholic principles… from beginning to end of scripture there is not a single passage that warrants the transfer of weekly public worship from the last days of the week to the first**" (Catholic Press, Sydney, Australia, August 1900).

The *Catechismus Romanus* was commanded by the Council of Trent and published by the Vatican Press by order of Pope Pius V in 1566. This catechism for priests says, "it pleased the church of God, that the religious celebration of the Sabbath day should be transferred to the Lord's Day" [*Catechism of the Council of Trent (Donovan's translation, 1867)*, part 3, chap. 4, p. 345).

Of course, the Catholic Church claims that the change of the Sabbath to Sunday was her act and a mark of her ecclesiastical power. The papacy also removed the second commandment, which forbids idol worship. In order to still have ten commandments, they divided the tenth one into two parts.

The Great Persecution

"**[H]e... shall wear out the saints of the most High.**" Daniel stated that they would make war with the saints and kill them. It is true that the Church of Rome has shed more innocent blood than any other institution that has ever existed among mankind. Some historians estimated that more than 100 million people were killed by the Roman Church during the Inquisition. Under a veil of Christianity, she persecuted and killed the true followers of God, as well as others who would not conform to her rule.

Time, Times, and Half a Time

The prophet said they would exercise their power for "**a time and times and the dividing of time.**" A "time" in the Bible is a year, while "times" is plural, thus two years, and "the dividing of time" is half a year. The total is three and a half years. A lunar year is 354 days and a solar year is 365 days. A biblical lunar-solar average year is 360 days. The 1,260 days are made up of forty-two months, which is the same as three and a half years, and these prophetic time periods equal 1,260 literal years. Note that in Bible prophecy, one prophetic day is one literal year. "**And when thou hast accomplished them, lie again on thy right side, and thou shalt bear the iniquity of the house of Judah forty days: I have appointed thee each day for a year**" (Ezek. 4:6; see also Num. 14:34).

> *Under a veil of Christianity, she persecuted and killed the true followers of God, as well as others who would not conform to her rule*

The Papal Captivity

The papacy was to rule supreme for exactly 1,260 years (from 538 to 1798). In 1798, General Berthier of France made his entrance into Rome, abolished the papal government, and established a secular one. The pope was stripped of authority by a civil power and taken into captivity. This was the ultimate humiliation. The pontiff of the Roman Church, Pope Pius VI, was driven out of Rome by the French armies in 1798, and in the following year was taken captive by them and dragged back to France, where he died. General Berthier abolished the papal government.

Summary

Let's quickly summarize Daniel 7. The first beast, the lion, had <u>one head</u>. The second beast, the bear, also had <u>one head</u>; the third beast, the leopard, had <u>four heads</u>; and the fourth beast, the very last beast in Daniel 7, had <u>one head</u> and ten horns.

1. Head One—Babylon
2. Head Two—Medo-Persia
3. Head Three—Grecian Seleucid
4. Head Four—Grecian Cassandra
5. Head Five—Grecian Ptolemy
6. Head Six—Grecian Lysimachus
7. Head Seven—Rome

Speaking further, the angel said to Daniel, "**As concerning the rest of the beasts, they had their dominion taken away: yet their lives were prolonged for a season and time**" (7:12). At the time of the reign of the fourth beast, the dominions of the other three previous beasts had already been taken away, but their lives were still prolonged under the reign of the fourth beast. That is to say, the reign of the Roman Empire was actually the extension of the influence of the other three previous kingdoms that ruled before it. With this understanding, let's move to the book of Revelation.

CHAPTER 9

BREAKING THE SECRET CODE

In Revelation, all the other books of the Bible meet their end. Here is the complement of the book of Daniel. One is a prophecy; the other a revelation. The book that was sealed was not Revelation, but the portion of the prophecies of Daniel relating to the last days. The angel commanded, **"But thou, O Daniel, shut up the words, and seal the book,** *even* **to the time of the end"** (Dan. 12:4).

However, in this chapter, we shall unlock the sealed book, break its secret code, and take a shocking glimpse into the future. Friends, in continuation of our study in Daniel, I wish to ask the following question: What further description was given by John, in the book of Revelation, concerning the seven heads and ten horns of Daniel? **"And there appeared another wonder in heaven; and behold a great red dragon, having seven heads and ten horns, and seven crowns upon his heads"** (Rev. 12:3).

As already established before, the seven heads are derived from the four beasts of Daniel 7—Babylon, Medo-Persian, Greece, and Rome. However, notice specifically the picture displayed in Revelation 12. The seven heads and ten horns were bound together upon one dreadful creature—the dragon. What prophetic symbolism does this portray?

Here the Bible gives us a picture of a beast, a reptile for that matter, with seven heads and ten horns. If you look at the seven heads, they each had a crown. The crown is a symbol of a kingdom. The seven heads are all tied to that reptile; that is to say, they have one thing in common—they derive their lives from the great dragon. Having established this fact, who does this dragon, in a primary sense, represent? **"And the great dragon was cast out, that old serpent, called the Devil, and Satan, which deceiveth the whole world: he was cast out into the earth, and his angels were cast out with him"** (v. 9).

Here the Bible says the dragon is Lucifer, the devil. Thus, God is here telling us that all these kingdoms mentioned by Daniel were satanic kingdoms. Can you see why the prince of Persia was standing in the way of the angel Gabriel when he came to minister to Daniel? Nevertheless, God intervened by sending Michael to help His covering cherub. Here is what Gabriel said he would go back to do after ministering to Daniel: "**Then said he, Knowest thou wherefore I come unto thee? and now will I return to fight with the prince of Persia: and when I am gone forth, lo, the prince of Grecia shall come**" (Dan. 10:20).

He said he would fight with the prince of Persia. This is to confirm to us that these empires are under the control of Satan, who works through principalities and powers in his efforts to destroy the people of God. Now let's look at this scenario in more detail.

Warfare Against the Church

How did Jesus, through John the revelator, describe the spiritual warfare the dragon would wage against God's people through history? Looking at it squarely, what was the main action the dragon took as soon as he noticed he was cast out of heaven?

> **And there appeared a great wonder in heaven; a woman clothed with the sun, and the moon under her feet, and upon her head a crown of twelve stars: And she being with child cried, travailing in birth, and pained to be delivered. And there appeared another wonder in heaven; and behold a great red dragon, having seven heads and ten horns, and seven crowns upon his heads.** (Revelation 12:1–3)

Woman Clothed with the Sun

A woman clothed with the sun was standing on the moon and had a crown of twelve stars on her head. She was pregnant and already in labor, and soon she delivered a man-child who was to rule the nations of the earth with a rod of iron. Many have assumed that this woman is the virgin Mary, but is that true? The Bible says:

> **Before she travailed, she brought forth; before her pain came, she was delivered of a man child. Who hath heard such a thing? who hath seen such things? Shall the earth be made to bring forth in one day?** *or* **shall a nation be born at once? for as soon as Zion travailed, she brought forth her children. Shall I bring to the birth, and not cause to bring forth? saith the LORD: shall I cause to bring forth, and shut** *the womb*? **saith thy God. Rejoice ye with Jerusalem, and be glad with her, all ye that love her: rejoice for joy with her, all ye that mourn for her.** (Isaiah 66:7–10)

Zion and Jerusalem

The woman that brought forth a man child was not Mary, but rather Zion or Jerusalem; but which Jerusalem? Paul says, "**But Jerusalem which is above is free, which is the mother of us all**" (Gal. 4:26). Additionally, "**I John saw the holy city, new Jerusalem, coming down from God out of heaven, prepared as a bride adorned for her husband**" (Rev. 21:2).

The woman represents the Holy City, the heavenly Jerusalem. She, the bride of God, is the one in labor. She has a crown of twelve stars on her head. What do the stars represent? The Bible says, "**The mystery of the seven stars which thou sawest in my right hand... The seven stars are the angels of the seven churches**" (Rev. 1:20).

The Twelve Stars

First of all, I want you to note that in Bible prophecy, a star is a symbol of an angel. Therefore, the crown of twelve stars implies that God, in a spectacular way, would station twelve angels around the Holy City. John states:

> **And there came unto me one of the seven angels which had the seven vials full of the seven last plagues, and talked with me, saying, Come hither, I will shew thee the bride, the Lamb's wife. And he carried me away in the spirit to a great and high mountain, and shewed me that great city, the holy Jerusalem, descending out of heaven from God, Having the glory of God: and her light** *was* **like unto a stone most precious, even like a jasper stone, clear as crystal; And had a wall great and high, [and] had twelve gates, and at the gates twelve angels, and names written thereon, which are** *the names* **of the twelve tribes of the children of Israel: On the east three gates; on the north three gates; on the south three gates; and on the west three gates. And the wall of the city had twelve foundations, and in them the names of the twelve apostles of the Lamb.** (Revelation 21:9–14)

The Church of the Firstborn

The woman was not the virgin Mary, but the Holy City of God, the heavenly Jerusalem. Paul further added, "**But ye are come unto mount Sion, and unto the city of the living God, the heavenly Jerusalem, and to an innumerable company of angels, To the general assembly and church of the firstborn, which are written in heaven, and to God the Judge of all, and to the spirits of just men made perfect**" (Heb. 12:22, 23).

The woman is the general assembly, the church of the firstborn. God is the husband of His church. The church is the bride, the Lamb's wife. Every true believer is a part of the body of Christ. The big question is, Who is her firstborn? **"And again, when he bringeth in the firstbegotten into the world, he saith, And let all the angels of God worship him. And of the angels he saith, Who maketh his angels spirits, and his ministers a flame of fire. But unto the Son** *he saith,* **Thy throne, O God,** *is* **for ever and ever: a sceptre of righteousness** *is* **the sceptre of thy kingdom"** (Heb. 1:6–8).

The woman represents God's children throughout history. In our new covenant dispensation, she represents the church, while her firstborn child is Jesus. We are Jesus' brethren. He is our elder brother. The dragon, in a primary sense, is Satan, the great enemy and persecutor of the church in all ages.

Principalities and Powers

The devil works through principalities and powers in his efforts to destroy the people of God. Therefore, in a secondary sense, the dragon represents all the pagan kingdoms that have made war with God's children through the ages. At the time of John the revelator, the dragon represented Rome. It was through a Roman king, Herod, that the devil sought to destroy Christ as soon as He was born. And it was through the Roman government that nearly all the apostles were put to death.

> *The devil works through principalities and powers in his efforts to destroy the people of God*

"As concerning the rest of the beasts, they had their dominion taken away: yet their lives were prolonged for a season and time" (Dan. 7:12). Rome indeed prolonged the life of the prior fallen kingdoms through her adoption of their religiopolitical cultures. Therefore, the crowns on the seven heads are an indication of the reign of paganism. The ten horns without crowns are the ten barbarian tribes that made up the Roman Empire. The fact that these horns are crownless implies that they've not yet become independent kingdoms. When does the Bible say the horns would become kingdoms?

The Ten Horns

"And the ten horns which thou sawest are ten kings, which have received no kingdom as yet; but receive power as kings one hour with the beast" (Rev. 17:12). The ten horns or kings were to receive power for one hour with the beast. That is to say, after the emergence of the ten kingdoms from the breakup of the old Roman Empire, the next kingdom that came up with the other ten was identified as the beast from whom the Bible warns us not to receive its mark.

The big question is, Who is this beast? A careful study of Daniel 7 reveals that after the emergence of the ten horns, there was another little horn that also emerged. We identified this little horn, earlier in our study, as the papal religious/political kingdom, so with this understanding, let's go to Revelation 13.

Revelation Thirteen

> **And I stood upon the sand of the sea, and saw a beast rise up out of the sea, having seven heads and ten horns, and upon his horns ten crowns, and upon his heads the name of blasphemy. And the beast which I saw was like unto a leopard, and his feet were as *the feet* of a bear, and his mouth as the mouth of a lion: and the dragon gave him his power, and his seat, and great authority.** (Revelation 13:1, 2)

The Composite Beast

The beast has a body like a leopard. You know from Daniel that the leopard represented **Greece**. This means it would take after the culture of **Greece**. The government of **Greece** was built by philosophers. In fact, it was a philosopher who inspired Alexander to be a great hero. Therefore, this government would take after Greek components.

John said the beast had the feet of a bear (the symbol for **Medo-Persia**; it would have **Medo-Persian components**). The **Medo-Persians** are known for one thing: once they made a law, it stuck and could never be reversed. Their power to make laws was considered infallible. That means this beast government would also have the notion of infallibility.

It had the mouth of a lion, which equated to **Babylon**, so this beast government would mimic **Babylon** in some way. **Babylon** was known for making religious laws and forcing people to worship their gods, rather than the God of heaven. Those who said "no" were cast into a burning furnace where they would burn to death (see Dan. 3). As such, this beast government would take after **Babylon** in religious persecution.

The Roman Empire

What did the composite beast specifically inherit from the dragon? The Bible says, **"and the dragon gave him his power, and his seat, and great authority"** (Rev. 13:2b). Having identified the dragon as Pagan Rome in our previous explanation, in Revelation 13 we are told that the dragon gave the composite beast his seat, power, and authority. The big question is when, how, and why?

Seat

First note that after the union of Christianity, Judaism, and paganism was successfully achieved under the reign of Constantine, the religion of the Roman government was changed from paganism to Catholic Christianity.

> The year was A.D 330; some remarkable event of history took place, something that alters the culture and history of Europe forever. Having dominated the mighty Roman Empire for more than four centuries, the centre of the Roman power was move from Rome to Constantinople by Emperor Constantine.
>
> This event of great historic significance set the Papacy on course for ultimate political power. As the Roman Catholic historian and apologist Henry Edward Manning wrote,
>
> But from the hour when Constantine, in the language of the Roman law, "Deo jubente", by the command of God, translated the seat of power to Constantinople, from that moment there never reigned in Rome a temporal prince to whom the Bishops of Rome owed a permanent allegiance. (*The Temporal Power of the Vicar of Jesus Christ*, 2nd ed. London: Burns & Lambert, pp. 11,12)

The removal of the capital of the Roman Empire from Rome to Constantinople in AD 330 left the Church of Rome practically free from imperial power to develop its own form of organization. In Greek, the word for "seat" is *chavrah*, meaning "a region." In this context, it applies to "an administrative division of a country or kingdom." History confirms that the papacy took over the seat of the pagan Roman government. The capital of the papal system was the same as that occupied by the Roman Empire at its height.

Power

We also noted that the dragon gave the first beast its power. When we look up "power" in the Greek, the word used was *dunamis*. This word applies to spiritual power, miraculous ability, and abundance. In other words, the power that was given to the first beast by the dragon was, in this context, a religious power.

History confirms that "Pontifex Maximus" was not only a title, but also a religious office that oversaw all the religious rituals and powers of the

Roman pagan religion. The title "Pontifex Maximus" was held by the head administrator of this religion. Eventually, the Caesars envied this title and office of high spiritual honor and power, so Julius Caesar and Augustus Caesar made the title and office their own, as did later emperors. Thus, they developed a religiopolitical power well-suited to their aim and ambition.

However, in AD 375, Emperor Gratian declined to accept this title, believing its pagan origins unsuited it for a Christian monarch. The bishop of Roma, Pope Damasus I, appropriated the title "Pontifex Maximus" to himself. Therefore, the religiopolitical power of the Caesars passed without objection to the papacy, together with its implied union of church and state, and prophecy was fulfilled.

Authority

The apostle John was also told that the dragon (Rome) gave its "authority" to the first beast (papacy). In Greek, the word used for "authority" here was *exousia*, which means "ability to make law, magistrate—act as a judge and execute judgment." In summary, it means political power. In 538, the emperor of the Eastern Roman Empire, Justinian, bestowed the title "Universal Bishop" upon Pope Vigilius, thus giving him the authority to exercise control in matters of politics and religion over the consciences of people.

The politics of the papacy take place in a framework of an absolute, theocratic, elective monarchy in which the head of the Catholic Church, the pope, exercises ex-officio supreme legislative, executive, and judicial power over the religiopolitical kingdom of the papacy. The term "Holy See" refers to the composite of the authority, jurisdiction, and sovereignty of the pope and his advisers to direct the worldwide Roman Catholic Church.

As a central government of the Roman Catholic Church, the Holy See has a legal personality that allows it to enter into treaties as the juridical source equal to a state and send and receive diplomatic representatives. All this constituted the authority he received from pagan Rome.

The Dark Ages

> Christians were forced to choose either to yield their integrity or accept the papal ceremonies and worship; or to wear away their lives in dungeons or suffer death by the rack, the fagot, or the headsman's ax....
>
> ...The accession of the Roman Church to power marked the beginning of the Dark Ages. As her power increased, the darkness deepened. Faith was transferred from Christ, the true foundation, to

the pope of Rome. Instead of trusting in the Son of God for forgiveness of sins and for eternal salvation, the people looked to the pope, and to the priests and prelates to whom he delegated authority. (White, *The Great* Controversy, p. 54)

Now were fulfilled the words of Jesus: **"And ye shall be betrayed both by parents, and brethren, and kinsfolks, and friends; and *some* of you shall they cause to be put to death. And ye shall be hated of all *men* for My name's sake"** (Luke 21:16, 17). Persecution opened upon the faithful with greater fury than ever before, and the world became a vast battlefield. This was the period about which the Bible speaks: **"And there was given unto him a mouth speaking great things and blasphemies; and power was given unto him to continue forty *and* two months"** (Rev. 13:5).

Forty-two Months

Forty-two months is the same as time, times, and half a time spoken of in Daniel's prophecy and equivalent to three and a half years. Every Jewish year is 360 days, so three and a half years, or 1,260 prophetic days, equals 1,260 literal years. The reason why we are changing the months to their equivalent in days is that when God gave time prophecies, He sometimes equated a day for a year (see Ezek. 4:6; Num. 14:34). Therefore, the Bible predicted that for 1,260 years, the papacy would rule before receiving a mortal wound. Now it's just a matter of basic mathematics.

AD 538 to 1798

In AD 538, the papacy, working through the civil government, broke the power of the Ostrogoths, leaving the pope's claim of ecclesiastical supremacy unchallenged. The Roman Church now exercised her full authority. In 1798, General Berthier of France made his entrance into Rome, abolished the papal government, and established a secular one. The papacy ruled supreme for exactly 1,260 years.

"In **1798** General Berthier made his entrance into Rome, **abolished the papal government**, and established a secular one" (*Encyclopedia Britannica*, 1941 edition). Therefore, through Napoleon, one of the seven heads of the beast received a fatal wound and temporally ceased to exist politically.

The Eighth Beast

1. Babylon
2. Medo-Persia

3. **Grecian Seleucid**
4. **Grecian Cassandra**
5. **Grecian Ptolemy**
6. **Grecian Lysimachus**
7. **Rome**
8. **Papacy**

Where is this beast in the sequence of significant world powers? Here is the clue the Bible gives: "**And the beast that was, and is not, even he is the eighth, and is of the seven, and goeth into perdition**" (Rev. 17:11). The beast that received power with the ten kingdoms is the eighth. Why does the Bible say the papacy is the eighth beast and at the same time of the seven? It's because it took many features from the past pagan kingdoms and maintained the seventh head, which was Rome. It was its connection with Rome, the seventh head, which made it of the seven. The seventh head was known as Rome and was occupied by the papacy all through the Dark Ages. Therefore, when the papacy got the fatal wound in 1798 from Napoleon, prophecy states that it "was not."

The angel said to John, "**And I saw one of his heads as it were wounded to death; and his deadly wound was healed: and all the world wondered after the beast. And they worshipped the dragon which gave power unto the beast: and they worshipped the beast, saying, Who *is* like unto the beast? Who is able to make war with him**" (Rev. 13:3, 4)? The infliction of the deadly wound points to the downfall of the papacy in 1798. However, at some point, the deadly wound would be healed. The angel plainly states that Rome would continue to rule the world until Christ's second coming.

Chapter 10

AMERICA IN PROPHECY

"And I beheld another beast coming up out of the earth; and he had two horns like a lamb, and he spake as a dragon. And he exerciseth all the power of the first beast before him, and causeth the earth and them which dwell therein to worship the first beast, whose deadly wound was healed" (Rev. 13:11, 12). John saw a beast coming up out of the earth, which is the opposite of the sea. In a previous chapter, we found that the water or sea represents **"peoples, and multitudes, and nations, and tongues."**

If the sea represents peoples, multitudes, nations, and tongues, then the earth simply represents a thinly populated area. As we all know, a beast in Bible prophecy represents a kingdom. The great kingdoms that have ruled the world were presented to the prophet Daniel as beasts of prey, rising when **"the four winds of the heaven strove upon the great sea."**

The Silent Seed

However, the beast with two horns like a lamb was seen coming up out of the earth. Like a silent seed, it grew up gradually and peacefully into a mighty nation. Now which nation in our human history was seen rising into power, giving promise of strength and greatness, and attracting the attention of the world around 1798 when the papacy was seen going into captivity?

The application of this symbol points to no other nation but one— the United States of America. Note that in 1798, the very year the pope was taken prisoner by Berthier, the United States of America was recognized by France as a world power. The same power that inflicted the wound upon the papacy acknowledged the US as coming into the scene as a world power.

The Two Lamblike Horns

This beast had two horns like that of lamb. In Bible prophecy, a horn is a symbol of a king or kingdom. When a horn is crowned, it represents a monarchy, but these two little horns had no crowns. This is what the Bible says about this type of imagery: "And *his* brightness was as the light; he had horns *coming* out of his hand: and there *was* the hiding of his power" (Hab. 3:4).

Horns are symbols of power, and the two horns that had an appearance like that of a lamb have particular significance:

> **The lamblike horns indicate youth, innocence, and gentleness, fitly representing the character of the United States when presented to the prophet as "coming up" in 1798. Among the Christian exiles who first fled to America and sought an asylum from royal oppression and priestly intolerance were many who determined to establish a government upon the broad foundation of civil and religious liberty....Republicanism and Protestantism became the fundamental principles of the nation. These principles are the secret of its power and prosperity. The oppressed and downtrodden throughout Christendom have turned to this land with interest and hope. Millions have sought its shores, and the United States has arisen to a place among the most powerful nations of the earth.** (White, *The Great Controversy*, p. 441)

The Dragon and the First Beast

With that said, the angel told John that this unique beast with two horns like a lamb would change. The two-horned beast spoke as a dragon and exercised the power of the first beast. Here we are told that America would speak like the papacy. The founding fathers of this unique nation sought civil and religious freedom. They wanted a government and religion of their choosing.

In the course of time, they discovered that the only way they could have both of these inestimable blessings was to keep church and state separated. The state was to be free and progressive, while the church was also to be free and open to advancing light.

ARTICLE IV, SECTION 4, OF THE CONSTITUTION SAYS, *"The United States shall guarantee to every state in this union a republican form of government."*

That means a representative government—democracy—since every person has a right to choose one's own religion without the price of discrimination.

ARTICLE VI SAYS, *"no religious test shall ever be required as a qualification to any office or public trust under the United States."*

Thus, a citizen was free to profess any religion or no religion. Then to guard the future more securely, certain amendments were added. These are known as the Bill of Rights. The first of these vital amendments reads, *"Congress shall make no law respecting an establishment of religion, or prohibiting the free exercise thereof."*

These men lived with a lingering memory of persecution in Europe. They had an acute recollection and actual observation of the human tendency to civil and religious tyranny, and they wanted to protect the United States. However, the prophecy says, **"he spake as a dragon. And he exerciseth all the power of the first beast before him."** How does a nation speak?

"The 'speaking' of the nation is the action of its legislative and judicial authorities....The prediction that it will speak 'as a dragon,' and exercise 'all the power of the first beast' plainly foretells a development of the spirit of intolerance and persecution that was manifested by the nations represented by the dragon and the leopardlike beast" (White 1911, p. 442).

The Spirit Intolerance

Note that the reference to "nation" in the above quote is in the plural, implying it's not just one nation, but many nations. The final sentence suggests that the dragon, in this context, is a reference to all the nations of our modern world. It also proves that at the time when America was seen speaking like the dragon, the spirit of intolerance and persecution had already pervaded the nations of the earth.

Radical and fundamental Islam no longer tolerates any other person except its fellow, radical Muslims, thus resulting in radical Muslims killing liberal Muslims; Muslims against Christian and Christians fighting Muslims; Muslims hating Jews; Shiites versus Sunnis; Sihks against Hindus; black killing white and white killing black. The spirit of intolerance and persecution is everywhere. It is at this point in human history that the United States of America was seen coming up and exhibiting the same spirit of intolerance and persecution.

The Union of Two

The prophet revealed that the United States would make laws like that of the papacy, which implies that the voice of the papacy, its principles, commands, enforcement, and authority will once again be heard domestically. Religious dogmas will be enforced by civil law; the policeman's power supplants the preacher's persuasion. As religionists lead the government to enact laws to support their plan through legislation, their dogma will be imposed on the people. The Bible further says, **"and he causeth the earth and them which dwell therein to worship the first beast, whose deadly wound was healed"** (Rev. 13:12b).

The United States shall cause the earth's inhabitants to worship the papacy. These two great powers shall unite in purpose to oppose God's law and persecute His people as our sinful planet's history comes to a close. These two powers, the United States and the Vatican, shall dominate and control the inhabitants of the earth. **"And he doeth great wonders, so that he maketh fire come down from heaven on the earth in the sight of men"** (v. 13).

Military Might

The United States is unchallengeable when it comes to military might. They are the great military power in our present time, whose air and ground campaigns start simultaneously. They launch a massive early blitz that always demoralizes their foes, signaling the start of the final march towards war.

They don't plead; they don't beg; you're either with them or not. Their military campaign is their chief instrument of diplomacy. Their war begins with a regime-shattering thunderclap. Their satellite-guided drones, known as joint-direct-attack munitions, find their targets automatically. Unimpeded by smoke or bad weather, their B-2 bombers fly beyond the reach of their foes' guns. Their speed bumps drive around flaming, oil-filled ditches or other defensive measures.

They make fire come down from heaven or the sky through their drones and B-2 and C-130 cargo plane bombs. These are satellite-guided, massive air burst bomb ordnances. These gigantic, nine-and-a-half-ton bombs are packed with the power of a small nuclear weapon, complete with mushroom clouds, and the trump, six-and-a-half-ton daisy cutter creates a feeling of absolute hopelessness in its foes.

Besides this, there were to be wonders in religious realms. The agencies of evil, by their false miracles, will secure the allegiances of the people of the earth.

Mary's Apparition

The Mary phenomenon is just a prelude to what is yet to come. It will be interesting to note that on May 13, 1917, at the Cova da Iria in Fatima,

Portugal, an unusual happening took place. Three children, Francisco, Jacinta, and Lucia, while tending sheep, encountered a flash of lightning that suddenly produced an apparition. Frightened, the children were about to flee when a beautiful young woman encouraged them to stay. She introduced herself as the virgin Mary and explained that she had a mission and message from God for them, the church, and the world.

The Miracle of the Sun

After the word of this appearance spread, there was another appearance that involved a supernatural manifestation. This one occurred on October 13, 1917. The night before, it rained torrentially into the morning. As almost 75,000 people turned out to see the miracle of the apparition, they watched the sun as it began to grow pale, like a silver disk in the sky. Rays of many colors shone from the sun in every direction—red, blue, yellow, green—all the colors of the light spectrum.

Suddenly the sun turned into a giant wheel of fire spinning madly on its axis. It danced wildly in the sky and appeared to break loose from its orbit and fall towards the earth. It turned blue, then yellow. Soon yellow spots began falling all over the landscape. All these were what took place in Fatima in 1917.

Pope John Paul's Dream

It is interesting to note that on May 13, 1981, Pope John Paul II and many other Catholics gathered to celebrate the sixty-fourth anniversary of the apparitions of Mary in Fatima in St. Peter's Square, in the presence of approximately 75,000 people and before the eyes of an estimated 11 million television viewers. The pope spied a little girl wearing a small picture of Mary. Just as he bent from his slow-moving car in a spontaneous gesture to the child, hired assassin Mamet Ali Agca squeezed off two bullets, aimed precisely where his head had been. As two pilgrims fell wounded to the ground, two more shots rang out, this time hitting the pope. His blood stained his white papal cassock.

It took the pope six months to recover, but three months after that injury, he had his first and only vision of the future. Martin Malachi, a Jesuit priest and Vatican insider, confirmed in his book *The Keys of This Blood* that the vision of the pope affirmed his deliverance from the shootings and his adoration of the virgin Mary.

In the pope's vision, he said he was told by God that the event of that supernatural manifestation of the apparition in Fatima would repeat itself just before the second coming of Christ. In a very marked manner, many of the inhabitants of the world will see it and believe. In fact, he was told in a vision that Mary would play the role of John the Baptist and be the very one who would usher in the second coming of Christ.

The Final Deception

The Bible says, **"And deceiveth them that dwell on the earth by *the means of* those miracles which he had power to do in the sight of the beast; saying to them that dwell on the earth, that they should make an image to the beast, which had the wound by a sword, and did live"** (v. 14). The Greek word for "power" in this verse is *didomi*. It is used in various applications and means "adventure, bestow, commit, and deliver."

The word "miracles" in this verse comes from the Greek *semeion*, meaning "miracle, wonder, sign, and token." Please note that the Bible states, ***"those miracles which he had power to do in the sight of the beast."*** The miracle was done in the sight of the beast. It is America's ability to exercise papal authority, jurisdiction, and sovereignty in deceiving the world by persuading them to make an image to the beast.

These miracles will deceive people to believe that the new world order of the antichrist is of the Lord. It is the lying wonders of the devil that will take the world captive. This miracle-working power shall sweep the whole world into the cage of the evil one. Satan has for many years been subtly setting the stage for his last master delusion.

Image of the Beast

America will persuade the inhabitants of the earth to make an image to the first beast. Here is presented a form of government in which the people are given the opportunity to participate (democracy). This is the most striking evidence that the United States is the nation denoted in the prophecy. What is the "image to the first beast," and how is it to be formed?

> **By this first beast is represented the Roman Church, an ecclesiastical body clothed with civil power, having authority to punish all dissenters. The image to the beast represents another religious body clothed with similar power….When the churches of our land, uniting upon such points of faith as are held by them in common, shall influence the State to enforce their decrees and sustain their institutions, then will Protestant America have formed an image of the Roman hierarchy. Then the true church will be assailed by persecution, as were God's ancient people.** (White, *The Spirit of Prophecy*, vol. 4, p. 278)

The United States shall make the image to the first beast. An image is a resemblance, similarity, or likeness. The first beast was a union of church and state—the papacy. The image is the union of church and state.

In John F. Kennedy's address, he solemnly affirmed the following:

> I believe in an America where the separation of church and state is absolute, where no Catholic prelate would tell the president (should he be Catholic) how to act, and no Protestant minister would tell his parishioners for whom to vote; where no church or church school is granted any public funds or political preference...
>
> I believe in an America that is officially neither Catholic, Protestant nor Jewish; where no public official either requests or accepts instructions on public policy from the Pope, the National Council of Churches or any other ecclesiastical source; where no religious body seeks to impose its will directly or indirectly upon the general populace or the public acts of its officials; and where religious liberty is so indivisible that an act against one church is treated as an act against all. ("Transcript: JFK's Speech on His Religion," http://1ref.us/pj, accessed 9/6/2018)

The above affirmation has always been the position of the American founding fathers. However, prophecy reveals that there will be a change to this position in the latter days. In fact, there was an illustrative picture titled "At it Again" by artist Eugene Zimmerman (1862–1935).

> [The] Illustration shows Pope Leo XIII climbing through a ballot box in an effort to get to the a sign on the wall that states "Congress shall make no law respecting an establishment of religion – Constitution"; other notices pasted on a wall in the background state "Every Catholic should rigidly adhere to the teachings of the Roman pontiffs ...", "All Catholics should do all in their power to cause the Constitutions of States and legislation to be modeled in the principles of the true church", and "All Catholics ... must penetrate wherever possible in the administration of civil affairs", each is noted as a "Papal Encyclical". (http://1ref.us/pk, accessed 9/6/2018)

Constitutional Convention

Efforts are already being made to secure an amendment in the American Constitution. The leader of this movement is Mark Meckler. The demand is now being urged in Congress. The following reports show that the call for an amendment to the United States Constitution is getting louder and gaining momentum.

A newly proposed bill in Arkansas calls for a constitutional convention in order to amend the United States Constitution so as to ban same-sex marriage all together across the country. The bill, which was introduced on Thursday by State Senator Jason Rapert (R), would serve as an application to Congress to call a convention "for the purpose of proposing an amendment prohibiting the United States Constitution or the Constitution or Laws of any state from defining or construing the definition of 'marriage' to mean anything other than the union of one man and one woman....

...This week, Sen. Rapert also filed a bill asking for an additional constitutional convention to ban abortion in the U.S. The Senate is scheduled to have a hearing on the same sex marriage bill on February 7th. ("New Bill Proposes Constitutional Convention to Amend Constitution to Ban Gay Marriage All Together," http://1ref.us/pl accessed 9/6/2018)

"For decades now the federal government has grown out of control, it has increasingly abandoned the constitution; it has stiff-armed the states; and ignored its very own citizens," said Abbott.

"Now this isn't a problem caused by just one president and it's not a problem that can be solved by one president. It must be fixed by the people themselves," Abbott continued to a standing ovation. "That is why we need a Convention of States – authorized in the constitution – to propose amendments to fix America."

Successfully assembling a Convention of States would require approval from 34 states. Over the past four decades, more than two dozen states have endorsed the idea at one time or another. ("Texas Governor Abbott Declares Convention Of States An 'Emergency Item," http://1ref.us/pm, accessed 9/6/2018)

All these people zealously striving to change the American Constitution have one thing in common: they all have a mindset of making religious laws.

NOW, THEREFORE, I, GREG ABBOTT, Governor of Texas, pursuant to the authority vested in me by the Constitution and Statutes of the State of Texas, do hereby proclaim Sunday, September 3, 2017, as a Day of Prayer in Texas. I urge Texans of all faiths and religious traditions and backgrounds to offer prayers on that day for the safety of our first responders, public safety officers, and military personnel, healing of individuals, rebuilding of communities and the restoration of the entire region struck by this disaster. (Office of the Texas Governor, http://1ref.us/qk, accessed 10/24/2018)

Power to Give Life

"**And he had power to give life unto the image of the beast, that the image of the beast should both speak, and cause that as many as would not worship the image of the beast should be killed**" (Rev. 13:15). What does it mean to give life to the image of the beast? It means the power to enforce or decree. What threat will hang over those who refuse to conform to this law? The Bible says they will be killed.

Here we are told that laws will be made. "**New controversies will arise. The scenes to be enacted in our world are not even dreamed of. Satan is at work through human agencies. Those who are making so great efforts to change the Constitution and secure a law enforcing the first day of the week little realize what will be the result. A crisis is just upon us**" ("Our Present Duty and the Coming Crisis," The Review and Herald, January 11, 1887).

As **Pope Pius XII** said: "It is reserved then to the public power to deprive the condemned man of the benefit of life, in expiation of his fault, when already, by his crime, he has dispossessed himself of the right to life."

Third, the death penalty can sometimes support the common good. St Thomas Aquinas makes this point: "**Therefore if a man be dangerous and infectious to the community, on account of some sin, it is praiseworthy and advantageous that he be killed in order to safeguard the common good.**" (Catholic Herald, http://1ref.us/ql, accessed 10/24/2018)

"**And he causeth all, both small and great, rich and poor, free and bond, to receive a mark in their right hand, or in their foreheads: And that no man might buy or sell, save he that had the mark, or the name of the beast, or the number of his name**" (vs. 16, 17).

The Mark of the Beast

Please note that there are three important things the Bible warned us not to receive:

1. The mark of the beast
2. The name of the beast
3. The number of the beast

No person will buy or sell without having the mark of the beast. What is the mark of the beast? What did the papacy claim as its mark? This is one of the papal claims: "**Sunday is our mark of authority...The church is** above the Bible, and this transference of the Sabbath observance is proof of that fact" (*Catholic Record Ontario*, September 1, 1923).

Sunday, a Mark of Authority

That was why Pope Francis, who has framed climate change as an urgent moral crisis, has stated that nations must enforce a Sunday rest to care for the environment, as well as the poor. This is contained in his new encyclical *Laudato Si'*. Laid out in the pope's encyclical is one of his chief solutions for addressing climate change, which is mandatory Sunday observance. Politicians and religious teachers alike will assert that the calamities which they consider judgments from God are befalling humanity because of their desecration of Sunday.

> *Politicians and religious teachers alike will assert that the calamities which they consider judgments from God are befalling humanity because of their desecration of Sunday*

Today the Roman Catholic Church and Pope Francis are already packaging Sunday, not only as the solution to climate change, but as a global family day—a day every family on earth will set aside for rest. As Sunday is being pushed today for global legislation, prophecy reveals that it will eventually become a global day of worship, replacing every other day of religious services, including the Sabbath day.

Global Climate Movement

Can you see the reason why it is now proposed by climate movement managers that Earth Day should be observed once a week and that we should give our beautiful planet a day of rest, thus making Earth Day a "green sabbath"?

> It's in this context of the World Environment Day that the UN Environmental Sabbath was launched, specifically designed to fall on the weekend closest to the WED. As one writer for the Earth Island Institute noted, "The approach of world Environment Day also signals the return of another unique UN- conceived event – the Earth Sabbath – a day of worship that transcends denominations and welcomes all faiths to participate in a day of global reverence for the Earth." ("Cult of Green: The United Nations Environmental Sabbath and the New Global Ethic," http://1ref.us/pe, accessed 9/6/2018).

As I am speaking to you right now, there is already agitation around the world for a Sunday law. Activists in twelve different European countries call for a Sunday law (see http://1ref.us/o7, accessed 9/6/2018). **"It should also be noted that in Austria, Germany, Norway, Switzerland, France, Great Britain, Greece, Belgium, Denmark, there is either a total ban on Sunday trading or it is limited depending on the region, the season, or the size of the store"** (FOR, http://1ref.us/qm, accessed 9/24/2018).

An Austria court supports a ban on a Sunday shop opening; retail stores in Austria still stay closed on Sundays (see http://1ref.us/oo, accessed 9/6/2018).

The Reformed Political Party in The Netherlands "wants to close all shops on Sundays in order for citizens 'to go to church'" (http://1ref.us/po, accessed 9/6/2018).

"Poland's president [Andrzej Duda] signed into law a bill that largely limits trade on Sundays, saying it will benefit employees' family life" (http://1ref.us/o1, accessed 9/5/2018).

Stores remained shuttered all over Poland as the country's new Sunday shopping ban went into effect on March 11.

The new law will be introduced in stages. From now until 2019, stores will be allowed to open two Sundays a month. In 2019, they will be allowed to open for only one Sunday. But in 2020, they will be shut every Sunday, with the exception of a few Sundays falling before Easter and Christmas....

...Ironically, **Sunday shopping began only when democracy and capitalism returned to Poland**. Kwiatkowski, who was already an adult when **the Berlin Wall fell**, said that he has missed the old Sunday....

...The partial restoration of Sunday as a day of rest was proposed by *Solidarność* ("Solidarity"), the trade union founded in the Gdańsk shipyard under the leadership of Lech Wałęsa....

...**The new law was put into effect by Poland's ruling *Prawo i Sprawiedliwość* ("Law and Justice") party government and welcomed by the Catholic Church.**

Some Poles object to the measure as bad for business, while others complain that it does not go far enough in freeing Poles from pressures to work on Sunday. (Life Site, http://1ref.us/qn, accessed 10/24/2018)

The new Italian government will introduce a ban on Sunday shopping in large commercial centres before the end of the year.

The right-leaning government will move to tighten trading rules in an effort to defend family traditions, deputy Prime Minister Luigi Di Maio said on Sunday.

Former Italian PM Mario Monti liberalised Sunday trading in 2012 in a bid to spur economic growth during the eurozone crisis. **He faced pressure from the Roman Catholic Church and unions who said the country needed to keep its traditional day of rest.** (Daily Mail, http://1ref.us/qo, accessed 10/24/2018)

Sunday opening hours were liberalised in 2012 by the then prime minister, Mario Monti, in an effort to prompt economic growth, despite pressure from the Catholic church, unions and small businesses to maintain the traditional day of rest....

They propose that trading should be curbed on Sundays and national holidays...

"Blocking [Sunday shopping] at a time when the world is going in a different direction is laughable," said Pugliese. **"I always worry when the state starts telling you when to shop."** (The Guardian, http://1ref.us/qp, accessed 10/24/2018)

Hundreds of people protested shops opening on Sunday in Athens, Greece and blocked access to the shops. Representatives in Hungary passed a controversial Sunday shopping ban affecting large-sized retailers, initiated by Christian Democrats (see http://1ref.us/ot, accessed 9/5/2018).

German unions and churches won the Sunday shopping fight to tighten rules and demanded limits on online shopping on Sundays to protect workers.

"The debate about opening businesses on Sunday - both online and physically - has been raging on recently with major department stores arguing that to compete with internet commerce on such a significant day of shopping, they should have more flexibility to open on the Christian day of rest....

...Religious leaders, meanwhile, argue that the protection of Sunday runs much deeper within the country's values, pointing to Article 139 of the German Constitution, which states: "Sundays and holidays recognized by the state shall remain protected by law as days of rest from work and of spiritual improvement."

The Protestant Church of Germany argues that Sundays belong to the people and not to merchants.

"Therefore the Constitution protects the day," said a church spokesman. (http://1ref.us/o2, accessed 9/5/2018)

The Lord's Day Alliance regards "Sunday as a Mark of Christian Unity" (http://1ref.us/ou, accessed 9/5/2018).

The mark of the beast is Sunday sacredness. Bible prophecy reveals that the United States of America will, through legislative arms, pass a decree enforcing the observance of Sunday as a day of worship, and it will become a global issue.

Rulers of various nations shall, through legislative enactments, enforce Sunday law, and God's people will be brought into great peril. As the nations, in their legislative councils, enact laws to bind the consciences of people in regards to their religious privileges and enforce Sunday observance, bringing oppressive power to bear against those who keep the seventh-day Sabbath, the law of God will, for all intents and purposes, be made void, and national apostasy will be followed by national ruin.

The Number of the Beast

No one will buy or sell except those who have the name of the beast. The name of the beast is a blasphemous name. Receiving it in the hand or forehead indicates that its blasphemous character will be thoroughly developed in the life of men and women who live in these last days.

Can you imagine a recent movie that was released, projecting Jesus as a homosexual? What an abomination! The Bible says, **"Here is wisdom. Let him that hath understanding count the number of the beast: for it is the number of a man; and his number *is* Six hundred threescore *and* six"** (Rev. 13:18).

Men and women, young and old, shall be forced to receive the number of the beast's name. On the pope's official miter has been seen the title **"VICARIOUS FILII DEI,"** which means "Vicar of the son of God." The claim that this is his official title has been stated publicly through the years. The April 18, 1915 issue of *Our Sunday Visitor* states, **"the letter inscribed in the popes MITRE are these VICARIOUS FILII DEI,"** which is Latin for **"Vicar of the son of God."** Adding up the Roman numerals in this title will give us 666.

> V = 5 (there are two, when you count the "U")
> I = 1 (six)
> C = 100 (one)
> L = 50 (one)
> D = 500 (one)
> **Remaining letters = 0**
> 5 + 1 + 100 + 1 + 5 + 1 + 50 + 1 + 1 + 500 + 1 = 666

Do you know that with the advent of modern technology, it's now possible to issue this number to the people?

The Biometric Identification

Biometrics is an automated method of identifying a living person through biological features unique to the individual through the use of advanced computerized recognition techniques. This system was set up by the United States government for security. It was meant to be implemented in the form of a chip-based identification card that includes demographic data and biometric information such as a retinal scan, fingerprints, DNA data, and radio frequency.

This card is not only a means of certifying your identity; it will serve as drivers' license, voters' card, health insurance card, tax payment card, and an international travel document. The card can also be used for financial transactions such as buying and selling. Finally, when the national ID card has been fully implemented, it will be swapped to Radio Frequency Identification (RFID). This is the last phase of the national ID card implementation.

The Real ID Act

That's why various states are already responding to this new order.

> Gov. Wolf on Friday signed legislation **that brings Pennsylvania into compliance with the 2005 Real ID law enacted following the Sept. 11 terror attacks.**…
>
> …The federal Real ID Act stemmed from a recommendation by the 9/11 Commission to help curb the use of fake identification by terrorists by setting minimum standards all states should follow when issuing ID cards such as driver's licenses. Among the things the act required that licenses and IDs have are: full legal name; features that prevent tampering, counterfeiting, or duplication; **and an RFID chip or machine readable technology that can be used to pull up biographical or biometric data.** (The Inquirer, http://1ref.us/o8, accessed 9/5/2018).
>
> **"Under the provisions of this existing bill, everyone will have their biometric data collected, whether they are requesting the REAL ID compliant, or noncompliant,"** Dahm said. **"They will still have their biometric data not only collected, but then shared with other states and potentially, then, with other foreign governments."**
>
> The Federal REAL ID Act was passed in 2005 as a counterterrorism measure, and sets standards for issuing identification.
>
> Fallin signed the bill on March 2, 2017. In a statement, Fallin said she appreciated the work of legislative leaders who crafted the bill and guided it to passage.

"Our citizens let us know they wanted action on this legislation so they wouldn't be burdened with the cost and hassle of providing additional identification to gain entrance to federal buildings, military bases or federal courthouse. And they most certainly didn't want to have to pay for additional identification, such as a passport, in order to board a commercial airliner beginning in January," Fallin said. (http://1ref.us/on, accessed 9/5/2018)

Indian ID System

Many nations are already adopting this new identification system. For instance:

India is building a biometric database for 1.3 billion people — and enrollment is mandatory…

…Into the office stepped Vimal Gawde, an impoverished 75-year-old widow dressed in a floral print sari. **She had come to secure her ticket to India's digital future — to enroll in the identity program, called Aadhaar, or "foundation," that aims to record the fingerprints and irises of all 1.3 billion Indian residents.**

Nearly 9 out of 10 Indians have registered, each assigned a unique 12-digit number that serves as a digital identity that can be verified with the scan of a thumb or an eye. But Gawde came to the enrollment office less out of excitement than desperation: **If she didn't get a number, she worried that she wouldn't be able to eat.**…

…Indians now need an Aadhaar number to pay taxes, collect pensions and obtain certain welfare benefits.…

…Supporters say the program, which has cost about $1 billion to implement, will save multiples of that by curbing tax evasion and ensuring that welfare subsidies are not stolen by middlemen.…

…**This month lawyers opposing Aadhaar argued before the Supreme Court that the government could not force Indians to share their biometric data. Atty. Gen. Mukul Rohatgi countered that Indians had no constitutional right to privacy and could not claim an "absolute right" over their bodies.** (http://1ref.us/oa, accessed 9/5/2018)

UK Biometric System

Biometric banking is very popular in the UK. Less than half of people surveyed trusted fingerprint recognition (see http://1ref.us/o6, accessed 9//2018).

The **horrible attack in Manchester,** coupled with the recent release of **the Department of Homeland Security's Visa Overstay Report, should again force us to ask the question, are we doing everything we can to properly vet those seeking to come to the United States?**

The answer is as clear today as it was two years ago when I served as chief of staff to the secretary of homeland security — more needs to be done. (http://1ref.us/om, accessed 9/5/2018)

JetBlue Facial Recognition

Starting in June, passengers on the airline's Boston-Aruba route will be photographed at the gate prior to boarding and checked against the images on their passport or visa photos on file with U.S. Customs and Border Protection. If the computer affirms their identity, they will be allowed to board without showing any documentation.

JetBlue customers can opt out of using the facial recognition system and scan their boarding passes as usual, if they wish....

..."Self-boarding eliminates boarding pass scanning and manual passport checks. Just look into the camera and you're on your way....

...The partnership with Customs and Border Protection is just part of a broader trend of biometric technology being used at airports to increase security and expedite passengers through the security process. (http://1ref.us/oe, accessed 9/5/2018)

The Final Crisis

As all the nations of the earth today are fast moving toward a cashless society and electronic money system, you can now see how easy a world power, such as the one mentioned in Revelation 13, with this new technology, can identify and enforce its agenda by prohibiting certain people from buying or selling. Inspiration reveals that the church shall appeal to the strong arm of civil power, and by this work, the law shall be invoked against God's people.

Brethren, get ready! From here onward, our world shall not remain the same again. Soon great trouble will arise among the nations—trouble that will not cease until Jesus comes. God has always given people warnings of coming judgment. Those who had faith in His message during their time, and acted out their faith in obedience to His commandments, escaped the judgments that fell upon the disobedient and unbelieving.

The word came to Noah: **"Come thou and all thy house into the ark; for thee have I seen righteous before me"** (Gen. 7:1). Noah obeyed and was saved. The message came to Lot: **"Up, get you out of this place; for**

the Lord will destroy this city" (19:14). Lot placed himself under the guardianship of the heavenly messengers and was saved.

Christ gave the disciples warnings of the destruction of Jerusalem. Those who watched for the signs of the coming ruin and fled from the city escaped. Now we are given warnings of Christ's second coming and the devastation to fall upon the world. Those who will heed the alerts will be saved. No matter which way you look at this thing, a great crisis is stealing upon our planet. This global conflict will be like nothing we've ever dreamed before. Our wildest imaginations have never pictured it.

Chapter 11

THE DRUNKEN HARLOT

And there came one of the seven angels which had the seven vials, and talked with me, saying unto me, Come hither; I will shew unto thee the judgment of the great whore that sitteth upon many waters: With whom the kings of the earth have committed fornication, and the inhabitants of the earth have been made drunk with the wine of her fornication. (Revelation 17:1, 2)

In a prophetic vision, one of the seven angels that had the vials came to John to reveal to him the judgment that would shortly befall the woman that sat on many waters.

One of the Seven Angels

The identification of this angel as one of the seven angels bearing the last plagues of Revelation 15 and 16 implies that the information about to be imparted to John is related to the time and period when they will be poured upon the earth. John wrote, **"And the seventh angel poured out his vial into the air... And the great city was divided into three parts, and the cities of the nations fell: and great Babylon came in remembrance before God, to give unto her the cup of the wine of the fierceness of his wrath. And every island fled away, and the mountains were not found"** (16:17–20). The event that John was called to behold is connected with the judgment of the last days.

The Great City

Who does the angel say the whore is? **"And the woman which thou sawest is that great city, which reigneth over the kings of the earth"** (17:18). A city is a highly organized and integrated association of human beings. John further tells us several things about this whore. She is an international power, since she sits on many waters (see v. 15).

She is not only a city, but one that influences many nations, languages, and peoples. John said the woman is corrupt and commits fornication with the kings of the earth. In Jeremiah 13:27, the idea of nations or systems committing "adultery" is a symbol for turning away from God and the true faith, as well as following after false beliefs. Committing adultery with the kings of the earth shows how worldwide this harlot is.

The Wilderness

"So he carried me away in the spirit into the wilderness: and I saw a woman sit upon a scarlet coloured beast, full of names of blasphemy, having seven heads and ten horns" (v. 3). This sensation of motion was doubtless designed to aid John in making the mental transition from his own time and place to those of the vision. The absence of the definite article in the Greek term for "in spirit" stresses the quality or nature of the experience.

John said he saw the woman in the wilderness. Prophetically, what does a wilderness denote? The Greek word *eremos* means "a desolate place." The related verb used in Revelation 17:16 means "to desolate," "to lay waste," to stripe bare," "to abandon." A wilderness is an uninhabited region where life is sustained only amid difficulty and danger. A wilderness denotes obscurity; a state of concealment and seclusion from the public gaze.

At what time in history did the "woman" phase into the wilderness experience? This question will be answered as soon as we unravel the true identity of the woman. Having said that, who is this shameless seductress who has inflamed the dwellers of earth with her fornication? Who does the angel say the whore is? John, in the Spirit, was taken far into the future to behold the life and activities of the "woman" during this period. The whore has **"a golden cup in her hand full of abominations and filthiness of her fornication: And upon her forehead** *was* **a name written, "MYSTERY, BABYLON THE GREAT, THE MOTHER OF HARLOTS AND ABOMINATIONS OF THE EARTH"** (vs. 4, 5).

Babylon the Great

It is interesting to note that the name "Babylon" was derived from an ancient city. The Bible says:

> **And the whole earth was of one language, and of one speech. And it came to pass, as they journeyed from the east, that they found a plain in**

> the land of Shinar; and they dwelt there. And they said one to another, Go to, let us make brick, and burn them thoroughly. And they had brick for stone, and slime had they for mortar. And they said, Go to, let us build us a city and a tower, whose top *may reach* unto heaven; and let us make us a name, lest we be scattered abroad upon the face of the whole earth" (Genesis 11:1–4).

Their primary desire was to build a gateway to heaven. Unfortunately for them, the Bible continues:

> And the LORD came down to see the city and the tower, which the children of men builded. And the LORD said, Behold, the people *is* one, and they have all one language; and this they begin to do: and now nothing will be restrained from them, which they have imagined to do. Go to, let us go down, and there confound their language, that they may not understand one another's speech. So the LORD scattered them abroad from thence upon the face of all the earth: and they left off building the city. Therefore is the name of it called Babel; because the LORD did there confound the language of all the earth: and from thence did the LORD scatter them abroad upon the face of all the earth. (Genesis 11:5–9)

In their cause of building, God confused their language and scattered them all over the earth, and they abandoned their project and called the uncompleted city "Babel," which means "confusion." The most interesting thing about this uncompleted city was that it was not abandoned permanently. The project was completed by King Nebuchadnezzar. In the Holy Scriptures, we read, "At the end of twelve months he walked in the palace of the kingdom of Babylon. The king spake, and said, Is not this great Babylon, that I have built for the house of the kingdom by the might of my power, and for the honour of my majesty" (Dan. 4:29, 30)?

Wine of Fornication

What evil has this city carried out against God since its completion? "Babylon *hath been* a golden cup in the LORD'S hand, that made all the earth drunken: the nations have drunken of her wine; therefore the nations are mad" (Jer. 51:7). Babylon made the nations of the earth drunk, and this drunkenness has caused many to be mad. If the Bible says she made the inhabitants of the earth drunk with the wine of her spiritual fornication, then what does this wine prophetically represent?

> Stay yourselves, and wonder; cry ye out, and cry: they are drunken, but not with wine; they stagger, but not with strong drink. For the

LORD hath poured out upon you the spirit of deep sleep, and hath closed your eyes: the prophets and your rulers, the seers hath he covered. And the vision of all is become unto you as the words of a book that is sealed, which *men* deliver to one that is learned, saying, Read this, I pray thee: and he saith, I cannot; for it [is] sealed: And the book is delivered to him that is not learned, saying, Read this, I pray thee: and he saith, I am not learned. Wherefore the Lord said, Forasmuch as this people draw near *me* with their mouth, and with their lips do honour me, but have removed their heart far from me, and their fear toward me is taught by the precept of men. (Isaiah 29:9–13)

The wine is spiritual blindness. The Bible says she made the inhabitants of the earth drunk with the wine of her false doctrine. God predicted that this city would be destroyed and never rebuilt, and it came to pass. If ancient Babylon was destroyed permanently, who is the whore spoken of in the book of Revelation?

Early Fathers and Babylon

We all know that the Babylon spoken of here isn't the ancient kingdom of Babylon, for that was destroyed a long time ago. In fact, it is well known that the early church fathers referred to Pagan Rome as Babylon. Therefore, we are talking about spiritual Babylon. Not only is she a city, but the city is apparently the headquarters of a vast international system. Let me prove to you without any doubt that this Babylon is also connected to Christianity. **"And the light of a candle shall shine no more at all in thee; and the voice of the bridegroom and of the bride shall be heard no more at all in thee"** (Rev. 18:23).

Now, to be a "shining light" to the world and have the voice of the "bridegroom," what does it need to proclaim? Jesus Christ of course! The light is the gospel message and Jesus is the Bridegroom. Therefore, this modern Babylon has to be a professing Christian institution. For the candle to shine no more and the voice of the bridegroom to be heard no more, they had to be in effect at some point. Additionally, it must be located in Rome.

There can be only one conclusion: the Vatican is the mysterious Babylon of Revelation. It is this false religious system that has deceived the people of the world and will be destroyed at the time of Armageddon.

> *The wine is spiritual blindness. The Bible says she made the inhabitants of the earth drunk with the wine of her false doctrine*

The Seven Mountains

About which city are we talking here? Here is the clue the Bible gives: **"The seven heads are seven mountains, on which the woman sitteth"** (Rev. 17:9). Which city in the history of nations is built on seven hills? Only one city has, for more than 2,000 years, been known as the City on the Seven Hills. The hills or mountains are:

- **Palatine**
- **Capitoline**
- **Aventine**
- **Caelian**
- **Esquiline**
- **Viminal**
- **Quirinal**

"The historic site of Rome on the famous seven hills… was occupied as early as the Bronze Age" (*Encyclopedia Britannica*, 1990, vol. 10, p. 162). One Catholic resource acknowledges the following: **"it is within the city of Rome, called the city on seven hills, that the entire area of Vatican, State Proper is now confined"** (*The Catholic Encyclopedia*, p. 529). Therefore, the seven heads in this context are the Seven Hills of Rome, and the woman is the Vatican. This is the very city that rules over the kings of the earth.

A Royal Whore

The Vatican is the seat of the Roman Church. John continued, **"And the woman was arrayed in purple and scarlet colour, and decked with gold and precious stones and pearls, having a golden cup in her hand full of abominations and filthiness of her fornication"** (Rev. 17:4). She is rich, for she is decked with gold, precious stones, and pearls. Here we see the woman is connected with royalty since she is dressed in the royal color purple. When the Bible says she was clothed with purple, scarlet, and decked with gold, this is what one Catholic source states: **"The colour for bishops and other prelates is purple, for cardinals scarlet…the pectoral cross should be made of gold and… decorated with gems…"** (*Our Sunday Visitor's Catholic Encyclopaedia*, 1991, pp. 175, 178, 466).

Drunk with Blood

What else did she do? **"And I saw the woman drunken with the blood of the saints, and with the blood of the martyrs of Jesus: and when I** saw her, I wondered with great admiration" (Rev. 17:6). History confirms that the Catholic Church, more than any other institution, has shed much innocent blood of the saints during the Dark Ages. A time when the papal government and church controlled these civil authorities was what John saw and marvelled at when the angel said to him, **"Wherefore didst thou marvel? I will tell thee the mystery of the woman, and of the beast that carried her, which hath the seven heads and ten horns"**. (v. 7).

The Scarlet-colored Beast

The angel said to John that he would tell him the mystery about the woman and the beast that was carrying her. After this, what other revelation did the angel deliver to John? Here is what the Bible says: **"The beast that thou sawest was, and is not; and shall ascend out of the bottomless pit, and go into perdition: and they that dwell on the earth shall wonder, whose names were not written in the book of life from the foundation of the world, when they behold the beast that was, and is not, and yet is"** (v. 8).

The focus here was the beast that **once existed** in the past, yet **is not**, which means it ceased to exist, but the angel told John this beast would eventually come back to life again, and all those whose names are not written in the book of life from the foundation of the world shall wonder after it. There is only one beast that fulfills this prophecy, and that is the first beast of **Revelation 13**. **"And I saw one of his heads as it were wounded to death; and his deadly wound was healed: and all the world wondered after the beast.... And all that dwell upon the earth shall worship him, whose names are not written in the book of life of the Lamb slain from the foundation of the world"** (vs. 3, 8).

From our study of Revelation 13:1–10, we identified this beast as papal Rome. Do you remember the angel told John? **"And the ten horns which thou sawest are ten kings, which have received no kingdom as yet; but receive power as kings one hour with the beast"** (17:12). At first, when the papal political government emerged as a kingdom in AD 538, there were other kingdoms that emerged with it from the ruin of the old Roman Empire. What did the angel say those kingdoms would do? **"These have one mind, and shall give their power and strength unto the beast"** (v. 13).

Romans' Shadow

It continued for 1,260 years, dominating all the kingdoms that once made up the old Roman Empire. Its manner of operation was like an empire. To clarify the definition of an **empire, it is a group of countries or states that are controlled by one ruler or government.**

The fact that the first beast of Revelation 13 had seven heads and ten crowned horns suggests that this papal political kingdom did not only inherit the old Roman Empire but continued its reign in a different dimension. A Catholic historian, Francis P.C. Hays, rightly stated, **"When the Roman Empire became Christian and the peace of the Church was guaranteed, the Emperor left Rome to the Pope, to be the seat of authorities of the Vicar of Christ, who should reign there independent of all human authority, to the consummation of ages, to the end of time"** (*Papal Rights and Privileges*, 1889, pp. 13, 14).

Dr. Alexander C. Flick stated, in confirmation, the following: **"the removal of the capital of the empire from Rome to Constantinople in 330 left the Western Church particularly free from imperial power, to develop its own form of organization. The Bishop of Rome, in the seat of Caesars, was now the greatest man in the West, and was soon forced to become the political as well as the spiritual heads"** (*The Rise of the Medieval Church*, p. 168). The very name "Catholic" means universal, which shows her worldwide influence and therefore goes on to prove that the woman sitting on the beast was actually sitting on all the nations of Western Europe that were once under the reign of old Roman Empire.

The City was Divided

Having identified this woman as the Vatican, with her religious arm being the Catholic Church, there is another point I want you to carefully examine: **"And the great city was divided into three parts, and the cities of the nations fell: and great Babylon came in remembrance before God, to give unto her the cup of the wine of the fierceness of his wrath"** (Rev. 16:19).

The apostle John says Babylon the great city was divided into three parts. You may ask, 'In what way?' Let's look at it from this angle: **"And he cried mightily with a strong voice, saying, Babylon the great is fallen, is fallen, and is become the habitation of devils, and the hold of every foul spirit, and a cage of every unclean and hateful bird"** (18:2). Please note that Babylon is compartmentalized into three sections:

1) The habitation of devils
2) The hold of every foul spirit
3) The cage of every unclean and hateful bird

Shedding more light, John said, **"And I saw three unclean spirits like frogs *come* out of the mouth of the dragon, and out of the mouth of the beast, and out of the mouth of the false prophet"** (16:13). These devils have their habitation in Babylon, and John saw the three divisions operating through the dragon, beast, and false prophets. The dragon fits very well with today's role of the United Nations under the Vatican's global influence on politics, religion, and economy. This corrupt system (spiritual Babylon) uses religion, economy, and political power to achieve its global agenda through the UN.

Also, the false prophet is our modern charismatic/Pentecostal movement of the United States of America. John also saw an unclean spirit like frogs coming out of it. This is the system that will be molded into the image of the beast.

The third unclean spirit was seen coming out from the very beast that was carrying the woman. This beast is divided Western Europe that was once under the reign of the old Roman Empire. All three powers came together under Babylon working to bring about a one world government and the religion of the antichrist.

Heads, Horns, and Crowns

Revelation 12 talks about a beast with seven heads and ten horns. We noticed that the seven heads had **crowns**, while the ten horns had none. Then in 13:1, the horns had **crowns**, but the seven heads had none. In chapter 17, both the heads and horns were identified without crowns. What prophetic significance does all this symbolism imply?

Why is it that the seven heads and ten horns of the beast of Revelation 17 have no crowns on them? The answer is that they've fulfilled their place in prophetic history. As history now repeats before our very eyes, we are not only to look at these prophetic symbols from their historical application, but also consider them in the light of the present, unfolding, world events.

The Two Sitting Position

The woman was seen sitting on **many waters and a scarlet-colored beast.** This differentiation was designed to show the two phases of the **papal government**. We saw before that the water stands for people, tongues, multitudes, and nations. This is the area that has to do with her religious influence. While the beast is the government of papal Rome, a reference to the very geographical region in which the seven hills are located, this very region is not only Europe, but Rome in particular, where we presently have Vatican City.

The angel said to John that at a certain point, the woman was seen sitting on the sea, and later she was found sitting on the beast, and all this took place in the wilderness. One of the big questions many would like to ask is, In what year did the woman and beast go into the wilderness?

Papal Captivity

With the rise to power of Napoleon Bonaparte, the cause of the papacy worsened. Indeed, by 1797, Napoleon had determined to exterminate the papal line. **"One of the first measures of the new government** [The Directory] **was to dispatch an order to Joseph Bonaparte at Rome, to promote, by all the means in his power, the approaching revolution in the papal states; and, above all things, to take care that, at the pope's death** [he was ill, 1797], **no successor should be elected to the chair of St. Peter"** (Hales 1958, pp. 37, 38).

Contrary to all expectations, Pius made a remarkable recovery. With this, Napoleon lost patience. By 1798, he felt it was time for decisive action to implement his will, despite the pope's compliance with the harsh Treaty of Tolentino forced upon him in 1797.

Napoleon Bonaparte sent General Louis Alexander Berthier and his army into Rome, and Berthier abolished **the papal government** on February 10, 1798, and established a secular one. Then Napoleon banished and exiled Pope Pius VI to Valence, France.

> **It was decreed that he should go; an on the morning of the 20th of February [1798], about seven o'clock, he left Rome, accompanied by three coaches of his own suites, and a body of French cavalry, to escort him safely into Tuscany; and on the 25th arrived at Siena, where he was requested to remain till further orders** (Duppa, *A Brief Account of the Subversion of the Papal Government*, pp. 46, 47)
>
> **An earthquake having taken place Siena in the Month of May, the Pope was removed to a Carthusian Covent with two miles of Florence...he was suffered to remain in the Carthusian Covent until the 27 of March, 1799. He was then removed to Parma; from whence he was conducted to Briancon in France, and afterward to Valence, where he died on the 29th of August of the same years.** (ibid., pp. 50–54)

Therefore, the year 1798 marks the beginning of the wilderness experience for both the political arm of Rome and the church herself. Furthermore, the wilderness experience of the Catholic Church came to weigh on her in a profound way, from an entirely unexpected direction—Italy, her own backyard. Here is the background for the harsh and arid realities of life that the Catholic Church faced in Italy in the nineteenth century.

The Roman Question

After the second and final defeat of Napoleon in 1815, Italians found their peninsula divided into duchies and papal states. Metternich, the stout Austrian leader at that time, used to refer to Italy as a mere geographical expression, reflecting the absence of a united country. This odd situation gave rise to nationalistic attempts to unify Italy into one country. However, these attempts were met with much suspicion and resistance from the Catholic Church. Over time, the conviction grew in the minds of these nationalistic leaders that the Catholic Church was indeed a considerable obstacle to the fulfillment of their national aspirations. Nevertheless, the move to unite Italy passed a crucial milestone when the papal states were usurped in 1860 by force.

> **The combined armies of Piedmont and France defeated the Austrians. With the fall of Austria, the Papal States were at the mercy of Piedmont. On September 20, 1860, Victor Emmanuel's army occupies Rome and declared it as capital of Italy. He gave the pope the rights of a sovereign and an annual remuneration of 3.25 million lire. But the Pope did not accept the offer.** (Thomas, *A Compact History of the Popes*, p. 168)

Understandably, the pope refused to recognize the new kingdom and went into voluntary captivity in protest. This unprecedented situation came to be known historically as the Roman Question. It remained unresolved for fifty-nine years, during which time all succeeding popes confined themselves to movement within the few buildings within the Vatican, refusing to leave Rome. Indeed, the Catholic Church in the nineteenth century was engulfed in a very hostile wilderness setting.

The Path to Reconciliation

This unresolved tension between the Italian state and the church had significantly undermined the new country internationally, as well as domestically. A solution for the Roman Question had to be found. Both sides of the conflict were eager for an end to this lingering problem. In 1922, Benito Mussolini, the Duke, and Pope Pius XI came to power.

By 1929, they had at last found a solution to the thorny Roman Question that had lasted fifty-nine years. On February 11, 1929, three sets of documents, known collectively as the Lateran Accords, were signed in Rome at the Lateran Palace by Cardinal Gasparri, representing Pope Pius XI, and Mussolini, representing King Victor Emmanuel III. **"Heal a wound of 59 years"** [*The Catholic Advocate (Australia)*, April 18, 1929, p. 16].

Recovery from this deadly wound has been a slow yet steady process. In 1929, the papacy managed to highly accelerate her recovery efforts when she, together with the kingdom of Italy, signed the Lateran Treaty, which essentially made the pope king of the Vatican city-state. Although this was a far cry from what the Vatican used to be in the Dark Ages, the despotic papacy was pleased to accept the agreement, as it was a necessary step in her recovery.

The Jesuit Connection

It's interesting to note that the Jesuits work like the papacy's secret worldwide police.

> [T]he members of the Jesuit society are divided into four classes the first class as the Professed, the second class as the coadjutors, the third class as the Scholars, and the fourth class as the Novices.
>
> There is also a secret fifth class, known only to the general and a few faithful Jesuits, which, perhaps more than any other contributes to the dreaded and mysterious power of the order. It is composed of laymen of all ranks both educated uneducated, male and female.
>
> From the minister to the humble shoe-boy, these are affiliated connected to the society, but not bound by any vows, they are persons who will make themselves useful, they act as the spies of the order, and observers, often unwittingly, as the tools, and accomplices in dark and mysterious crimes. According to Jesuits Father Francis Pelico who candidly confesses that the many of the illustrious friends of the society remain Occult, and they are obliged to be silent. (Nocolini, *History of the Jesuits: Their Origin, Progress, Doctrines, and Designs*, p. 42)

To many it is extreme to claim that the Jesuits infiltrate Protestant and other churches. Why should it be considered extreme to claim that they would do so? Does not the Bible warn us that we must watch for infiltrators who will creep into the true church of Jesus Christ, "not sparing the flock"? **"For I know this, that after my departing shall grievous wolves enter in among you, not sparing the flock"** (Acts 20:29). **"For there are certain men crept in unawares, who were before of old ordained to this condemnation"** (Jude 4).

Nino Lo Bello, in his book *The Vatican Papers*, published by New English Library in 1982, in the nineteenth chapter entitled "The Vatican's Spy Network," makes it very clear that the Vatican has the most efficient and widespread spy network in the whole world. It outclasses even the Russian KGB. He states that this group of espionage agents came to be known by the popes as Sodalitium Pianum, and it includes every priest, nun, and monk anywhere on earth. He calculates the pope's spy network to be approximately 1.6 million people, consisting of Diocesan priests, regular priests, seminarians, religious males and nuns that are indeed full-time trained agents.

Now what do agents do but infiltrate other organizations, and what organizations would Catholic spies infiltrate if not other churches, especially the true church of Jesus Christ? Permit me to quote a passage from an old, reliable, Protestant classic:

"There was no disguise they (the Jesuits) could not assume, and therefore, there was no place into which they could not penetrate. They could enter unheard the closet of the Monarch, or the Cabinet of the Statesman. They could sit unseen in convocation or General Assembly, and mingle unsuspected in the deliberation and debates.

There was no tongue they could not speak, and no creed they could not profess, and thus there was no people among whom they might not sojourn and no church whose membership they might not enter and discharge. They could execrate the Pope with the Lutheran, and swear the Solemn League with the Covenanter. (Wylie, *The History of Protestantism*, vol. II, p. 412)

The Seven Kings

Now having identified the seven heads as the seven hills of Rome, in this second phase of prophetic meaning, what other prophetic insight did the angel give to John? **"And there are seven kings: five are fallen, and one is,** *and* **the other is not yet come; and when he cometh, he must continue a short space"** (Rev. 17:10). Many scholars have assumed that these kings are not in addition to the heads and mountains, but presumably identified with them. How much distinction, if any, is intended between the kings and the heads? This verse begins with the conjunction "and," which practically tries to put demarcation between the seven heads and seven kings.

It is interesting to note that Revelation 17 does not only take us through the period of the papal wilderness experience, but also highlights some of the key events of prophetic history, some of which will be repeated as the Papacy regains her once lost glory. With that said, the seven kings and ten horns of Revelation 17 may very well point to another application different from the old meaning. Therefore, could these seven kings point to the bishop of Rome, the supreme head of the Catholic Church, as many modern scholars are suggesting?

We all know that the bishop of Rome is not only the spiritual head of the Roman Church, but also the indisputable, temporal king over Vatican City. The wilderness context of Revelation 17:3 demands that we focus attention on the time when the papacy was in the wilderness. This took place when the papacy received the deadly wound in 1798.

Two-phase Experience

As we earlier stated, there are two sitting positions the woman assumed in the wilderness: first, on many waters, and second, on the scarlet-colored beast. Water in prophecy represents multitudes of people and tongues, while the beast represents a kingdom, empire, or state. The book of Revelation reveals that the first sitting position of the woman was on many waters, while the second position was on the beast.

There are two phases of experience of the Church of Rome in the wilderness. The first phase was between 1798 and 1929, a period of 131 years in which the Church of Rome existed without the beast, the political arm of the church, because the beast was deposed by both Napoleon and the Italian state. However, after her political arm was restored, then came the second phase between 1929 and 2013, a period of eighty-four years in which the Church of Rome existed with a political arm—the Vatican.

It is interesting to note that the Italian state recognized the sovereignty of the Catholic Church and regarded it as an independent member of the international community. By this agreement, the church obtained an independent state in Rome with an area of about forty-four hectares (over 100 acres). The Bible says, **"And there are seven kings: five are fallen, and one is,** *and* **the other is not yet come; and when he cometh, he must continue a short space. And the beast that was, and is not, even he is the eighth, and is of the seven, and goeth into perdition"** (Rev. 17:10, 11).

Having established the fact that these seven kings could point to the kings of the Vatican, how do we identify these kings? How are they numbered? The papal procedure in making a king is different from the secular approach. When a pope is appointed, he drops his name, which signifies that he has dropped his personality to take up a new, royal personality. The choice of name signals to the world who the new pontiff wants to emulate, policies he will seek to enact, or even the length of reign. Since 1798, to date there have only been eight pontifical titles adopted by any of the elected popes:

> **PIUS**
> **LEO**
> **GREGORY**
> **BENEDICT**
> **JOHN**
> **PAUL**
> **JOHN PAUL**
> **FRANCIS**

Here are the total numbers of popes that took each title in history:

> **PIUS**—12 POPES TOOK THIS NAME IN HISTORY
> **LEO**—13
> **GREGORY**—16
> **BENEDICT**—16
> **JOHN**—23
> **PAUL**—6
> **JOHN PAUL**—2
> **FRANCIS**—1 **(current)**

Please note that these names are carefully arranged in their order as they reigned. Also, to those of you who may not have been familiar with the history of the popes and may be wondering why Benedict was placed fourth instead of seventh, the reason is that the pope that placed the number on the fourth list is Pope Benedict XV. He was the fourth after 1798, the one on the papal throne when World War I was fought.

Therefore, when Pope Benedict XVI came, he only increased the number of the years of the reign of the fourth pontific title "Benedict." Thus, Pope John Paul remains the seventh. How long did the Bible say the seventh king would rule? **"And there are seven kings: five are fallen, and one is,** *and* **the other is not yet come; and when he cometh, he must continue a short space"** (v. 10).

The seventh king in this line of understanding was Pope John Paul. This is the only name that was adopted so rarely (besides Francis). Other names have higher numbers of popes who adopted them, so when you put together the years of service of each, that would determine how long each title or king has ruled.

At the termination of the reign of the seventh king, the pope that came after the death of Pope John Paul II did not continue with the name

John Paul, but instead took the fourth name in the list, Benedict. It was Pope Benedict XV that placed the name on the fourth list. Therefore, when Cardinal Joseph Ratzinger took the name Benedict XVI, he did not add a new name to the list, but only continued one of the names on the list. He increased the number of years of Benedict, so the reign of Benedict XVI did not only peg the number of kings to seven, but also serve as a transition between the seventh king, John Paul, and the eighth king, Francis.

Five Are Fallen

Why did the Bible say five are fallen, and one is? To answer this question, we must identify the five that are fallen:

> **Pius**
> **Leo**
> **Gregory**
> **Benedict**
> **John**

When the apostle John was taken in a vision to the future, he was taken to the time of the reign of the sixth king (Paul). Why was the angel specific about the sixth king? It was because of the role the sixth king will play in the recovery of the deadly wound of the beast. It is interesting to note that after the emergence of Cardinal Roncali, the Patriarch of Venice, on November 4, 1958, he took the name Pope John XXIII.

On October 11, 1962, he called for the Second Vatican Council but was unable to superintend it. His life was cut short by sudden death. Giovanni Batista Montini, Archbishop of Milan and former Vatican diplomat, was elected as the new pope. He took the name Pope Paul VI and became the sixth king. He turned out to be a history-making pope and superintended the three last sessions of the Vatican II. It was in this council that the agenda for ecumenism and the new world order was officially entrenched into universal papal policy.

Ecumenical Policy

It was in this council that the Church of Rome grouped all the various religions, both Christian denominations and pagan sects, into units. In fact, all the religions were classified and divided into four major groups called provincial globalists. After this was done, the missionary servants of the Roman Church were entrusted with the task of evangelizing each group by way of infiltration to pull each group together under one ecumenical fold that will be subject to the Roman See, when the one world government shall be established. What did the Bible say the eighth beast would do when it comes?

The Eighth Beast

Who is this eighth beast? We identified the eighth beast as the papal religiopolitical kingdom of the Dark Age. In Daniel 7, we saw seven heads, each representing a government:

Kingdoms	Heads	Horns
Babylon	1	0
Medo-Persia	1	0
Greece	4	0
Rome	1	10
Totals	7	10

When the heads of these four kingdoms are added up together, we get seven kingdoms, but when pagan Rome gave its seat, power, and authority to papal Rome, it became the eighth, yet of the seven prophetically. Why was it so? Because the government of papal Rome was not established in a different geographical territory, but rather it maintained the same geographical territory of pagan Rome.

The Great Martyrdom

Having established the fact that the eighth beast is papal Rome, what did the angel say it was doing during those dark years of its spiritual supremacy? **"And I saw the woman drunken with the blood of the saints, and with the blood of the martyrs of Jesus: and when I saw her, I wondered with great admiration"** (v. 6). It is estimated that between 50 and 100 million of God's followers were martyred at the hand of the papacy for daring to stand up to this wicked institution. That is why the Bible says, **"And it was given unto him to make war with the saints, and to overcome them: and power was given him over all kindreds, and tongues, and nations"** (13:7).

The Span of Reign

For how long did the prophecy say the papacy would exercise its power? **"And there was given unto him a mouth speaking great things and** blasphemies; and power was given unto him to continue forty *and* two months" (v. 5). This is the period the Bible says the beast ruled supremely, and it was the world's despot from 538 to 1798 until it was not. The prophecy states, **"The beast that thou sawest was, and is not; and shall ascend out of the bottomless pit, and go into perdition: and they that dwell on the earth shall wonder, whose names were not written in the book of life from the foundation of the world, when they behold the beast that was, and is not, and yet is"** (17:8).

The "is not" period was from 1798 to 2013. Then the prophecy added **"yet is,"** a period when it had fully come out of its political isolation to regain its once-lost global, political domination as it was in the Dark Ages. As stated earlier, there were two sitting positions the woman assumed in the wilderness: first, on many waters, and second, on the scarlet-colored beast. The first phase was between 1798 and 1929, a period of 131 years. The Church of Rome existed without its political arm.

If you apply the prophecy of the seven kings to this first phase, using the pontifical titles, you will notice that Francis is the eighth title, which automatically makes him the eighth king. Though the Bible did not use the term "eighth king," but rather "eighth beast," it therefore shows that the focus of the biblical prophecy is the reemergence of the beast that was not. The appointment of Pope Francis and his new title was designed to show that under him, the eighth beast would fully recover from its deadly wound.

Looking at the time maker, the **second phase of prophetic application spans from 1929 to 2013, a period of eighty-four years in which the Church of Rome existed** with a developing political arm—the Vatican. We also notice that there were seven literal popes who mounted the seat of St. Peter from 1929 to 2013, after which came the eighth pope, who happens to be Francis.

Prophetic Principle

When applying the seven-kings prophetic principle in a literal form, Pope Francis still remains in the position of the eighth, therefore confirming that his reign is the prophetic time maker that is really pointing us to the fullness of time when the eighth beast shall fully emerge from the bottomless pit as predicted by the book of Revelation. Therefore, looking at it from 1929, here are the literal popes that mounted the throne of the papacy:

No	Name	Month	Date	Year	Month	Date	Years
1	PIUS 11	Feb	11	1929	Feb	10	1939
2	PIUS 12	Mar	2	1939	Oct	9	1958
3	JOHN 23	Oct	28	1958	June	3	1963
4	PAUL 6	June	21	1963	Aug	6	1978
5	JOHN PAUL 1	Aug	26	1978	Sep	28	1978
6	JOHN PAUL 2	Oct	16	1978	April	2	2005
7	Benedict 16	April	19	2005	Feb	11	2013
8	FRANCIS 1	Mar	13	2013	-	-	=

In this literal position, the retired Pope Benedict is the seventh on the list, while Pope Francis is the eighth. Friends, we are now living under the reign of the eighth king. We wish to share with you in all humility and seriousness the critical fulfillment of its emergence.

The Signing of Document

"New book says Vatican II key to understanding Pope Francis…[Giacomo] Galeazzi argues that Jorge Mario Bergoglio, the future pope, came of age as a leader in the Catholic Church in the period immediately following the [Vatican II] council. He served as a Jesuit superior in Argentina from 1973 to 1979, when implementing the council's directives was every religious order's top priority" (Crux, http://1ref.us/o9, accessed 9/5/2018).

Pope Francis stated the following as his mission: **"I am Vatican II"** (National Catholic Reporter, http://1ref.us/pp, accessed 9/6/2018).

On October 31, 2017, Catholics and Protestants commemorated the 500th anniversary of the Reformation. **"Somewhere in Pope Francis's office is a document that could alter the course of Christian history**. It declares an end to hostilities between Catholics and Evangelicals and says the two traditions are now 'united in mission because we are declaring the same Gospel'" (Catholic Herald, http://1ref.us/pq, accessed 9/6/2018).

Pope Francis and all Protestant leaders signed the text on October 31, 2017. Although it was a simple act, a work of a few moments, it triggered an epic era of political and religious convulsions that change the religious shape of the world.

"Francis is convinced that the Reformation is already over. He believes it ended in 1999, the year the Catholic Church and the Lutheran World Federation issued **a joint declaration on justification, the doctrine at the**

heart of Luther's protest....In 1999, after extensive talks, **Catholic and Lutheran theologians concluded that the two communions now shared 'a common understanding of our justification by God's grace through faith in Christ'"** (Ibid.).

Since the election of Pope Francis to the papal throne, he has been working aggressively to bring back and unite all Christian faiths with Rome. Revelation 17 foretold that there would be seven kings, followed by an eighth. It is during the reign of this eighth that the papacy will fully recover from its deadly wound inflicted by the French civil power in 1798. Speaking of this event, the apostle John said, **"And the ten horns which thou sawest are ten kings, which have received no kingdom as yet; but receive power as kings one hour with the beast"** (Rev. 17:12).

It is interesting to note that the entire, then-known world had been divided, through the fall of Rome in AD 476, into ten regions or kingdoms. The Bible says that the world's ten rulers shall, in the end times, be of one mind and briefly reign together with the emerging eight beasts.

This shows how unified and planned the strategy is for world dominion. There will be a universal bond, one great harmony, a confederacy of satanic forces. The forces of darkness will unite with human agents who have given themselves into the control of the devil, and the same scenes that were exhibited at the trial, rejection, and crucifixion of Christ will be revived.

"These shall make war with the Lamb, and the Lamb shall overcome them: for he is Lord of lords, and King of kings: and they that are with him *are* called, and chosen, and faithful" (Rev. 17:14). How will the activities of the great whore be brought to an end just before Christ's second coming? **"And the ten horns which thou sawest upon the beast, these shall hate the whore, and shall make her desolate and naked, and shall eat her flesh, and burn her with fire"** (v. 16)

The Bible clearly states that when the kings of the earth finally realize the true nature of the whore, that she has no true connection with God,

> *The forces of darkness will unite with human agents who have given themselves into the control of the devil, and the same scenes that were exhibited at the trial, rejection, and crucifixion of Christ will be revived*

is a deceiver, and has led the entire world into damnation, they will hate her, violently strip her naked, and devour her flesh. However, at first we are told, **"For God hath put in their hearts to fulfil his will, and to agree, and give their kingdom unto the beast, until the words of God shall be fulfilled"** (v. 17).

Chapter 12

THE ABOMINATION OF DESOLATION

From the Mount of Olives, Jesus looked into the future and beheld the storms that were to fall upon the apostolic church. In a few brief utterances of awful significance, He foretold the portion that the rulers of this world would mete out to the church of God. **"Then shall they deliver you up to be afflicted, and shall kill you: and ye shall be hated of all nations for my name's sake"** (Matt. 24:9).

Jesus, in a prophetic warning, tells of a time of trouble that will befall the world just before His second coming:

> **When ye therefore shall see the abomination of desolation, spoken of by Daniel the prophet, stand in the holy place, (whoso readeth, let him understand:) Then let them which be in Judaea flee into the mountains: Let him which is on the housetop not come down to take any thing out of his house: Neither let him which is in the field return back to take his clothes.** (Matthew 24:15–18)

What is an abomination? What does He have in mind? Is it the one associated with His generation, the following generation, or the last days? What is the connection between the prophecies of Daniel and Jesus? Who is **"the reader,"** and what should he or she understand? In what sense should readers **"flee to the mountains"**? Should they obey literally or spiritually?

It is interesting to note that the above warning has three prophetic applications in history:

1. The period within Christ's generation
2. The period that follows Christ's generation
3. The last generation of earth's history

The Abomination of Desolation | 143

What is this prophecy all about, and how does it affect us? These verses come in the context of the Olivet Discourse, which begins with Jesus warning about the destruction of Jerusalem. We shall unravel these periods in this study. First of all, let's start with Christ's immediate generation.

The Period Within Christ's Generation

Jesus had warned His disciple, saying, **"when ye shall see Jerusalem compassed with armies, then know that the desolation thereof is nigh. Then let them which are in Judaea flee to the mountains; and let them which are in the midst of it depart out; and let not them that are in the countries enter thereinto"** (Luke 21:20, 21). He was referring to the destruction of Jerusalem in AD 70 and said that when the followers of Christ were to see the idolatrous standards of the Romans set upon the holy ground, which extended some furlongs outside the city walls, then they should find safety in flight. When the warning signs should be seen, those who would escape must make no delay.

Throughout the land of Judea, as well as in Jerusalem itself, the signal for flight must be immediately obeyed. He who chanced to be upon the housetop must not go down into his house, even to save his most valuable treasures. Those who were working in the fields or vineyards must not take time to return for the outer garment laid aside while they were toiling in the heat of the day. They must not hesitate a moment, lest they become involved in the general destruction.

Nearly forty years after Christ predicted these events, in AD 66, the Jews rebelled against the Roman Empire. Cestus withdrew his troops in October of 67. On May 10, 70, Titus besieged the city, and it fell in August. **"The prophecy which [Christ] uttered was twofold in its meaning: while foreshadowing the destruction of Jerusalem, it prefigured also the terrors of the last great day"** (White 1911, p. 25).

The Period That Follows Christ's Generation

Jesus tells us that our study of the abomination of desolation should be focused on the book of Daniel. The key that unlocks the mystery of this prophetic event is found in the following passage:

> **For the ships of Chittim shall come against him: therefore he shall be grieved, and return, and have indignation against the holy covenant: so shall he do; he shall even return, and have intelligence with them that forsake the holy covenant. And arms shall stand on his part, and they shall pollute the sanctuary of strength, and shall take away**

the daily *sacrifice*, **and they shall place the abomination that maketh desolate.** (Daniel 11:30, 31)

I carefully highlighted seven key points from these two verses:

1) The ships of Chittim, coming against
2) Grievances and indignation against the holy covenant
3) Intelligence with those who forsake the holy covenant
4) Arms standing on their part
5) Pollution of the sanctuary of strength
6) Taking away of the daily sacrifice
7) Setting up the abomination of desolation

As we start to evaluate history in connection with the above prophetic prediction, let's begin with some questions. In prophecy, what do all of the above features represent? What are the ships of Chittim?

The Ship of Chittim

In the Hebrew language, the name "Chittim" referenced all the coasts and islands of the Mediterranean. These coasts and islands are located around the area between the Middle East and North Africa. The power precisely addressed is the Vandals, whose political influence and jurisdiction spread across the Middle East to North Africa, having its base in Carthage, which is present-day Tunisian.

Which power is the subject of this prophecy?

> **The prophetic narrative still has reference to the power which has been the subject of the prophecy from the sixteenth verse; namely, Rome. What were the ships of Chittim that came against this power, and when was this movement made?…Was ever a naval warfare with Carthage as a base of operations, waged against the Roman Empire?… we have but to think of the terrible onslaught of the Vandals upon Rome under the fierce Genseric, to answer readily in the affirmative.** (Smith, *Daniel and Revelation*, p. 281)

Daniel said he saw the ships of Chittim approaching. Before we can correctly understand this inspired statement, it would be better if we first define "ship." In prophecy, what do ships represent? Here is a clue the Bible gives: **"They that go down to the sea in ships, that do business in great waters"** (Ps. 107:23).

> **For in one hour so great riches is come to nought. And every shipmaster, and all the company in ships, and sailors, and as many as trade by sea, stood afar off…And they cast dust on their heads, and cried,**

weeping and wailing, saying, Alas, alas, that great city, wherein were made rich all that had ships in the sea by reason of her costliness! for in one hour is she made desolate. (Revelation 18:17, 19)

It is interesting to note that in the days of old, ships constituted one of the world's major transportation systems, mostly for merchants who used these means for easy conveyance of goods and services. Back then they were the driving force of commerce, and that's why in Bible prophecy ships were employed to represent economy. By extension, the clause "coming against" could mean economic crisis. Particular areas of the Roman Empire were attacked, destroyed, and controlled by barbarian tribes, namely the Vandals, under General Genseric, who also waged economic warfare against Rome. The war brought about the collapse of Rome in AD 476.

He Shall Be Grieved and Return

This may reference the desperate efforts that were made to dispossess Genseric of the sovereignty of the seas—the first by Majorian, the second by Leo—both of which proved to be utter failures. Rome was obliged to submit to the humiliation of seeing its provinces ravaged, and its 'eternal city' pillaged by the enemy" (Smith, p. 282).

Indignation Against the Holy Covenant

What is the meaning of "holy covenant"? And who in the Scriptures is connected with it? Here is what the Bible says:

> **And his father Zacharias was filled with the Holy Ghost, and prophesied, saying, Blessed *be* the Lord God of Israel; for he hath visited and redeemed his people, And hath raised up an horn of salvation for us in the house of his servant David; As he spake by the mouth of his holy prophets, which have been since the world began... To perform the mercy *promised* to our fathers, and to remember his <u>holy covenant</u>; The oath which he sware to our father Abraham. (Luke 1:67–73)**

The holy covenant is the covenant made with Abraham and confirmed in Christ.

> **Now to Abraham and his seed were the promises made. He saith not, And to seeds, as of many; but as of one, And to thy seed, which is Christ. And this I say, *that* the covenant, that was confirmed before of God in Christ, the law, which was four hundred and thirty years**

after, cannot disannul, that it should make the promise of none effect. (Galatians 3:16, 17)

How Was the Covenant Made with the People?

"This *is* the covenant that I will make with them after those days, saith the Lord, I will put my laws into their hearts, and in their minds will I write them" (Heb. 10:16). Christ is called the prince of the covenant, which is God's plan of salvation. By death, Christ confirmed and became the prince of the covenant. That was why the Bible states, **"But now hath he obtained a more excellent ministry, by how much also he is the mediator of a better covenant, which was established upon better promises"** (8:6).

Indignation against the holy covenant represents the hatred against and effort to destroy the divinity of Christ and plan of salvation, as was established under the new covenant. History documents that in the fourth century AD, a controversy arose concerning the teachings of Arius, a Christian priest of Alexandria, Egypt. Please read the following comments regarding the teachings of Arius:

> **It affirmed that Christ is not truly divine but a created being. Arius basic premise was the uniqueness of God, who is alone self-existent and immutable; the Son, who is not self-existent, cannot be God. Because the Godhead is unique, it cannot be shared or communicated, so the Son cannot be God…According to its opponents, especially the bishop Athanasius, Arius teaching reduced the Son to a demigod, reintroduced polytheism, and undermined the Christian concept of redemption since only he who was truly God could be deemed to have reconciled man to the Godhead.** (*Encyclopedia Britannica*, "Arianism")

It is interesting to note that **"The Heruli, Goths, and Vandals, who conquered Rome, embraced the Arian faith, and became enemies of the Catholic Church"** (Smith 1897, p. 281).

Intelligence with Those who Forsake the Holy Covenant

Daniel revealed that pagan Rome had **"intelligence with them that forsake the holy covenant."** Why did Emperor Justinian, the leader of the Roman Empire, join with the church to overthrow the Vandals? The following historical account gives us a clue:

> [I]t was especially for the purpose of exterminating this heresy that Justinian decreed the pope to be the head of the church and the corrector of heretics… And the emperors of Rome, the eastern division of which still continued, had intelligence, or connived with

the Church of Rome, which had forsaken the covenant...The man of sin was raised to his presumptuous throne by the defeat of the Arian Goths, who then held possession of Rome, in A.D.538. (Smith, *Daniel and Revelation*, p. 281)

The Roman Catholic Church (led by the pope) was the very institution that forsook the holy covenant and gave intelligence to the pagan Roman emperor Justinian.

Arm Shall Stand on Their Part

The Roman Empire joined with the Catholic Church, who had forsaken God's holy covenant. The Bible says, **"And arms shall stand on his part."** According to Daniel 11:31, the Roman Empire gave arms to support popery in the overthrow of the barbarian-terrorist tribes. After this, the Bible says, **"and they shall pollute the sanctuary of strength."**

Pollution of the Sanctuary of Strength

What is the sanctuary of strength? Let's first define "sanctuary." God said to Moses, "And let them make me a sanctuary; that I may dwell among them" (Ex. 25:8). The sanctuary is the dwelling place of God. Please note that the sanctuary that Moses built had three compartments: the outer court, Holy Place, and Most Holy Place. You will notice that in the outer court or courtyard, we have two articles of furniture: the altar of sacrifice and laver, which is a basin of water.

The Holy Place

In the first apartment of the sanctuary, there were three articles of furniture. The first was the table of a showbread standing on the north side with twelve loaves of bread arranged in two heaps. They were to be eaten only by the priests. It was called the bread of His presence because it was continually before the face of Jehovah.

On the south was the seven-branched golden candlestick. There were no windows in the tabernacle, and the light of the lamps was never extinguished but shined day and night. Just in front of the inner veil, which separated the Holy Place from the Most Holy Place, stood the golden altar of incense. Upon this altar, the priest burned incense every morning and evening at the hours of prayer.

The Most Holy Place

The Most Holy Place, or the second apartment in the sanctuary, contained only one article of furniture: the ark of the covenant (or testament). This was a wooden chest overlaid with gold. In it were the two tables of stone upon which was written the law of God, the Ten Commandments. At the dedication of Solomon's temple, as the priests where bringing the ark with the law into the sanctuary, there was an expression made: **"Now therefore arise, O LORD God, into thy resting place, thou, and the ark of thy strength: let thy priests, O LORD God, be clothed with salvation, and let thy saints rejoice in goodness"** (2 Chron. 6:41).

"Arise, O LORD, into thy rest; thou, and the ark of thy strength" (Ps. 132:8). On top of the ark was a solid piece of fine gold, and on each end stood the figure of an angel, or covering cherub. These angels stood with uplifted wings, as if in worship. Above the mercy seat, between the cherubim, appeared the supernatural bright light known as the Shekinah glory, the visible manifestations of Jehovah's presence among His people.

***"There was* nothing in the ark save the two tables of stone, which Moses put there at Horeb, when the LORD made *a covenant* with the children of Israel, when they came out of the land of Egypt"** (1 Kings 8:9). Solomon's use of the phrase "the ark of thy strength" was connected to the presence of God's law and bright glory. Since the glory of God dwelt within the Most Holy Place, a thick, elegant curtain or veil was place as a partition between the two apartments. It veiled the priests from the consuming presence of God while they fulfilled their various responsibilities in the Holy Place.

It would seem from the expressions the Lord made to Moses concerning the sanctuary that not only did He show him a mere pattern, but a real sanctuary in heaven. This earthly sanctuary was built after a heavenly one and therefore a shadow of the one that God built Himself. Now here is the lesson God wants us to learn: **"If any man defile the temple of God, him shall God destroy; for the temple of God is holy, which *temple* ye are"** (1 Cor. 3:17).

Here the Bible is saying we are also God's sanctuary and dwelling place. Just as Moses' sanctuary had three apartments, so we have three dimensions. The outer court is our **physical body;** the holy place is **our spirit;** and the most holy place is **our soul,** or more specifically, **our mind and heart**. This is where God's law is written. This is the sanctuary of strength, and strength in this context is the law of God. Under the new covenant, God said, **"For this *is* the covenant that I will make with the house of Israel after those days, saith the Lord; I will put my laws into their mind, and write them in their hearts: and I will be to them a God, and they shall be to me a people"** (Heb. 8:10; see also Obasi, *The Final Atonement*).

Under the new covenant, the law of God is "the strength" written in our hearts, the most holy place of our sanctuary. **"The sting of death *is* sin; and the strength of sin *is* the law"** (1 Cor. 15:56). The Bible says the strength of sin is the law. What is the primary function of the law concerning sin? **"What shall we say then? *Is* the law sin? God forbid. Nay, I had not known sin, but by the law: for I had not known lust, except the law had said, Thou shalt not covet"** (Rom. 7:7).

The angel told the prophet Daniel that the antichrist would strive to **pollute the sanctuary of strength.** Pollution of the sanctuary of strength implies corrupting the human mind with satanic dogmas that undermine faith in God's commandments. They will make war against the commandments of God, which will consummate in them **taking away the daily sacrifice.**

Taking Away of the Daily Sacrifice

The "daily" is mentioned in five verses of the Bible, all in the book of Daniel:

> **Yea, he magnified [himself] even to the prince of the host, and by him the daily *sacrifice* was taken away, and the place of his sanctuary was cast down. And an host was given *him* against the daily *sacrifice* by reason of transgression, and it cast down the truth to the ground; and it practised, and prospered. Then I heard one saint speaking, and another saint said unto that certain *saint* which spake, How long *shall be* the vision *concerning* the daily *sacrifice*, and the transgression of desolation, to give both the sanctuary and the host to be trodden under foot?** (Daniel 8:11–13)
>
> **And arms shall stand on his part, and they shall pollute the sanctuary of strength, and shall take away the daily *sacrifice*, and they shall place the abomination that maketh desolate.** (Daniel 11:31)
>
> **And from the time *that* the daily *sacrifice* shall be taken away, and the abomination that maketh desolate set up, *there shall be* a thousand two hundred and ninety days"** (Daniel 12:11)

A study of this word reveals that it was used in connection with the many activities the priests performed in their daily work in the sanctuary. It is usually used as an adjective before the various, continuous activities within this priestly work, or as an adverb following said activities.

Thus, we see that the reference to **"taking away the daily"** is filled with sanctuary language. The "daily" was conducted in the earthly sanctuary. In the days of old, under the old covenant, the priest would offer a sacrifice in the morning and again in the evening, confessing the sins of Israel and reconciling them with their Maker.

However, under the new covenant relationship in which believers are recognized as priests, the Bible says, **"Let my prayer be set forth before thee *as* incense; *and* the lifting up of my hands *as* the evening sacrifice"** (Ps. 141:2).

> *The sacrifice we offer unto God is our prayers and worship. Taking away the daily sacrifice means taking away our freedom of worshipping God in purity and holiness*

And another angel came and stood at the altar, having a golden censer; and there was given unto him much incense, that he should offer *it* with the prayers of all saints upon the golden altar which was before the throne. And the smoke of the incense, *which came* with the prayers of the saints, ascended up before God out of the angel's hand. (Revelation 8:3, 4)

The sacrifice we offer unto God is our prayers and worship. Taking away the daily sacrifice means taking away our freedom of worshipping God in purity and holiness. This is the final act that breaks the camel's back. This is the very act that prepares the world for the setting up of the abomination of desolation.

Who Does the Bible Call the "Abomination"?

And there came one of the seven angels which had the seven vials, and talked with me, saying unto me, Come hither; I will shew unto thee the judgment of the great whore that sitteth upon many waters: With whom the kings of the earth have committed fornication, and the inhabitants of the earth have been made drunk with the wine of her fornication. So he carried me away in the spirit into the wilderness: and I saw a woman sit upon a scarlet coloured beast, full of names of blasphemy, having seven heads and ten horns. And the woman was arrayed in purple and scarlet colour, and decked with gold and precious stones and pearls, having a golden cup in her hand full of abominations and filthiness of her fornication: And upon her forehead *was* a name written, MYSTERY, BABYLON THE GREAT, THE MOTHER OF HARLOTS AND ABOMINATIONS OF THE EARTH. And I saw the woman drunken with the blood of the saints,

and with the blood of the martyrs of Jesus: and when I saw her, I wondered with great admiration. (Revelation 17:1–6)

In Revelation 17, the abomination of desolation is represented as a woman, a figure which is used in the Scriptures as a symbol of a church or religious entity. A virtuous woman represents a pure church; a vile woman, an apostate church. The abomination of desolation is said to be a harlot, and the prophet beheld her drunken with the blood of saints and martyrs. This, thus described, represents Papal Rome, the apostate church that has so cruelly persecuted the followers of Christ. What is meant by the phrase **"stand in the holy place"**?

The words **"stand up"** are used in Scripture to denote someone is about to rule. **"And a mighty king shall stand up, that shall rule with great dominion, and do according to his will"** (Dan. 11:3). The setting up of the abomination of desolation is the global enthronement of the papacy. Its reign commenced from 538 to 1798.

For the papacy to rule in the holy place, which means to stand in the position of God, signifies that it would receive the worship that only He deserves. The Bible says, **"Let no man deceive you by any means: for *that day shall not come*, except there come a falling away first, and that man of sin be revealed, the son of perdition; Who opposeth and exalteth himself above all that is called God, or that is worshipped; so that he as God sitteth in the temple of God, shewing himself that he is God"** (2 Thess. 2:3, 4). This prediction was fulfilled in the exaltation of the man of sin in AD 538.

The Last Generation of Earth's History

> We have no time to lose. Troublous times are before us. The world is stirred with the spirit of war. Soon the scenes of trouble spoken of in the prophecies will take place. The prophecy in the eleventh of Daniel has nearly reached its complete fulfillment. Much of the history that has taken place in fulfillment of this prophecy will be repeated. In the thirtieth verse a power is spoken of that "shall be grieved, and return, and have indignation against the holy covenant: so shall he do; he shall even return, and have intelligence with them that forsake the holy covenant." [Verses 31-36, quoted.]
>
> Scenes similar to those described in these words will take place. We see evidence that Satan is fast obtaining the control of human minds who have not the fear of God before them. Let all read and understand the prophecies of this book, for we are now entering

upon the time of trouble spoken of: [Daniel 12:1-4, quoted.] (White, *Manuscript Releases*, vol. 13, p. 394).

From the perspective of the last generation, how does prophecy repeat in our time? By looking at previous fulfillments, we can learn more about what to expect in the future. **"The prophecy which He uttered was twofold in its meaning; while foreshadowing the destruction of Jerusalem, it prefigured also the terrors of the last great day**" (White 1911, p. 25).

Referring to the last days, when He would return to the earth the second time, Jesus said:

> **When ye therefore shall see the abomination of desolation, spoken of by Daniel the prophet, stand in the holy place, (whoso readeth, let him understand:) Then let them which be in Judaea flee into the mountains: Let him which is on the housetop not come down to take any thing out of his house: Neither let him which is in the field return back to take his clothes.** (Matthew 24:15–18)

Daniel, the prophet to whom Jesus referred, was told in a vision that the words he had been given were **"sealed till the time of the end"** (Dan. 12:9). **"And from the time *that* the daily *sacrifice* shall be taken away, and the abomination that maketh desolate set up, *there shall be* a thousand two hundred and ninety days"** (v. 11).

This time, which the angel declares with a solemn oath, is not the end of the world or probationary time, but of the prophetic time that led to the opening of the judgment in the autumn of 1844. (see Obasi, *The Final Atonement*). Daniel presents a succession of events, many of which were fulfilled in the past, while those that are yet to come in their order will be in the last remnant of time. The teachings of this book are definite, not mystical or unintelligible. Some prophecies have repeated, thus showing that importance must be given to them. The Lord does not repeat things that are of no great consequence. Yet there can be no definite tracing of the prophetic time. The longest reckoning reaches to the autumn of 1844.

Modern Ships of Chittim

Modern ships of Chittim are the activities of Islamic fundamentalism. In fact, Daniel stated that there would be a crisis in the last moments of earth's history that will spring up from around North Africa and the Middle East, and this crisis would trigger a global economic recession and aim to terrorize and collapse the world system of government. As you can see today, the news media outlets are already broadcasting the activities of these barbaric terrorist groups who are attacking, destroying, and controlling various parts of the globe. This indeed is our modern ship of Chittim that will come against our civilized world.

Modern Indignation Against the Holy Covenant

Today, history is being repeated before our very eyes. The divinity of Christ, His eternal pre-existence and creatorship, Messianic prophecies, miraculous birth, incarnation, gospel of salvation, resurrection, ascension, and second coming are all under attack. Undoubtedly this very attack is in part carried out by Islamic fundamentalists who are not only denying the aforementioned biblical realities, but also killing those who believe in them.

Among the people of God today there's a strong contention about the Godhead. The question is about how many divine beings really compose the Godhead. Is it the Father, Son and Holy Spirit? While this doctrinal agitation is going on among God's people, it is interesting to note that the Vatican has expanded its definition of fundamentalism.

News media have reported the following: "In an unusually strongly worded editorial, L'Osservatore Romano said… **'This, too, is terrorism. It's terrorism to launch attacks on the Church… It's terrorism to stoke blind and irrational rage against someone who always speaks in the name of love, love for life and love for man'"** (Reuters, http://1ref.us/op, accessed 10/24/2018).

Pope Francis said, "freedom of expression has limits" (http://1ref.us/ov, accessed 9/5/2018).

He also said, **"religion should not be confined to 'personal conscience, The orderly development of a civil, pluralistic society requires that the authentic spirit of religion not be confined to personal conscience but that its significant role in the construction of society is recognized,"** said Pope Francis in his remarks to the Italian president (http://1ref.us/ps, accessed 9/6/2018).

"Fundamentalist terrorism is the fruit of a profound spiritual poverty, and often is linked to significant social poverty," the Pope said. **"It can only be fully defeated with the joint contribution of religious and political leaders"** (http://1ref.us/qh, accessed 10/24/2018).

"A fundamentalist group, although it may not kill anyone, although it may not strike anyone, is violent. The mental structure of fundamentalists is violence in the name of God" (http://1ref.us/qi, accessed 10/24/2018).

Arms Shall Stand on Their Part

According to Daniel 11:31, the Roman Empire gave arms to support popery in the overthrow of the barbarian-terrorist tribes. As history repeats in our modern time, what should we expect? In the process of time, the next event will be that the nations will unite with popery to fight the "terrorists." These nations will despise God's holy covenant by enacting laws that are contrary to His laws.

Once the nations fully unite with popery to fight so-called terrorism, who will they persecute next? The Bible says, **"And the dragon was wroth with the woman, and went to make war with the remnant of her seed, which keep the commandments of God, and have the testimony of Jesus Christ"** (Rev. 12:17). **"Then shall they deliver you up to be afflicted, and shall kill you: and ye shall be hated of all nations for my name's sake"** (Matt. 24:9).

Is the idea of giving to popery the backing of the leading nations to fight "terrorists" a reality today? The answer is yes. Take note of this:

> Former Israeli President Shimon Peres has said that **Pope Francis is more powerful than the United Nation** when it comes to advocating peace....
>
> ...Peres said the United Nations and its peacekeepers "do not have the force or the effectiveness of any one of the Pope's homilies, which can draw half a million people just in St Peter's square alone.
>
> "So given that the United Nations has run its course, what we need is an organisation of United Religions," Mr. Peres said, as "the best way to counteract these terrorists who kill in the name of their faith." (Catholic Herald, http://1ref.us/o5, accessed 9/5/2018)

Just as it was specifically for the purpose of exterminating heresy that Justinian decreed the pope to be the head of the universal church and corrector of heretics, so likewise nations will today appropriate to the bishop of Rome arms and armies to fight "terrorists." Soon those arms and armies will turn against God's people who will be labeled "terrorists."

> **Those who honor the Bible Sabbath will be denounced as enemies of law and order, as breaking down the moral restraints of society, causing anarchy and corruption, and calling down the judgments of God upon the earth. Their conscientious scruples will be pronounced obstinacy, stubbornness, and contempt of authority. They will be accused of disaffection toward the government.** (White, *The Great Controversy*, p. 592)

This is the time Jesus warned His followers to flee out of Judea to the mountains. What is Judea? The Bible says, **"Judah was his sanctuary *and* Israel his dominion"** (Ps. 114:2).

Judea here represents the sanctuary, the church that has made merchandise of people's souls and has not warned them of impending doom. What about the mountains? Do you know what the mountains represent? This is what the Bible says:

> **But in the last days it shall come to pass, *that* the mountain of the house of the LORD shall be established in the top of the mountains, and it shall be exalted above the hills; and people shall flow unto it. And many nations shall come, and say, Come, and let us go up to the mountain of the LORD, and to the house of the God of Jacob; and he will teach us of his ways, and we will walk in his paths: for the law shall go forth of Zion, and the word of the LORD from Jerusalem.** (Micah 4:1, 2)

The mountains in this context represent the secret place of God, the court of His presence and divine domain. We are meant to understand that as soon as the abomination of desolation is set up, many faithful souls in these false denominations will separate themselves from those churches in which the love of this world has supplanted love for God and His Word. Many, both of ministers and laypeople, will gladly accept the great truths which God has caused to be proclaimed at this time to prepare people for the Lord's second coming. At that time, people shall flee to this mountain for divine security.

What does it mean when the Bible says that those on the housetop are not going to come down? **"What I tell you in darkness, *that* speak ye in light: and what ye hear in the ear *that* preach ye upon the housetops"** (Matt. 10:27). Those on the housetops are those proclaiming the message of Christ's saving grace. Those in the field are those in the vineyard of service. The time of the great tribulation is when, like the early disciples, we shall be forced to seek refuge in desolate and solitary places of the earth.

> *The followers of Christ must tread the same path of humiliation, reproach, and suffering that their Master trod. The enmity that burst forth against the world's Redeemer would be manifested against all who should believe on His name*

The followers of Christ must tread the same path of humiliation, reproach, and suffering that their Master trod. The enmity that burst forth against the world's Redeemer would be manifested against all who should believe on His name. In every age, His chosen messengers have been reviled and persecuted, yet through their affliction, the knowledge of God has been spread abroad. Likewise, the children of God will in these last days be triumphant.

> **Blessed are they which are persecuted for righteousness' sake: for theirs is the kingdom of heaven. Blessed are ye, when *men* shall revile you, and persecute *you*, and shall say all manner of evil against you falsely, for my sake. Rejoice, and be exceeding glad: for great *is* your reward in heaven: for so persecuted they the prophets which were before you.** (Matthew 5:10–12)

CHAPTER 13

THE KINGS OF THE NORTH AND SOUTH

Troublous times are before us. The world is stirred with the spirit of war. Soon the scenes of strife spoken of in Daniel's prophecies will take place. **"The prophecy of the eleventh chapter of Daniel has nearly reached its complete fulfillment"** (White 1909, p. 14). Much of the history that has taken place in fulfillment of this prophecy will be repeated. There is no time for us now to assimilate with the world. The prophecies of Daniel and John are to be understood.

> *Troublous times are before us. The world is stirred with the spirit of war. Soon the scenes of strife spoken of in Daniel's prophecies will take place*

What event did Daniel say will mark the time of the end? "And at the time of the end shall the king of the south push at him: and the king of the north shall come against him like a whirlwind, with chariots, and with horsemen, and with many ships; and he shall enter into the countries, and shall overflow and pass over" (Daniel 11:40). The expression **"time of the end"** appears only in the book of Daniel. The context in each case indicates that it refers to the final period of history before the second coming of Christ. Daniel said that at that time, **"many shall run to and fro, and knowledge shall be increased"** (12:4). Inspiration reveals that **"since 1798 the book of Daniel has been unsealed, knowledge of the prophecies has increased, and many have proclaimed the solemn message of the judgment near"** (White 1911, p. 356).

King of the North

Now the big question is who is this king of the north at the time of the end? From Judea's point of view, Babylon is considered to be on the side of the north, but prophetically, in this time of the end, the focus is on spiritual Babylon. Babylon is the code name for papal Rome, in concert with the world political powers who are seeking to establish a one world system of government and religion.

The Bible states that at that time of the end, the king of the south will push at the king of the north. From Judea's point of view, the south refers to the arid desert towards Egypt. Prophetically, which nation or power fulfills these criteria?

If the north represents modern Babylon, the papacy, and her allies, then Egypt, the opposing power, can spiritually be referred to as all the powers that have ever opposed the papacy. The first nation to have publicly opposed the papacy, leading even to the deposition of the pope in 1798, is France. Giving further prophetic clarification about this nation, John leads our minds to the story of the two witnesses in Revelation 11.

The Two Witness

> **And I will give *power* unto my two witnesses, and they shall prophesy a thousand two hundred *and* threescore days, clothed in sackcloth.... And when they shall have finished their testimony, the beast that ascendeth out of the bottomless pit shall make war against them, and shall overcome them, and kill them. And their dead bodies *shall lie in the street of* the great city, which spiritually is called Sodom and Egypt, where also our Lord was crucified.** (Revelation 11:3, 7, 8)

From our study of both Daniel and Revelation, we noted that it was the papacy that for 1,260 years persecuted the followers of Christ, and this period was known in history as the Dark Ages when the common people were not permitted to read the Bible. The only people who had access to the Bible were the bishops and prelates. Both the Old and New Testaments become the only witnesses that have the access to speak directly to these cruel men. Their witness ended shortly before 1798.

Spiritual Sodom

The following inspired account, which ties to the passage above, has this to say:

> "The great city" in whose streets the witnesses are slain, and where their dead bodies lie, is "spiritually" Egypt. Of all nations presented

in Bible history, Egypt most boldly denied the existence of the living God and resisted his commands. No monarch ever ventured upon more open and highhanded rebellion against the authority of Heaven than did the king of Egypt. When the message was brought him by Moses, in the name of the Lord, Pharaoh proudly answered, "Who is Jehovah, that I should hearken unto his voice to let Israel go? I know not Jehovah, and moreover I will not let Israel go." Exodus 5:2, A.R.V. This is atheism, and the nation represented by Egypt would give voice to a similar denial of the claims of the living God and would manifest a like spirit of unbelief and defiance. "The great city" is also compared, "spiritually," to Sodom. The corruption of Sodom in breaking the law of God was especially manifested in licentiousness. And this sin was also to be a pre-eminent characteristic of the nation that should fulfill the specifications of this scripture. (White, *The Great Controversy*, p. 269)

Proscription of the Bible

This prophecy has received a most exact and striking fulfillment in the history of France. During the Revolution, in 1793, **"the world for the first time heard an assembly of men, born and educated in civilization, and assuming the right to govern one of the finest European nations, uplift their united voice to deny the most solemn truth which man's soul receives, and renounce unanimously the belief and worship of a Deity."** --Sir Walter Scott, *Life of Napoleon*, vol. 1, ch. 17. **"France is the only nation in the world concerning which the authentic record survives, that as a nation she lifted her hand in open rebellion against the Author of the universe....by the decree of her Legislative Assembly, pronounced that there was no God, and of which the entire population of the capital, and a vast majority elsewhere, women as well as men, danced and sang with joy in accepting the announcement."** (White, *The Great Controversy*, pp. 269, 270)

The atheistical power that ruled in France during the Revolution and the reign of terror, did wage such a war upon the Bible as the world had never witnessed. The Word of God was prohibited by the national assembly. Bibles were collected and publicly burned with every possible manifestation of scorn. The law of God was trampled underfoot. The institutions of the Bible were abolished. The weekly rest-day was set aside, and in its stead every tenth day was devoted to reveling and blasphemy. Baptism and the communion were prohibited. And announcements posted conspicuously over the burial-places declared death to be an eternal sleep. (White, *The Great Controversy*, pp. 273, 274)

France presented the characteristic which especially distinguished Sodom. During the Revolution, there was manifested a state of moral debasement and corruption similar to that which brought destruction upon the cities of the plain. The Bible says, **"where also our Lord was crucified."** This specification of the prophecy was also fulfilled by France. In no land had the spirit of enmity against Christ been more strikingly displayed in the person of His professed followers.

It is interesting to note that before France openly denounced the existence of God and proscribed the Bible, she had first, under the influence of Romanism, set up the first stake at the opening of the Reformation, whereby many of God's followers were murdered in cold blood. On the very spot where the first martyrs of the Protestant faith were burned in the sixteenth century, the first victims of the French revolution were guillotined in the eighteenth century. History now takes us back to that former event.

Killing of St. Bartholomew

In fact, on August 24, 1572, there was a secret mass killing of the Huguenots, who were French Calvinist Protestants, by the Roman Catholics. It originated in Paris and spread throughout France for two months until almost 100,000 Protestants were killed and the Huguenots were nearly extinguished from the face of the earth.

> **"The pope, Gregory XIII., received the news of the fate of the Huguenots with unbounded joy. The wish of his heart had been gratified, and Charles IX, was now his favorite son. Rome rang with rejoicings. The guns of the castle of St. Angelo gave forth a joyous salute; the bells sounded from every tower; bonfires blazed throughout the night; and Gregory, attended by his cardinals and priests, led the magnificent procession to the church of St. Louis, where the cardinal of Lorraine chanted a *Te Deum*. The cry of the dying host in France was gentle harmony to the court of Rome. A medal was struck to commemorate the glorious massacre; a picture, which still exists in the Vatican, was painted, representing the chief events of St. Bartholomew. The pope, eager to show his gratitude to Charles for his dutiful conduct, sent him the Golden Rose; and from the pulpits of Rome eloquent preachers celebrated Charles, Catherine, and the Guises as the new founders of the papal church."** [White, *The Great Controversy* (1888), pp. 272, 273]

South Pushes the North

The Bible states that in the time of the end, the kings of the South and North would engage in some sort of warfare. It was atheistic France to which the Bible referred as the king of South that would push against the king of North in the time of the end. In prophecy, what does "push" signify? "Push" signifies war. Daniel tells us that at the time of the end, there would be an attack made first by the king of the South. Thus, our question is, Was there an attack made by France against the papacy in 1798? The answer is yes.

On February 10, Napoleon Bonaparte sent General Louis Alexander Berthier and his army into Rome, Italy. **"In <u>1798</u> General Berthier made his entrance into Rome, <u>abolished the papal government</u>, and established a secular one"** (*Encyclopedia Britannica*, 1941, "General Berthier").

What is meant by "come against him like a whirlwind"? A whirlwind is a fearful storm. It describes how the papal powers, in a mighty tumult, would sweep away her foes and recover her lost dominion. History recorded that before the papacy first ascended the world throne, she first subdued three geographical obstacles, namely **the Heruli, Goths, and Vandals.** As it was in history, so shall it be now; she must vanquish three obstacles before ascending the world throne. The three modern barriers, represented as the king of the South, are:

1. **Atheistic France**
2. **Soviet Union (Communism)**
3. **Islamic Extremism**

The conquest of these three papal enemies began in 1798 and still continues. The last of this enemy is Islamic fundamentalism. These radical, Islamic fundamentalists and their temporal victory in this war of terror become the papacy's stepping stone to world dominion. The prophet said they would accomplish this through the strength of their **chariots** and **horsemen** and with **many ships. What are chariots and horsemen in prophecy?** They symbolize military strength. Ships symbolize economic strength. Therefore, through the combination of economic power and military might, the axis of evil will succumb to the power of the new world order.

The Glorious Land

What are countries? The countries spoken of here represent those that were under the control of the king of the south. The Bible says the king of the north shall overflow and pass over them. This means victory. Daniel continued, **"He shall enter also into the glorious land, and many *countries* shall be overthrown: but these shall escape out of his hand, *even* Edom, and Moab, and the chief of the children of Ammon"** (11:41). Daniel spoke of a "glorious land" twice in chapter 11, the first being in verse 16. When this reference was first made, it pointed to Jerusalem.

If you have been carefully following our study in this book, you will note that we prophetically identified Jerusalem under the new covenant as the general assembly, the church of the Firstborn. Speaking about Christ's great objective for the church, we are told that His desire is **"That he might present it to himself a <u>glorious church</u>, not having spot, or wrinkle, or any such thing; but that it should be holy and without blemish"** (Eph. 5:27).

Christ's great objective is to have a glorious church. Describing God's plan of redemption for His people:

> **And in that day there shall be a root of Jesse, which shall stand for an ensign of the people; to it shall the Gentiles seek: and his <u>rest shall be glorious</u>....And he shall set up an ensign for the nations, and shall assemble the outcasts of Israel, and gather together the dispersed of Judah from the four corners of the earth....they shall lay their hand upon Edom and Moab; and the children of Ammon shall obey them.** (Isaiah 11:10, 12, 14)

This prophecy speaks about God's final work in the church when its rest (the Sabbath) shall be glorious. On that day, Edom, Moab, and the chief children of Ammon shall obey God's people. The term **"glorious,"** as you can see, is closely connected to the church. Therefore, when Daniel says the king of the North, the papacy, will enter the glorious land, he's saying that the papacy will enter the territory of the church through the state. As the dignitaries of church and state unite, they bribe, persuade, or compel all classes to honor Sunday.

Many People Overthrown

The Bible says, **"and many *countries* shall be overthrown."** In this verse, the word "countries" is supplied and not found in the original Hebrew text. What was actually written there was "people," not "countries." Who are the people who will be overthrown? Paul said, **"Let no man deceive you by any means: for *that day shall not come*, except there come a falling away first, and that man of sin be revealed, the son of perdition; Who opposeth and exalteth himself above all that is called God, or that is worshipped;**

so that he as God sitteth in the temple of God, shewing himself that he is God" (2 Thess. 2:3, 4).

The apostle Paul told us that the antichrist would take over the church, and then the church will be sifted by fiery trials, and a heftier proportion than we now anticipate will give heed to seducing spirits and doctrines of devils. "In the absence of persecution, there have drifted into the ranks some who appear sound, and their Christianity unquestionable, but who, if persecution should arise, would go out from us" (White 1976, p. 28). Did you notice there were some who escaped?

Edom, Moab, and Ammon

"[B]ut these shall escape out of his hand, *even* Edom, and Moab, and the chief of the children of Ammon" (Dan. 11:41). It is interesting to note that the Edomites are descendants of Esau, while the Moabites and Ammonites are descendants of Lot, both of whom are the distant relatives of the children of Israel. Prophetically, these are God's children in the various religious bodies who would escape the hand of the antichrist. With that said, the big question is, As they are escaping, into whose hand shall they fall?

Inspiration reveals that as the servants of God, endowed with power from on high, with their faces lighted up and shining with holy consecration, went forth to proclaim His final warning message to the inhabitant of the earth, souls that were scattered all through the religious bodies answered the call. These precious souls were hurried out of the doomed churches, just as Lot was hurried out of Sodom before its destruction. Isaiah also uses Ammon, Moab, and Edom to symbolism those who respond to the loud-cry message.

> **And it shall come to pass in that day, [that] the Lord shall set his hand again the second time to recover the remnant of his people, which shall be left, from Assyria, and from Egypt, and from Pathros, and from Cush, and from Elam, and from Shinar, and from Hamath, and from the islands of the sea. And he shall set up an ensign for the nations, and shall assemble the outcasts of Israel, and gather together the dispersed of Judah from the four corners of the earth. The envy also of Ephraim shall depart, and the adversaries of Judah shall be cut off: Ephraim shall not envy Judah, and Judah shall not vex Ephraim. But they shall fly upon the shoulders of the Philistines toward the west; they shall spoil them of the east together: they shall lay their hand upon Edom and Moab; and the children of Ammon shall obey them. (Isaiah 11:11–14)**

The Bible says Edom, Moab, and the chief children of Ammon shall fall into the hand of the spiritual children of Judah, whom the Lord has redeemed through the blood of Christ.

Egypt/the World

"He shall stretch forth his hand also upon the countries: and the land of Egypt shall not escape" (Dan. 11:42). In this context, what does Egypt represent? Egypt is more often used spiritually to symbolize the world, while Canaan or Israel symbolizes God's people. Therefore, Egypt in this context is the world. The verse says the world political power of the antichrist will stretch out its hand to the nations, and they would all conform to the new world order, for it states that "the countries…shall not escape."

Libya and Ethiopia

"But he shall have power over the treasures of gold and of silver, and over all the precious things of Egypt: and the Libyans and the Ethiopians *shall be* **at his steps"** (v. 43).

What this implies is that as soon as the antichrist appears, it will take charge of the financial structure of the world. However, before it can do this, the financial system of the world will collapse first, and that is what we have just experienced through the global economic crisis. The control of world finances by the papacy proves that it has fully returned to its once-held position of world dominance.

Who are the Libyans and Ethiopians? Ancient Egypt had two neighbors who had intriguing histories. The Libyans, to the west of Egypt, lived on the fringe of the desert and throughout their history cast a longing eye toward Egypt and the fertile Nile Valley. They attempted to invade Egypt several times but were repulsed. As Egypt symbolizes the world, Libya symbolizes what we call today the third world—the poor, downtrodden countries that long to move up to the standards of affluence.

Our next question is, Who does Ethiopia represent in this prophecy? Ancient Ethiopia included not only Nubia but also part of Western Arabia bordering the Red Sea. The Egyptians have always coveted Ethiopia because of the gold mines in its mountains and its wealth in cattle, ivory, hides, and ebony, and because products from Central Africa entered Egypt through Ethiopia traders.

As Egypt represents the world, Libya the poor, and Ethiopia the rich, so shall the rich and the poor be at his steps. To be at the steps of the antichrist is to march with it as it runs over the world. The whole world will be in companionship with it.

Tidings from the East

"**But tidings out of the east and out of the north shall trouble him: therefore he shall go forth with great fury to destroy, and utterly to make away many**" (v. 44). What are the tidings out of the east and north? In this verse, the tidings represent good news, the earth's final warning against the worshiping of the beast and its image and receiving its mark on the foreheads or right hands. This message will significantly disturb the antichrist to the point that it will launch a great persecution and killing campaign.

Glorious Holy Mountain

"**And he shall plant the tabernacles of his palace between the seas in the glorious holy mountain; yet he shall come to his end, and none shall help him**" (v. 45). Who is "he" in this verse? The "he" is the man who owns a palace. Therefore, "he" is a king. The verb "plant" means "establish." Another word for "tabernacle" is "temple," a place of worship that this symbol pinpoints to its religious aspect. A palace is a secular, civil, or political dwelling place. Therefore, another term for "tabernacle" with "palace" is "church and state," a mixture of religious characteristics with political characteristics.

He establishes religious power and political power between the seas. In Bible prophecy, "seas" represent "multitudes, nations, tongues, and people." The word "between" used in this verse is the same as "in the midst," which literally means "in the middle" or "center." The "glorious holy mountain," in a literal sense, is Mount Zion or Jerusalem, but this is symbolic. Please note that the Bible did not say he will plant it in, but rather between, the sea and mountain.

What does a mountain represent in prophecy? The glorious holy mountain is God's people, while the sea is the inhabitants of the earth. The Bible says the antichrist will place itself between the people who are in these last days giving the final warning message and the people who are to receive it. It will try at this point to block the message, but it will come to its end. It is at this time that the Bible says:

And at that time shall Michael stand up, the great prince which standeth for the children of thy people: and there shall be a time of trouble, such as never was since there was a nation *even* to that same

time: and at that time thy people shall be delivered, every one that shall be found written in the book. And many of them that sleep in the dust of the earth shall awake, some to everlasting life, and some to shame *and* everlasting contempt. And they that be wise shall shine as the brightness of the firmament; and they that turn many to righteousness as the stars for ever and ever. (Daniel 12:1–3)

Michael the Archangel

Who is Michael? "**Yet Michael the archangel, when contending with the devil he disputed about the body of Moses, durst not bring against him a railing accusation, but said, The Lord rebuke thee**" (Jude 9). The Bible says that Michael is the Archangel who contended with the devil and disputed over the body of Moses. We know Moses was resurrected because he appeared on the mount of transfiguration with Jesus.

Therefore, it was when Michael came to raise him up that Satan contended with Him. According to Daniel, Michael was associated with the awakening of those who slept in the dust of the earth. This is the resurrection.

The Power of Resurrection

Michael can raise the dead. Can the Archangel raise the dead? Can any angel raise the dead? According to the Bible, who alone has the authority and ability to raise the dead?

> *I am* **he that liveth, and was dead; and, behold, I am alive for evermore, Amen; and have the keys of hell and of death.** (Revelation 1:18)
>
> **Jesus said unto her, I am the resurrection, and the life: he that believeth in me, though he were dead, yet shall he live.** (John 11:25)
>
> **Verily, verily, I say unto you, The hour is coming, and now is, when the dead shall hear the voice of the Son of God: and they that hear shall live....Marvel not at this: for the hour is coming, in the which all that are in the graves shall hear his voice, And shall come forth; they that have done good, unto the resurrection of life; and they that have done evil, unto the resurrection of damnation.** (John 5:25, 28, 29)

Jesus, the Son of God, is the only One who can raise the dead. Therefore, who is this Michael, whom the Bible described as the Archangel who can equally raise the dead? First, I want you to understand that in Hebrew, the word "Michael" means "One who is like God," while "archangel" means "the commander in chief, leader of all the heavenly angels."

Captain of the Lord's Host

Throughout the entire Scriptures, Michael is the only being who is addressed as the Archangel, another word for "Lord of Hosts," which equally means the Captain of the heavenly host. When this Captain of the heavenly host appeared to Joshua, what transpired between them?

> And it came to pass, when Joshua was by Jericho, that he lifted up his eyes and looked, and, behold, there stood a man over against him with his sword drawn in his hand: and Joshua went unto him, and said unto him, *Art* thou for us, or for our adversaries? And he said, Nay; but *as* captain of the host of the LORD am I now come. And Joshua fell on his face to the earth, and did worship, and said unto him, what saith my lord unto his servant? And the captain of the LORD'S host said unto Joshua, Loose thy shoe from off thy foot; for the place where on thou standest *is* holy. And Joshua did so. (Joshua 5:13–15)

If we remember when God appeared before Moses in the burning bush, He asked him to pull off his shoes because he was on holy ground.

Angels Are Not Worshipped

When John wanted to worship the angel who was ministering to him, he said, "**And I fell at his feet to worship him. And he said unto me, See *thou do it* not: I am thy fellow servant, and of thy brethren that have the testimony of Jesus: worship God: for the testimony of Jesus is the spirit of prophecy**" (Rev. 19:10). This angel forbade John from worshipping him, instead referring him to God, so angels cannot be worshiped; only God is to be worshiped. However, you know the Commander of the heavenly host, Michael received worship from Joshua. Is Michael equal to God? Who did John say Michael is?

> **And there was war in heaven: Michael and his angels fought against the dragon; and the dragon fought and his angels, And prevailed not: neither was their place found any more in heaven....And I heard a loud voice saying in heaven, Now is come salvation, and strength, and the kingdom of our God, and the power of his Christ: for the accuser of our brethren is cast down, which accused them before our God day and night.** (Revelation 12:7, 8, 10)

Michael, in the book of Revelation, is said to be in charge of the angels. When He overcame the devil, and praises were sung to God, the verse states that He obtained victory through Christ. The Bible says Christ was the one who defeated Satan.

Voice of the Archangel

"**For the Lord himself shall descend from heaven with a shout, with the voice of the archangel, and with the trump of God: and the dead in Christ shall rise first**" (1 Thess. 4:16). The Archangel has a voice, and by that voice, the dead are to be raised. However, who is that Archangel? The Bible says in the book of Daniel that Michael will stand up. What does that mean?

Michael Stood Up

In the book of Daniel, the phrase "stand up" is used severally to mean "establishment of a new kingdom." Why and for whom does Michael stand up? The Bible says Michael stands up for God's people to deliver them from the time of trouble. Therefore, having learned from the account of Paul to the Thessalonians that Jesus came with the voice of the Archangel, our next question is, What was Michael doing before He stood up? Do we have any picture of Jesus sitting down?

> *As soon as Christ ceases His intercession on behalf of mankind before His Father in the heavenly sanctuary, He will lay off His priestly attire and clothe Himself with the garments of judgment*

Before he "stood up," he must have been sitting down first. "**Now of the things which we have spoken *this is* the sum: We have such an high priest, who is set on the right hand of the throne of the Majesty in the heavens; A minister of the sanctuary, and of the true tabernacle, which the Lord pitched, and not man**" (Heb. 8:1, 2). Jesus Christ went to heaven and sat down at the right hand of God in the heavenly sanctuary as our High Priest. Therefore, that is why when Michael stands up, it means His work as High Priest is over; His intercession is over; our probation is closed.

Then immediately He stands up and makes the following declaration: "**He that is unjust, let him be unjust still: and he which is filthy, let him be filthy still: and he that is righteous, let him be righteous still: and he that is holy, let him be holy still. And, behold, I come quickly; and my reward *is* with me, to give every man according as his work shall be**" (Rev. 22:11, 12). After Jesus walks out of the sanctuary, what was its condition? "**And the temple was filled with smoke from the glory of God,**

and from his power; and no man was able to enter into the temple, till the seven plagues of the seven angels were fulfilled" (15:8).

As soon as Christ ceases His intercession on behalf of mankind before His Father in the heavenly sanctuary, He will lay off His priestly attire and clothe Himself with the garments of judgment. Now stepping aside from the throne of mercy, the unmingled wrath of God is poured out on those who have rejected His truth and chosen to worship the beast and his image and receive his mark on their hands or foreheads.

Chapter 14

DOUSING ALLAH'S TORCH

Turning the pages of history backward, much of what we've discussed began with Abraham and his slave girl Hagar, who later became his concubine and the mother of his son Ishmael. This girl was purchased in Egypt and served as a maid to Abraham's childless wife, Sarah, who gave her to him to conceive an heir. When Hagar became pregnant, her meek manner changed to arrogance. With Abraham's reluctant permission, Sarah treated her so harshly that she fled into the wilderness. There, by a spring of water, she was found by an angel of the Lord, who told her she would have a son. **"And the angel of the LORD said unto her, Behold, thou *art* with child, and shalt bear a son, and shalt call his name Ishmael; because the LORD hath heard thy affliction"** (Gen. 16:11).

The angel told Hagar to return to Sarah, promising her that she would have many descendants through her son. Then the angel added, **"And he will be a wild man; his hand *will be* against every man, and every man's hand against him; and he shall dwell in the presence of all his brethren"** (v. 12). Ishmael fathered twelve princes whose descendants became the Arab world. In the origins of the Arabs, the majority of whom are Muslims, we see a prophetic description of later days.

Prophecy depicts that Ishmael would have two sides to his character—a spiritual side and an anti-God side—that would drive him to be against everyone. Although Islam often seems oppressive and violent, it is a deeply spiritual faith that has provided meaning and purpose for millions. Its faith is end-time oriented. Muslims live their lives in the consciousness of the final judgment and accountability for every thought and act. However, the two sides still clash within it. God's Word reveals that Ishmael would be like a wild donkey and in a constant struggle with everyone. One common thread through the global threats we face today is the connection to radical Islam.

Islamic Rule and the Jihad

Islam was created by Muhammad to be the army of God (Allah). Every single Muslim is a soldier in this army. Every single Muslim who dies in fighting for the spread of Islam is a *shaheed* ("martyr") no matter how he dies. What happens if Jews and Christians don't want to live under the rules of Islam? Islam has to fight them, and this fighting is called "holy jihad." Jihad means "struggle," but when applied in a radical context, it means "struggle against falsehood," which indirectly is a war against those people who don't want to accept the Islamic superior rule. That's jihad. They may be Jews; they may be Christians; they may be pagans. Militant Muslims believe the following verses from the Qur'an support their views:

> "Fighting is prescribed upon you" (2:216).
>
> "Fight and slay the pagan wherever ye find them" (9:5).
>
> "Fight those who believe not in Allah nor the Last Day nor hold that forbidden which hath been forbidden by Allah and his Apostle, nor acknowledge the religion of truth, from among the people of the book until they pay the Jizyah with willing submission and feel themselves subdued" (9:29).
>
> "Think not of those who are slain in Allah's way as dead: they live in the presence of the Lord" (3:169).
>
> "To him who fights in the cause of Allah soon shall we give him a reward" (4:74).

The philosophical roots of Islamic fundamentalism, with its global resurgence of

> *Many Christians and Jews today are struggling to make sense of the current hatred and now believe that all Muslims are either violent or supportive of violence against non-Muslims, but the truth is that the majority of Muslims are not terrorists. These wandering sons and daughters of Ishmael also long for a relationship with the God of Abraham*

ambition and worldwide spread of terror and bloodshed, are primarily the results of a conscious attempt to revive and restate the theoretical relevance of Islam in the modern world. Many Christians and Jews today are struggling to make sense of the current hatred and now believe that all Muslims are either violent or supportive of violence against non-Muslims, but the truth is that the majority of Muslims are not terrorists. These wandering sons and daughters of Ishmael also long for a relationship with the God of Abraham.

It has been Satan's settled determination to be at war with all of Abraham's descendants, both natural and spiritual. He infected Isaac's descendants, the children of Israel, with apostasy and idolatry. The devil also permeates Ishmael's descendants with his evil sophistry. The September 11, 2001 attacks on the United States placed the issue of Islamic terrorism on center stage. The highest numbers of incidents and fatalities caused by Islamic terrorism occur in Iraq, Afghanistan, Nigeria, Pakistan, and Syria.

"In 2015 four Islamic extremist groups were responsible for 74% of all deaths from terrorism: ISIS, Boko Haram, the Taliban and Al-Qaeda, according to the Global Terrorism Index 2016" (Global Terrorism Index 2016, Institute for Economics and Peace, 2016).

"In recent decades, such incidents have occurred on a global scale, affecting not only Muslim-majority states in Africa and Asia, but also Europe, Russia, Australia, Canada, France and the United States. Such attacks have targeted Muslims and non Muslims" (The Guardian, August 24, 2014).

Radical Islam and Peace

To the radical Muslim, peace can exist only within the Islamic world; only between a radical Muslim and another radical Muslim. With the non-Muslim world and opponents of Islam, there can just be one solution: a cease-fire until the radical Muslims can gain more power. They believe that their struggle is a continual war that continues until the end of days. Peace can only come when the Islamic side wins. What can make radical Islam accept a cease-fire? Only one thing: when the enemy is too strong. It is a tactical choice. Sometimes, it may have to agree to a cease-fire in the most humiliating conditions. It's allowed because Mohammed accepted a cease-fire under humiliating conditions. This was the statement of Arafat in Johannesburg.

It is interesting to note that every Muslim sees the world divided into two parts: those under Islamic rule are designated as *Dar al-Islam* ("the house of Islam"), and those who are supposed to come under Islamic rule in the future are designated as *Dar al-Harb* ("the house of war").

Please note that they are not called the "house of non-Muslims," but rather the "house of war." Why? Because it is expected that in the last days of earth's history, this house of war would be conquered by Islam. And that is exactly what we see today around the world through the increased activities of Islamic insurgency. Therefore, the world will continue to be in the house of war until it comes under the supreme control of Islamic rule. All Muslims believe that God has sent Mohammed with the true religion so that the truth will overcome all other religions.

The Army of Locusts

In Revelation 9, John saw an army of locusts come out of the smoke that issued out of the bottomless pit. These locusts had power, but it was limited. They were not to hurt the grass or trees; they were allowed to harm only those people who did not have the seal of God in their foreheads; they had the power to torment like a scorpion. John described their appearance with these words:

> **And the shapes of the locusts *were* like unto horses prepared unto battle; and on their heads *were* as it were crowns like gold, and their faces *were* as the faces of men. And they had hair as the hair of women, and their teeth were as *the teeth* of lions. And they had breastplates, as it were breastplates of iron; and the sound of their wings *was* as the sound of chariots of many horses running to battle. And they had tails like unto scorpions, and there were stings in their tails.** (Revelation 9:7–10)

What was John talking about when he described the army of locusts? Students of Bible prophecy understand this army of locusts as the rise and spread of Islam. "We have in the locusts a perfect description of the Saracens in a most remarkable blending of the literal and the figurative. These horsemen of the desert are well typified by the locusts for a country overrun by them was literally infested as by plague of locusts" (Rand 1985, p. 90).

Let's look at some of the details of John's vision and see how it describes the rise and spread of Islam. We are told that the army of locusts came forth from a dark cloud of smoke that rolled out of the bottomless pit. In Greek, "bottomless pit" is *abussos*, the source of our English word "abyss." That was why some English Bibles translate it simply as "the abyss."

It is remarkable that Abul A'la Mawdudi, one of Islam's most prominent scholars of the twentieth century, used the very word "abyss" when writing about the beginnings of Islam. In a book written to introduce English-speaking people to the basics of Islam, Mawdudi tells his readers that Mohammed and his message came out of Arabia—"the abyss of darkness" (1986, p. 63).

Why did an army of locusts represent an army of Arabs? About 900 years before John wrote Revelation, the prophet Joel symbolically described an invading, attacking army as a swarm of locusts. Any large, invading army might be compared to a swarm of locusts, but the Arabs and Muhammad have a unique connection to this critter:

"In the Bedoween romance Antar, the locust is introduced as the national emblem of the Ishmaelite [one the ancestors of the Arabs-DB]. And it is a remarkable coincidence that Muslim tradition speaks of locusts having dropped into the hands of Muhammad, bearing on their wings this inscription—'we are the army of the Great God'" (*Forster's Mohammedism Unveiled*, Vol i, p. 217).

As we just saw, a Muslim writer unwittingly connects Islam's beginnings to the abyss; now we see another Muslim writer unwittingly connect Islam to the locusts that come from the abyss. In the book of Revelation, God used the symbol of locusts and angry horses to represent the radical aspect of Islam in the past. As we can see today, Islamic armies are rising again and setting out once more to vex the world like a plague of locusts. Centuries ago they abandoned their lust for conquest and world domination to pursue literature and sciences. Now they have abandoned their love for literature and the sciences and have returned to their lust for conquest and world domination.

The Third Woes

"And I beheld, and heard an angel flying through the midst of heaven, saying with a loud voice, Woe, woe, woe, to the inhabiters of the earth by reason of the other voices of the trumpet of the three angels, which are yet to sound" (Rev. 8:13)! Between the thirteenth and eighteenth centuries, the world experienced the first and second woes of Revelation, otherwise known as the fifth and sixth trumpets.

Today we are experiencing the third woe, which is a repetition of the sixth trumpet and the fulfillment of the seventh trumpet. The Bible says, **"And the sixth angel sounded, and I heard a voice from the four horns of the golden altar which is before God, Saying to the sixth angel which had the trumpet, Loose the four angels which are bound in the great river Euphrates"** (9:13, 14). The Euphrates is the longest river in the Middle

East and runs from Armenia through Turkey, Syria, Iraq, Saudi Arabia, and Kuwait. In Bible prophecy, water represents multitudes, nations, and tongues. Therefore, the Euphrates represents the people of that region.

The Final Battle

In Islam's second holiest book, the Hadith, there is also a prophecy about the Euphrates River from the translation of Abu Huraira's report on Allah's messenger. It reads in English, **"The last hour will not come to pass unless you begin to see River Euphrates dries up in preparation for the final battle the River shall uncover its treasures for which men would fight. Whosoever sees it should not take anything from it"** (Abu Huraira report Allah's messenger, Sahih Muslim: book #041, Hadith #6918).

As far back as the 1980s, the Euphrates River was noticed drying up each year. As it kept receding, a lot of discoveries were made as it revealed ancient archaeological sites, some of which were unknown until now. Among the Muslims, this development is nothing but the sign of the end, and also an indication that the time for the final battle has come. They call this final war ***Al-malhama Alkubre***, Allah's great and final war against evil. It will be fought between the holy jihadists of Islam and unbelievers just before the end of the world.

Radical Islam, as we can see today through terrorism, is already stirring up the nations of the earth into global war. Inspiration reveals that **"As the angels of God cease to hold in check the fierce winds of human passion, all the elements of strife will be let loose. The whole world will be involved in ruin more terrible than that which came upon Jerusalem of old"** (White 1976, p. 265).

> But although the nations are mustering their forces for war and bloodshed, the command to the angels is still in force, that they hold the four winds until the servants of God are sealed in their foreheads....
>
> ...Then the powers of earth will marshal their forces for the last great battle....
>
> > ...Then I saw the four angels cease to hold the four winds. And I saw famine, pestilence and sword, nation rose against nation, and the whole world was in confusion. (White, *Maranatha*, p. 243)
> >
> > The present is a time of overwhelming interest to all living. Rulers and statesmen, men who occupy positions of trust and authority, thinking men and women of all classes, have their attention fixed upon the events taking place about us. They are watching the strained,

restless relations that exist among the nations. They observe the intensity that is taking possession of every earthly element, and they realize that something great and decisive is about to take place, that the world is on the verge of a stupendous crisis....

...In the last scenes of this earth's history, war will rage. There will be pestilence, plague, and famine. The waters of the deep will overflow their boundaries. Property and life will be destroyed by fire and flood. We should be preparing for the mansions that Christ has gone to prepare for all that love Him.... ...The restraining Spirit of God is even now being withdrawn from the world. Hurricanes, storms, tempests, disasters by sea and by land, follow one another in quick succession. The signs thickening around us, telling us of the near approach of the Son of God... (White, *Maranatha*, pp. 174, 175)

"And it was commanded them that they should not hurt the grass of the earth, neither any green thing, neither any tree; but only those men which have not the seal of God in their foreheads" (Rev. 9:4).

The Seal of God

A seal, in biblical times, as well as today, is used to guarantee security or indicate ownership. Ancient seals were often made of wax, embedded with the personalized imprint of their guarantor. This seal typically contained three elements:

1) **Name**
2) **Official position, title, or authority**
3) **Domain and jurisdiction**

With this understanding, let's answer the following question: What is the seal of God? The seal of God is a pledge of perfect security to His chosen ones. Sealing indicates you are God's chosen. He has appropriated you to Himself. The Bible says, **"Now it is God who makes both us and you stand firm in Christ. He anointed us, set His seal of ownership on us, and put his Spirit in our hearts as a deposit, guaranteeing what is to come"** (2 Cor. 1:21, 22, NIV).

The seal of God shows authentic ownership and evidence that we are His. He has approved of us as His children. As the sealed of God, we are Christ's purchased possession, and no one shall pluck us out of His hands.

With the above understanding, our next question is this: Upon what is God's seal placed? **"And I saw another angel ascending from the east, having the seal of the living God: and he cried with a loud voice to the four angels, to whom it was given to hurt the earth and the sea, Saying,**

Hurt not the earth, neither the sea, nor the trees, till we have sealed the servants of our God in their foreheads" (Rev. 7:2, 3).

The apostle John, in his prophetic vision, was shown that the seal of God is placed upon our foreheads. With what three elements are we sealed? "And I looked, and, lo, a Lamb stood on the mount Sion, and with him an hundred forty *and* four thousand, having his Father's name written in their foreheads" (14:1).

"Him that overcometh will I make a pillar in the temple of my God, and he shall go no more out: and I will write upon him the name of my God, and the name of the city of my God, *which is* new Jerusalem, which cometh down out of heaven from my God: and *I will write upon him* my new name" (3:12). We see from the above texts that the name of the Father, the new name from Christ, and the name of the city which all describe His position and domain of jurisdiction (Jerusalem), are the three elements of God's seal. Our next question is, What is this name of the Father?

> **And Moses said unto God, Behold, *when* I come unto the children of Israel, and shall say unto them, The God of your fathers hath sent me unto you; and they shall say to me, What *is* his name? what shall I say unto them? And God said unto Moses, I AM THAT I AM: and he said, Thus shalt thou say unto the children of Israel, I AM hath sent me unto you.** (Exodus 3:13, 14)

God saying "I AM THAT I AM" means His very character constitutes His name. The Bible says:

> **And the LORD descended in the cloud, and stood with him there, and proclaimed the name of the LORD. And the LORD passed by before him, and proclaimed, The LORD, The LORD God, merciful and gracious, longsuffering, and abundant in goodness and truth, Keeping mercy for thousands, forgiving iniquity and transgression and sin, and that will by no means clear *the guilty*; visiting the iniquity of the fathers upon the children, and upon the children's children, unto the third and to the fourth *generation*.** (Exodus 34:5–7)

The Lord passed by Moses and declared His name. And as you can see above, this isn't just a simple "name" that God is revealing. He is revealing His character—merciful, gracious, longsuffering, forgiving, and just. These attributes of character are referred to as the name of the Lord. That was why He told Moses to tell the children of Israel that His name is "I AM THAT I AM." "For **I** *am* **the LORD your God: ye shall therefore sanctify yourselves, and ye shall be holy; for I** *am* **holy**" (Lev. 11:44).

"Ye shall be holy: for I the Lord your God *am* holy" (19:2).

"He sent redemption unto his people: he hath commanded his covenant for ever: holy and reverend *is* his name" (Ps. 111:9).

God saying "I AM WHAT I AM" simply means that the state of His being describes His name. Holiness is a state of being holy. God's state of being, holy character, and name go hand in hand. The apostle John, in a revelation, saw this name placed on the foreheads of the believers as a seal. "**The seal of the living God will be placed upon those only who bear a likeness to Christ in character. As wax takes the impression of the seal, so the soul is to take the impression of the Spirit of God and retain the image of Christ**" (White 1958, p. 287).

Therefore, when it says in Bible prophecy that those who serve God will have a seal on their foreheads, it means that His attributes of character have become part of their thinking and action. This is why the forehead (our mind) is where we receive the seal of God. With what is God's seal connected? The Bible says, "**Bind up the testimony, seal the law among my disciples**" (Isa. 8:16). And what does this imprint make of God's people? "**I will put my laws into their mind, and write them in their hearts: and I will be to them a God, and they shall be to me a people**" (Heb. 8:10).

The law of God in our minds makes us God's people and Him our God. Which of the commandments publicly identifies us as His people? "**And hallow my sabbaths; and they shall be a sign between me and you, that ye may know that I *am* the LORD your God**" (Ezek. 20:20). The Sabbath is a sign of ownership and connecting link between God and us. The fourth commandment commences, "**Remember the sabbath day, to keep it holy**" (Ex. 20:8).

There is only one manner in which we can truly keep God's Sabbath holy, and that is in holiness. To keep the Sabbath holy, we ourselves must be holy.

Anti-terrorism Laws

Friends, much has changed in the world since September 11, 2001. While terrorism did not begin on that day, for many it was a wakeup call that marked a dramatic shift in both the reach of jihadism and how the world responds. The attacks themselves created a permanent change in global consciousness and transition in worldwide policies and attitudes. As a result of the attack, representatives of the world's organized religions were gathered to pray for peace and a reversal of the threat of terrorism. Each of them made solemn declarations in favor of peace.

The nature of the war against terrorism drove the rise of "big brother" surveillance platforms, including the proliferation of closed-circuit cameras and biometric recognition software. Perhaps the most tangible intrusions on privacy are the full-body scanners now being rolled out at airports around the world.

The impact of the 9/11 attacks, which killed nearly 3,000 people, is still being felt today. Industries have changed policies, and the governments of various nations have formed new agencies and signed new acts into law. After the attack on the United States, President George W. Bush signed into law an anti-terrorism bill that gives sweeping new powers to police forces and intelligence agencies.

The legislation gives the police and Federal Bureau of Investigation more leeway to secretly search people's homes and business records. It also gives them more power to eavesdrop on telephone conversations, share intelligence, and detain suspected terrorists who enter the United States.

The bill increases the number of crimes considered as terrorist acts and toughens the punishment for committing them, as well as imposing stronger penalties on those harboring or financing terrorists. It is interesting to note how the United Nations Security Council unanimously adopted Resolution 1373 after 9/11 mandating member states to pass wide-ranging counterterrorism laws.

Human Rights Watch

Today more than 160 countries have passed counterterrorism laws since the attacks of September 11, 2001, often with little regard for due process and other basic rights. Human Rights Watch has found out that many countries since September 11, 2001 have enacted or revised one or more counterterrorism laws. Reviewing 130 of those laws, they've found that all contained one or more provisions that opened the door to abuse of rights. For instance, Russia's newest anti-terror laws violate privacy and religious freedom in the following ways:

- Foreign guests are not permitted to speak in churches unless they have a "work permit" from Russian authorities
- If a friend or relative from outside Russia wishes to share his/her faith in your home the guest will be fined and expelled from Russia.
- Any discussion of God with non-believers is considered missionary activity and will be punishable.

- Missionary activity will be permitted by special government permission. Example: If one traveling on a train shares his faith without written permission the offender will be taken into police custody for the duration of the journey and will be fined 50,000 rubles ($1,000).
- Offenders from the age of 14-years-old will be subject to prosecution
- Religious activity is no longer permitted in private homes. Most churches in Russia meet in homes.
- Every citizen is obligated to report religious activity of neighbors to the authorities. Failure to be an informant is punishable by law.
- One may pray and read the Bible at home but not in the presence of a non-believing person. You will be breaking the law and be punished.
- If the church has purchased property it cannot be converted into a place of worship.
- In church buildings, it is not permitted to invite people to turn to God. Worship services are permitted but making a non-believer a follower of Christ is against the law. (CharismaNews, http://1ref.us/pt, accessed 9/6/2018)

Religious Censorship

The same kind of bill was also passed into law in Nepal. The new constitution signed by Nepal's president stated that "any act of converting another person from one religion to another or any act of behavior to undermine or jeopardize the religion of another," violates the constitution and is punishable by prison or fines. The government has been clamping down on evangelistic outreach, including the distribution of religious literature. Clearly, this fast-spreading bill is traveling around the nations of the world and specifically targeting some classes of Christians.

A Catholic missionary priest serving in Russia, who asked to be kept anonymous to protect his identity and parish, told CNA that the laws would have a much heavier impact on evangelicals and religious fundamentalists, both among Christians and non-Christians. He added that these new laws also target newer, less established Christian groups who are unregistered and always hold their meetings in private residences. The restrictions will additionally restrict groups considered extremist.

The majority of churches in the world are already registered with governments so they can get their tax-exempt status. However, this will come at a cost that which they will learn very soon. They will learn that they will have to submit to the rules of the government in other to continue, and how many churches and pastors will abide by this? For instance, the first-known victims of Russia's new anti-terrorism laws were two missionaries, one US citizen, and one Ghanaian. Both were heavily fined. In court, the US citizen was accused of posting notices in public places, inviting anyone interested in studying the Scriptures. He was accused of holding religious services in his home and advertising them on bulletin boards of nearby housing blocks.

The second set of victims was the Jehovah's Witnesses. The Russian Supreme Court, on Thursday, April 20, 2017, banned the Jehovah's Witnesses and declared them an extremist organization. The Supreme Court judge Yuri Ivanenko said Russia had decided to close down "the Administrative centre of Jehovah's Witnesses and the local organizations in its fold and turn their property over to the Russian Federation."

The Supreme Court argues that the Jehovah's Witnesses activities "violates Russia's law on combating extremism" and their pamphlets incited hatred against other groups. Several of its publications have been placed on a list of banned extremist literature, and prosecutors have long cast it as an organization that destroys families, fosters hatred, and threatens lives, descriptions that the organization says are false.

Anti-Extremism/Fundamentalism

Britain Forges Ahead With Anti-Extremism Commission…

…Prime Minister Theresa May announced the plan earlier this year [2017], but Christians and others are concerned about how the effort will affect their own civil liberties…

…When she was home secretary, Theresa May strongly supported the introduction of Prevent, stating, **"This strategy aims to tackle the whole spectrum of extremism, violent and nonviolent, ideological and non-ideological.…**

The Crown Prosecution Service defines hate crime as: "**Any criminal offense which is perceived by the victim or any other person to be motivated by hostility or prejudice based on a person's race or perceived race; religion or perceived religion; sexual orientation or perceived sexual orientation;** disability or perceived disability and any crime motivated by hostility or prejudice against a person who is transgender or perceived to be transgender." (http://1ref.us/ob, accessed 9/5/2018)

"People who repeatedly view terrorist content online could face up to 15 years behind bars in a move designed to tighten the laws tackling radicalisation the home secretary, Amber Rudd, is to announce on Tuesday" (http://1ref.us/ow, accessed 9/5/2018).

Pope Francis said, "A fundamentalist group, although it may not kill anyone, although it may not strike anyone, is violent. The mental structure of fundamentalists is violence in the name of God" (http://1ref.us/od, accessed 9/5/2018).

Here are the belief concepts of those they considered and described as extremists:

…religious concepts — such as end times prophecy, millennialism and the belief that the Second Coming of Jesus Christ was imminent — played a vital role in the recruitment, radicalization and mobilization of these Christian-inspired extremists and their illegal activities. For example, CSA members, the Weaver family and the Branch Davidians each embraced a lethal triad of end times prophecy, antigovernment conspiracy theories and an affinity for weapons.…Each also used their religious beliefs to justify engaging in "prepper" type activities, such as living off the land, isolating themselves from other family members and society, and stockpiling food, water and weapons to prepare for the end times and await — or even hasten — the apocalypse. (http://1ref.us/oi, accessed 9/5/2018)

France approves tough new anti-terror laws…

…The law will incorporate several measures first authorized under the emergency arrangement.

They include easier searches of homes and confining individuals to their home towns, without judicial approval.…

…A state of emergency was first introduced after the attacks of 13 November 2015, when militants from so-called Islamic State (IS) killed 130 people in gun and bomb attacks in Paris.…

…The bill was approved by 415 votes to 127, with 19 abstentions, **and is expected to become law before the latest state of emergency extension expires on 1 November**.

Interior Minister Gérard Collomb told parliament on Tuesday that the threat level was still "very serious", saying: **"We're still in a state of war.**…

…Mosques or other places of worship can be shut down if preachers there are found to be promoting radical ideology. (http://1ref.us/nz, accessed 9/5/2018)

The Mystery of God

"But in the days of the voice of the seventh angel, when he shall begin to sound, the mystery of God should be finished, as he hath declared to his servants the prophets" (Rev. 10:7). What is the meaning of the angel's affirmation that in the days when the seventh trumpet shall begin to sound, the mystery of God shall be finished? Please take note that the text does not say that the mystery of God shall be finished as soon as the seventh trumpet sounds, but rather the angel stated that it will happen in the days when the seventh trumpet *shall begin to sound*. We, therefore, conclude that the mystery is finished just before the ending of the seventh trumpet.

What is this mystery? **"To whom God would make known what *is* the riches of the glory of this mystery among the Gentiles; which is Christ in you, the hope of glory"** (Col. 1:27). The mystery of God is the manifestation of Christ in His church, a perfect reproduction of His character in the lives of believers. This is what John also identifies as the seal of God.

> *The mystery of God is the manifestation of Christ in His church, a perfect reproduction of His character in the lives of believers*

Chapter 15

THE TIME OF TROUBLE

A great crisis awaits the world. The most momentous struggle of all the ages is just before us. John wrote:

> **And the third angel followed them, saying with a loud voice, If any man worship the beast and his image, and receive *his* mark in his forehead, or in his hand, The same shall drink of the wine of the wrath of God, which is poured out without mixture into the cup of his indignation; and he shall be tormented with fire and brimstone in the presence of the holy angels, and in the presence of the Lamb.** (Revelation 14:9, 10)

The Bible says that when this great warning against receiving the mark of the beast has finished its work, and all have made up their minds, probation closes. God's people have received the outpouring of the Holy Spirit—the refreshing from the presence of the Lord—and they're prepared for the trying ordeal ahead. They are sealed with the seal of the Living God. The wicked are finally left to the master they have chosen. They've rejected God's mercy, despised His tender love, and trampled on His law.

Now unprotected from Satan's insane wrath, they have no shelter from his power. He will then plunge the entire world into one great, final trouble spoken of in Daniel 12. God's wrath poured out on this planet in rebellion will come in the form of the seven last plagues referenced in Revelation 16.

The First Plague

Just as the ten plagues of Egypt were against the gods that they worshiped, so the seven last plagues will be focused on those who worship the beast and its image. The Bible says, **"And I heard a great voice out of the temple saying to the seven angels, Go your ways, and pour out the vials of the wrath of God upon the earth. And the first went, and poured out his vial upon the earth; and there fell a noisome and grievous sore upon the men which had the mark of the beast, and *upon* them which worshipped his image"** (Rev. 16:1, 2).

Can you imagine sores all over your body? Just like the recent outbreak of Ebola, these gnawing, painful sores will afflict only those who have the mark of the beast and worship its image. What will it be like when this happens? Can you picture the evening news telling the shocking story of this gross epidemic?

The Second and Third Plagues

People by the thousands who have received the mark to save their jobs and comforts of life now find that these things are gone. Instead of becoming sober-minded, it causes them to blaspheme God and gnaw their tongues because of the pain. All of a sudden, the news breaks that the waters have turned to blood. **"And the second angel poured out his vial upon the sea; and it became as the blood of a dead [man]; and every living soul died in the sea. And the third angel poured out his vial upon the rivers and fountains of waters; and they became blood"** (Rev. 16:3, 4).

> *People by the thousands who have received the mark to save their jobs and comforts of life now find that these things are gone*

Look at the beaches. People are afraid. Where will they drink? They tried to shed the blood of the saints. Now they have blood to drink.

The Fourth Plague

Now something unbelievable happens. The atmospheric layer that shields the earth from the scorching heat fails. **"And men were scorched with great heat, and blasphemed the name of God, which hath power over these plagues: and they repented not to give him glory"** (v. 9). Horrible pain is now experienced by the wicked. The combination of scorching heat, raw sores, and lack of drinkable water is excruciating. Air conditioners will not be able to cope with the intense heat. The buildings will be like ovens. For the wicked, there will be no relief anywhere. In choosing to honor the beast and receive the mark instead of honoring God and receiving His seal, the people have opted for darkness. Again, God gives them what they have chosen.

The Fifth Plague

"And the fifth angel poured out his vial upon the seat of the beast; and his kingdom was full of darkness; and they gnawed their tongues for pain, And blasphemed the God of heaven because of their pains and their sores, and repented not of their deeds" (vs. 10, 11). Can you imagine that? I think the human mind is inadequate to conceive the horror that will engulf all of humanity. People of high society, the rich, scientists, and the ignorant masses will be paralyzed with pain, hate, and panic. The world will be in utter chaos. Of these scourges the Bible says:

> The field is wasted, the land mourneth; for the corn is wasted: the new wine is dried up, the oil languisheth. Be ye ashamed, O ye husbandmen; howl, O ye vinedressers, for the wheat and for the barley; because the harvest of the field is perished. The vine is dried up, and the fig tree languisheth; the pomegranate tree, the palm tree also, and the apple trees, *even* all the trees of the field, are withered: because joy is withered away from the sons of men....How do the beasts groan! the herds of cattle are perplexed, because they have no pasture; yea, the flocks of sheep are made desolate. (Joel 1:10–12, 18)

By the fifth plague, the whole wicked world is furious. They have decided that those who honor God's Sabbath of the Bible are the cause of the horrible convulsion of nature and determined to blot them from the earth. The date is set; when the clock strikes midnight on a certain day, God's obedient people will be sentenced to death. To all appearances, it seems that the doom of His people is fixed. Has He forsaken them? This very experience prepares them for the bliss of heaven as nothing else could.

The Sixth Plague

In the midst of the chaos, the sixth angel pours out his vial.

> And the sixth angel poured out his vial upon the great river Euphrates; and the water thereof was dried up, that the way of the kings of the east might be prepared. And I saw three unclean spirits like frogs *come* out of the mouth of the dragon, and out of the mouth of the beast, and out of the mouth of the false prophet. For they are the spirits of devils, working miracles, *which* go forth unto the kings of the earth and of the whole world, to gather them to the battle of that

great day of God Almighty....And he gathered them together into a place called in the Hebrew tongue Armageddon.** (Rev 16:12–14, 16)

This is the final battle between good and evil. In the global conflict of Armageddon, all have taken sides. The wicked are in the majority and seemingly have great advantages like Goliath over David. The people of God, some still in prison, some hidden in forests and mountains, plead for His protection, while companies of armed soldiers, hurried on by evil angels, are preparing to execute the death sentence.

The Seventh Plague

It is now in the darkest hour that the God of Israel will interpose to deliver His faithful people. The date has been set to strike one stunning blow that will wipe the hated sect from the face of the earth. At midnight the death decree goes into effect. Watch what happens:

> **And the seventh angel poured out his vial into the air; and there came a great voice out of the temple of heaven, from the throne, saying, It is done. And there were voices, and thunders, and lightnings; and there was a great earthquake, such as was not since men were upon the earth, so mighty an earthquake,** *and* **so great. And the great city was divided into three parts, and the cities of the nations fell: and great Babylon came in remembrance before God, to give unto her the cup of the wine of the fierceness of his wrath. And every island fled away, and the mountains were not found. And there fell upon men a great hail out of heaven,** *every stone* **about the weight of a talent: and men blasphemed God because of the plague of the hail; for the plague thereof was exceeding great.** (Revelation 16:17–21)

Angry Multitudes Arrested

With shouts of triumph, jeering, and imprecation, throngs of evil people are about to rush upon their prey, when lo, a dense blackness, deeper than the darkness of the night, falls upon the earth. Then a rainbow, shining with glory from the throne of God, spans the heavens and seems to encircle each praying company. The angry multitudes are suddenly arrested. Their mocking cries die away.

The objects of their murderous rage are forgotten. With fearful forebodings, they gaze upon the symbol of God's covenant and long to be shielded from its overpowering brightness. The streams cease to flow. Dark, heavy clouds come up and clash against each other. However, there is one clear place of settled glory from which comes the voice of God like many waters, shaking the heavens and earth. There is a mighty earthquake. The sky opens and shuts and is in commotion. The mountains shake like a reed in the wind and cast out ragged rocks all around. The sea boils like a pot and casts out stones upon the land.

God's Righteousness Declared

A marvelous change has come over those who have held fast their integrity in the very face of death. Their voices rise in triumphant song. While their words of holy trust ascend to God, the clouds sweep back, and the starry heavens are seen, unspeakably glorious in contrast with the black and angry firmament on either side. The glory of the celestial city streams from the gates ajar.

<u>Then there appears against the sky a hand holding two tables of stone folded together</u>. **"And the heavens shall declare his righteousness: for God *is* judge himself"** (Ps. 50:6). Soon appears the great white cloud, upon which sits the Son of man. When it first appears in the distance, this cloud looks very small.

Coming Signs of Christ

The angel says that it is the sign of the Son of man. As it draws nearer to the earth, we can behold the excellent glory and majesty of Jesus as He rides forth to conquer. A retinue of holy angels with bright, glittering crowns upon their heads escorts Him on His way.

The living righteous are changed **"In a moment, in the twinkling of an eye"** (1 Cor. 15:52). At the voice of God, they are glorified; now they are made immortal and with the risen saints caught up to meet their Lord in the air. Angels **"gather together his elect from the four winds, from one end of heaven to the other"** (Matt. 24:31). Little children are borne by holy angels to their mothers' arms. Friends long-separated by death are united, nevermore to part, and with songs of gladness ascend together to the City of God.

The world sees the very class whom they have mocked, derided, and desired to exterminate, pass unharmed through pestilence, tempest, and earthquake. They, on their part, recognize that they have been deluded. They accuse one another for being led to destruction, but all unite in heaping their bitterest condemnation upon the ministers.

A Global Bloodbath

The very hands that once crowned them with laurels will be raised for their destruction. The swords which were to slay God's people are now employed to destroy their enemies. Everywhere there is strife and bloodshed.

> **The whole city shall flee for the noise of the horsemen and bowmen; they shall go into thickets, and climb up upon the rocks: every city *shall be* forsaken, and not a man dwell therein.** (Jeremiah 4:29)
>
> **Therefore prophesy thou against them all these words, and say unto them, The LORD shall roar from on high, and utter his voice from his holy habitation; he shall mightily roar upon his habitation; he shall give a shout, as they that tread *the grapes*, against all the inhabitants of the earth. A noise shall come *even* to the ends of the earth; for the LORD hath a controversy with the nations, he will plead with all flesh; he will give them *that are* wicked to the sword, saith the LORD. Thus saith the LORD of hosts, Behold, evil shall go forth from nation to nation, and a great whirlwind shall be raised up from the coasts of the earth. And the slain of the LORD shall be at that day from *one* end of the earth even unto the *other* end of the earth: they shall not be lamented, neither gathered, nor buried; they shall be dung upon the ground.** (Jeremiah 25:30–33)
>
> **And the ten horns which thou sawest upon the beast, these shall hate the whore, and shall make her desolate and naked, and shall eat her flesh, and burn her with fire.** (Revelation 17:16)

Blotted from the Earth

At the coming of Christ, the wicked are blotted from the face of the whole earth, consumed with the spirit of His mouth and destroyed by the brightness of His glory. Christ takes His people to the City of God, and the earth is emptied of its inhabitants.

> **I beheld the earth, and, lo, *it was* without form, and void; and the heavens, and they *had* no light. I beheld the mountains, and, lo, they trembled, and all the hills moved lightly. I beheld, and, lo, *there was* no man, and all the birds of the heavens were fled. I beheld, and, lo, the fruitful place *was* a wilderness, and all the cities thereof were broken down at the presence of the LORD, *and* by his fierce anger. For thus hath the LORD said, The whole land shall be desolate; yet will I not make a full end. For this shall the earth mourn, and the heavens above be black: because I have spoken *it*, I have purposed *it*, and will not repent, neither will I turn back from it.** (Jeremiah 4:23–28)

Satan Banished

John the revelator foretells the banishment of Satan and the condition of chaos and desolation to which the earth is to be reduced, and declares that this condition will exist for 1,000 years. After presenting the scenes of the Lord's second coming and destruction of the wicked, the prophecy continues: **"And I saw an angel come down from heaven, having the key of the bottomless pit and a great chain in his hand"** (Rev. 20:1).

> **The earth is utterly broken down, the earth is clean dissolved, the earth is moved exceedingly. The earth shall reel to and fro like a drunkard, and shall be removed like a cottage; and the transgression thereof shall be heavy upon it; and it shall fall, and not rise again. And it shall come to pass in that day,** *that* **the LORD shall punish the host of the high ones** *that are* **on high, and the kings of the earth upon the earth. And they shall be gathered together,** *as* **prisoners are gathered in the pit, and shall be shut up in the prison, and after many days shall they be visited. Then the moon shall be confounded, and the sun ashamed, when the LORD of hosts shall reign in mount Zion, and in Jerusalem, and before his ancients gloriously.** (Isaiah 24:19–23)

Here is to be the home of Satan with his evil angels for 1,000 years. Limited to the earth, he will not have access to other worlds to tempt and annoy those who have never fallen. It is in this sense that he is bound; there are none remaining upon whom he can exercise his power. He is wholly cut off from the work of deception and ruin, which for so many centuries had been his sole delight.

Saints Now the Judge

During the millennium between the first and second resurrections, the judgment of the wicked takes place. The apostle Paul points to this judgment as an event that follows the second advent. **"Therefore judge nothing before the time, until the Lord come, who both will bring to light the hidden things of darkness, and will make manifest the counsels of the hearts: and then shall every man have praise of God"** (1 Cor. 4:5).

Daniel declares that when the Ancient of Days came, **"judgment was given to the saints of the most High; and the time came that the saints possessed the kingdom"** (7:22). At this time, the righteous reign as royal priests unto God. John says:

> **And I saw thrones, and they sat upon them, and judgment was given unto them: and** *I saw* **the souls of them that were beheaded for the witness of Jesus, and for the word of God, and which had not worshipped the beast, neither his image, neither had received** *his* **mark upon their foreheads, or in their hands; and they lived and reigned with Christ a thousand years....Blessed and holy** *is* **he that**

hath part in the first resurrection: on such the second death hath no power, but they shall be priests of God and of Christ, and shall reign with him a thousand years. (Revelation 20:4, 6)

This is the time Paul foretold. **"[T]he saints shall judge the world"** (1 Cor. 6:2). In union with Christ, they judge the wicked, comparing their acts with the statute book, the Bible, and deciding every case according to the deeds done in the body. Then the portion that the wicked must suffer is meted out according to their works, and it is recorded against their names in the book of death.

The End of the Thousand Years

"And when the thousand years are expired, Satan shall be loosed out of his prison" (Rev. 20:7). At the close of the millennium, Christ again returns to the earth. He is accompanied by the host of the redeemed and attended by a retinue of angels. As He descends in terrific majesty, He bids the wicked dead to arise and receive their doom. They come forth, a mighty host, numberless as the sands of the sea. The wicked bear the traces of disease and death.

Every eye in that vast multitude is turned to behold the glory of the Son of God. With one voice the wicked hosts exclaim, "Blessed is He that comes in the name of the Lord!" Christ descends upon the Mount of Olives from where, after His resurrection, He ascended, and where angels repeated the promise of His return. As the New Jerusalem, in its dazzling splendor, comes down from heaven, it rests upon the place purified and made ready to receive it, and Christ, with His people and the angels, enters the Holy City.

The Last Siege

"And [Satan] shall go out to deceive the nations which are in the four quarters of the earth, Gog and Magog, to gather them together to battle: the number of whom *is* as the sand of the sea. And they went up on the breadth of the earth, and compassed the camp of the saints about, and the beloved city" (Rev. 20:8, 9). Now Satan prepares for a last mighty struggle for supremacy. He marshals all the armies of the lost under his banner and through them endeavors to execute his plans. In that vast throng are multitudes of the long-lived race that existed before the flood; there are kings and generals who conquered nations, valiant men who never lost a battle, and proud, ambitious warriors whose approach made kingdoms tremble.

Satan consults with his angels, then with these kings, conquerors, and mighty men. They lay their plans to take possession of the riches and glory of the New Jerusalem. At last, the order to advance is given, and the countless host moves on—an army such as was never summoned by earthly conquerors; combined forces of all ages since warfare began on this planet that could never be equaled. Satan, the mightiest of warriors, leads the van, and his angels unite their forces for this final struggle.

Kings and warriors are in his train, and the multitudes follow in vast companies, each under its appointed leader. With military precision, the serried ranks advance over earth's broken and uneven surface to the City of God. Satan surrounds the city and makes ready for the onset.

The Final Panorama

> **And I saw the dead, small and great, stand before God; and the books were opened: and another book was opened, which is *the book* of life: and the dead were judged out of those things which were written in the books, according to their works. And the sea gave up the dead which were in it; and death and hell delivered up the dead which were in them: and they were judged every man according to their works.** (Revelation 20:12, 13)

In the presence of the assembled inhabitants of the earth and heaven, the final judgments of the wicked take place. The books of record are opened, and the whole depraved world stands arraigned at the bar of God on the charge of high treason against the government of heaven. They have none to plead their cause; they are without excuse, and the sentence of eternal death is pronounced against them. It is now evident to all that the wage of sin is not noble independence and eternal life, but slavery, ruin, and death. The wicked see what they have forfeited by their lives of rebellion.

As Satan looks upon his kingdom, the fruit of his toil, he sees only failure and ruin. He has led the multitudes to disobey God. Again, in the progress of the great controversy, he has been defeated and compelled to yield. He knows too well the power and majesty of the Eternal. The aim of the great rebel has ever been to justify himself and prove the divine government responsible for his rebellion.

To this end, he has bent all the power of his giant intellect. He has worked deliberately and systematically, and with marvelous success, leading vast multitudes to accept his version of the great controversy, which has been so long in progress. For thousands of years, this chief of conspiracy has pawned off falsehood for truth.

The Final Destruction

"And it shall come to pass in that day, *that* I will give unto Gog a place there of graves in Israel, the valley of the passengers on the east of the sea: and it shall stop the *noses* of the passengers: and there shall they bury Gog and all his multitude: and they shall call *it* The valley of Hamongog" (Ezek. 39:11). However, the time has now come when the rebellion is to be finally defeated and its history and character exposed. Fire comes down from God out of heaven. The earth is broken up. The weapons concealed in its depths are drawn forth. Devouring flames burst from every yawning chasm. The very rocks are on fire, **"For, behold, the day cometh, that shall burn as an oven; and all the proud, yea, and all that do wickedly, shall be stubble: and the day that cometh shall burn them up, saith the LORD of hosts, that it shall leave them neither root nor branch"** (Mal. 4:1).

"But the day of the Lord will come as a thief in the night; in which the heavens shall pass away with a great noise, and the elements shall melt with fervent heat, the earth also and the works that are therein shall be burned up" (2 Peter 3:10). The earth's surface seems one molten mass—a vast, seething lake of fire. It is the time of the judgment and perdition of ungodly people. **"For *it is* the day of the LORD's vengeance, *and* the year of recompenses for the controversy of Zion"** (Isa. 34:8).

While the earth is wrapped in the fire of destruction, the righteous abide safely in the Holy City. Upon those who had a part in the first resurrection, the second death has no power. While God is to the wicked a consuming fire, He is to His people both a sun and shield. The fire that consumes the wicked purifies the earth. Every trace of the curse is swept away.

> *While the earth is wrapped in the fire of destruction, the righteous abide safely in the Holy City. Upon those who had a part in the first resurrection, the second death has no power*

The New Beginning

No eternally burning hell is flashed before the ransomed as the fearful consequence of sin. Human language is inadequate to describe the reward of the righteous. It will be known only to those who behold it. No finite mind can comprehend the glory of the Paradise of God. In the Bible, the inheritance of the saved is called "a country."

> **For they that say such things declare plainly that they seek a country. And truly, if they had been mindful of that *country* from whence they came out, they might have had opportunity to have returned. But now they desire a better *country*, that is, an heavenly: wherefore God is not ashamed to be called their God: for he hath prepared for them a city.** (Hebrews 11:14–16)

There the heavenly Shepherd leads His flock to fountains of living waters. The tree of life yields its fruit every month, and the leaves of the tree are for the service of the nations. There are ever-flowing streams, clear as crystal, and beside them waving trees cast their shadows upon the paths prepared for the ransomed of the Lord. There the wide-spreading plains swell into hills of beauty, and the mountains of God rear their lofty summits. On those peaceful plains, beside those living streams, God's people, so long pilgrims and wanderers, shall find a home.

The great controversy is ended. Sin and sinners are no more. The entire universe is clean. One pulse of harmony and gladness beats through the vast creation. From Him who created everything flows life, light, and joy throughout the realms of illimitable space. From the minutest atom to the largest planet, all things, animate and inanimate, in their un-shadowed beauty and perfect delight, declare that God is love. "**And I heard another voice from heaven, saying, Come out of her, my people, that ye be not partakers of her sins, and that ye receive not of her plagues. For her sins have reached unto heaven, and God hath remembered her iniquities**" (Rev. 18:4, 5).

Dear friends, as God called the children of Israel out of Egypt, so He calls His people out of Babylon today, that they may not worship the beast or its image. Shall we hear the voice of God and obey, or shall we make a halfhearted commitment and try to serve God and mammon?

Time is running out for the earth and its inhabitants. This is the message that God is trying to share with each of us by His great prophecies: Jesus is soon coming to execute judgment and restore the dominion lost by Adam and Eve so long ago. He wants all of His children on earth to be a part of that kingdom and ready for that glorious moment when our Savior returns.

Bibliography

"A Call for Climate Justice — Release 7." The Salvation Army. http://1ref.us/pf (accessed September 6, 2018).

Abul A'la Mawdudi, *Towards Understanding Islam*, 8th ed. Riyadh, Saudi Arabia: National Offset Printing Press, 1986.

Allen, Jr., John L. "New book says Vatican II key to understanding Pope Francis." Crux. http://1ref.us/o9 (accessed September 5, 2018).

Arter, Melanie. "Jerry Brown: 3 Billion Will Die from Global Warming." CNS News. http://1ref.us/p4 (accessed September 6, 2018).

Bengali, Shashank. "India is building a biometric database for 1.3 billion people — and enrollment is mandatory." *Los Angeles Times*. http://1ref.us/oa (accessed September 5, 2018).

Bentz, Jan. "Asia Cardinal's Lenten message: Repent, an 'ecological apocalypse' is about to 'destroy Mother Earth.'" LifeSite. http://1ref.us/qe (accessed October 24, 2018).

Blackman, Daniel. "Britain Forges Ahead With Anti-Extremism Commission." *National Catholic Register*. http://1ref.us/ob (accessed September 5, 2018).

Bloomberg, Michael and Maroš Šefčovič. "Our new alliance unites 600m city dwellers in fight against climate change." *The Guardian*. http://1ref.us/oc (accessed September 5, 2018).

Blumberg, Antonia. "Pope Francis: 'The Mental Structure Of Fundamentalists Is Violence In The Name Of God.'" *Huffington Post*. http://1ref.us/od (accessed September 5, 2018).

Budetti, Varvara. "26 Retired Military Officers Sign Statement Lambasting Trump's Latest Transgender Ban." *Law and Crime*. http://1ref.us/pl (accessed September 6, 2018).

Bushnell, Dennis M. "Future Strategic Issues/Future Warfare." NASA Langley Research Center. http://1ref.us/p1 (accessed September 6, 2018).

Cook, Jeffrey. "JetBlue testing facial-recognition boarding system in Boston." ABC News. http://1ref.us/oe (accessed September 5, 2018).

Davenport, Coral. "Climate Change Deemed Growing Security Threat by Military Researchers." *The New York Times*. http://1ref.us/of (accessed September 5, 2018).

Devlin, Dory. "Rutgers Climate Scientists Find More Evidence Linking Arctic Warming to Jet Stream Movement." *Rutgers Today*. http://1ref.us/p3 (accessed September 6, 2018).

Dillard, Tom. "Baseball and blue laws." *Arkansas Democrat Gazette*. http://1ref.us/pi (accessed September 6, 2018).

Duppa, Richard. *A Brief Account of the Subversion of the Papal Government*. London: G.G and J. Robinson, 1799.

Feeney, Nolan. "Pope Francis Says World Nearing Climate-change 'Suicide.'" *Time*. http://1ref.us/og (accessed September 5, 2018).

"France approves tough new anti-terror laws." BBC News. http://1ref.us/nz (accessed September 5, 2018).

"Full text of Pope Francis' Interview with 'La Vanguardia.'" Catholic News Agency. http://1ref.us/o0 (accessed September 5, 2018).

Gilbert, Scott. "Environmental Warfare and US Foreign Policy." http://1ref.us/oz (accessed September 5, 2018).

Giuffrida, Angela. "Italian retailers warn of 50,000 job losses if Sunday trading curbed." *The Guardian*. http://1ref.us/qp (accessed October 24, 2018).

"Good ol' days' Poland limits Sunday shopping to benefit family life." *Daily Herald Tribune*. http://1ref.us/o1 (accessed September 5, 2018).

"Governor Abbott Issues A Proclamation For Day Of Prayer In Texas After Hurricane Harvey." Office of the Texas Governor. http://1ref.us/qk (accessed October 24, 2018).

"Green Sabbath." Climate CoLab. http://1ref.us/pd (accessed September 6, 2018).

"HAARP Poses Global Threat." Pravda.ru. http://1ref.us/p0 (accessed September 5, 2018).

Hales, E.E.V. *The Catholic Church in the Modern World*. New York: Hanover House, 1958.

Halstead, John. "Eight Ways Pagans Celebrate Earth Day." *HuffPost*. http://1ref.us/pb (accessed September 6, 2018).

"India co-hosts first solar alliance meet, PM Modi says 100 GW by 2022." *The Indian Express*. http://1ref.us/qd (accessed October 24, 2018).

Johnson, Daryl. "Hate In God's Name." Southern Poverty Law Center. http://1ref.us/oi (accessed September 5, 2018).

Josephus. *Antiquities of the Jews*.

Justice, Jessilyn. "7,000 Churches Fasting, Praying Over Terrifying New Persecution Law." Charisma News. http://1ref.us/pt (accessed September 6, 2018).

Kennedy, Eugene C. "Pope Francis to us: 'I am Vatican II.'" *National Catholic Reporter*. http://1ref.us/pp (accessed September 6, 2018).

Knapton, Sarah. "Bill Gates: Terrorists could wipe out 30 million people by weaponising a disease such as smallpox." *The Telegraph*. http://1ref.us/oj (accessed September 5, 2018).

Lalonde, Peter. *One World Under Antichrist*.

Lee, Martin A. "The CIA and the Vatican's Intelligence Apparatus." *Church and State*. http://1ref.us/ok (accessed September 5, 2018).

"Limit online shopping on Sundays to protect workers, demands Green Party." The Local. http://1ref.us/o2 (accessed September 5, 2018).

Longman Dictionary of Contemporary English. "Lord's Day Observance Society." http://1ref.us/pn (accessed September 6, 2018).

Lough, Richard and Michel Rose. "World is losing the battle against climate change, Macron says." Reuters. http://1ref.us/ol (accessed September 5, 2018).

Marrone, Christian. "Integrating biometrics into visitor screening." *The Washington Times*. http://1ref.us/om (September 5, 2018).

Martin, Malachi. *The Keys of This Blood*.

Mason, Marc. "Let's be honest: Catholic teaching doesn't always forbid the death penalty." *Catholic Herald*. http://1ref.us/ql (accessed October 24, 2018).

McCleland, Jacob and Nomin Ujiyediin. "Five Things That Happened During Oklahoma's 2017 Legislative Session." KGOU. http://1ref.us/on (accessed September 5, 2018).

McLean, Dorothy C. "Poland to reclaim 'day of rest' by phasing out Sunday shopping." LifeSiteNews.com. http://1ref.us/ph (accessed September 6, 2018).

McLean, Dorothy C. "'Time for God ... and rest': Catholic Poles rejoice as Sunday shopping ban comes into effect." LifeSiteNews.com. http://1ref.us/qn (accessed October 24, 2018).

McNamee, Dardis. "Opinion: To Sunday or not to Sunday." Metropole. http://1ref.us/oo (accessed September 5, 2018).

Mooney, Chris. "Global warming is now slowing down the circulation of the oceans — with potentially dire consequences." *The Washington Post*. http://1ref.us/p2 (accessed September 6, 2018).

"Natural solutions to climate change." Conservation International. http://1ref.us/o3 (accessed September 5, 2018).

New World Order Quotes. http://1ref.us/oy (accessed September 5, 2018).

"No Sunday Shopping: Dutch Vote Spawns Some Offbeat Ideas." Naharnet Newsdesk. http://1ref.us/po (accessed September 6, 2018).

Obasi, Chinedu Daniel. *The Final At-one-ment*. Fort Oglethorpe, GA: TEACH Services, 2018.

Petrulis, Geoff. "Texas Governor Abbott Declares Convention Of States An 'Emergency Item.'" CBS Dallas/Fort Worth. http://1ref.us/pm (accessed September 6, 2018).

Phillips, Francis. "The book that highlights the dangerous potential of secularist ideology." *Catholic Herald*. http://1ref.us/p6 (accessed September 6, 2018).

Pomeroy, Robin. "Vatican calls verbal attack on Pope 'terrorism.'" Reuters. http://1ref.us/op (accessed September 5, 2018).

Pope Francis. Encyclical Letter. "Laudato Si' of the Holy Father Francis on Care for Our Common Home." http://1ref.us/lc (accessed September 6, 2018).

"Pope Francis: Humanity's future is in the hands of the poor." Catholic News Agency. http://1ref.us/p8 (accessed September 6, 2018).

"Pope Francis: Jihadist attacks are 'homicidal madness.'" BBC News. http://1ref.us/o4 (accessed September 5, 2018).

"Pope Francis meets with Polish PM Morawiecki." *Vatican News*. http://1ref.us/pg (accessed September 6, 2018).

"Pope Francis: 'The Mental Structure Of Fundamentalists Is Violence In The Name Of God.'" *Huffington Post*. http://1ref.us/qi (accessed October 24, 2018).

"Pope's Environmental Encyclical On The Care Of Our Common Home." Verdexchange Conference. http://1ref.us/p9 (accessed September 6, 2018)

Prada, Luis. "Jesuits Controllers of Vatican and New World Order." Linear. http://1ref.us/oq (accessed September 5, 2018).

Rand, Howard B. *A Study in Revelation*, Merrimac, MA: Destiny Publishers, 1985.

Rice, Doyle. "Creating clouds to stop global warming could wreak havoc." *USA Today*. http://1ref.us/or (accessed September 5, 2018).

Scott, Romario. "Sabbath Agony – US State Department Report Highlights Job Challenges For Saturday Churchgoers." *The Gleaner*. http://1ref.us/os (accessed September 5, 2018).

"Shimon Peres: Francis is a more powerful peace advocate than UN." *Catholic Herald*. http://1ref.us/o5 (accessed September 5, 2018).

Smith, Helena. "Greeks plan protests against Sunday trading." *The Guardian*. http://1ref.us/ot (accessed September 5, 2018).

Smith, Uriah. *Daniel and Revelation*.

Stickings, Tim. "Italy BANS Sunday shopping: New deputy PM announces crackdown on trading laws he says are 'destroying families' since stores were allowed to open on the Sabbath in 2012." Daily Mail. http://1ref.us/qo (accessed October 24, 2018).

Teichrib, Carl. "Cult of Green: The United Nations Environmental Sabbath and the New Global Ethic." Forcing Change. http://1ref.us/pe (accessed September 6, 2018).

"The History of Earth Day." Earth Day Network. http://1ref.us/pa (accessed September 6, 2018).

"The United Nations and the New World Order." http://1ref.us/oh (accessed September 5, 2018).

Thomas, P.C. *A Compact History of the Popes*. Bandra, Mumbai: St. Paul Publications, 2003.

Tonias, Demetrios. "Sunday as a Mark of Christian Unity." The Lord's Day Alliance of the U.S. http://1ref.us/ou (accessed September 5, 2018).

Topping, Alexandra. "Pope Francis: freedom of expression has limits." *The Guardian*. http://1ref.us/ov (accessed September 5, 2018).

"Transcript: JKF's Speech on His Religion." NPR. http://1ref.us/pj (accessed September 6, 2018).

Travis, Alan. "Amber Rudd: viewers of online terrorist material face 15 years in jail." *The Guardian*. http://1ref.us/ow (accessed September 5, 2018).

"UK consumers want biometrics in banking." *Business Insider*. http://1ref.us/o6 (accessed September 5, 2018).

Vatican Radio. "Pope Francis on Monday called on people of every religious tradition to join in condemning the misuse of God's name to justify acts of violence." The Catholic Community Television Network. http://1ref.us/qh (accessed October 24, 2018).

Vidal, John and Helen Weinstein. "RAF rainmakers 'caused 1952 flood.'" *The Guardian*. http://1ref.us/ox (accessed September 5, 2018).

Wargas, Robert. "Why Catholics thrive in the CIA." *Catholic Herald*. http://1ref.us/p7 (accessed September 6, 2018).

"What's happening with Sunday work in Europe?" Eurofound. http://1ref.us/o7 (accessed September 5, 2018).

White, Ellen G. "A Time of Trouble." *The Review and Herald*, September 17, 1901.

White, Ellen G. "Our Present Duty and the Coming Crisis." *The Review and Herald*, January 11, 1887.

White, Ellen G. *Maranatha*. Washington, DC: Review and Herald Publishing Association, 1976.

White, Ellen G. *Testimonies for the Church*. Vol. 9. Mountain View, CA: Pacific Press Publishing Association, 1909.

White, Ellen G. *The Acts of the Apostles*. Mountain View, CA: Pacific Press Publishing Association, 1911.

White, Ellen G. *The Desire of Ages*. Mountain View, CA: Pacific Press Publishing Association, 1898.

White, Ellen G. *The Faith I Live By*. Washington, DC: Review and Herald Publishing Association, 1958.

White, Ellen G. *The Great Controversy*. Mountain View, CA: Pacific Press Publishing Association, 1911.

White, Ellen G. *The Great Controversy*. Mountain View, CA: Pacific Press Publishing Association, 1888.

White, Ellen G. *The Southern Work*. Washington, DC: Review and Herald Publishing Association, 1966.

White, Ellen G. *The Spirit of Prophecy*. Vol. 4. Battle Creek, MI: Seventh-day Adventist Publishing Association, 1884.

"Wolf signs Real ID law, expects new licenses in 2019." The Inquirer/Daily News/philly.com. http://1ref.us/o8 (accessed September 5, 2018).

"World see rapid upsurge in extreme weather: report." Phys.org. http://1ref.us/pu (accessed September 6, 2018).

Zavis, Alexandra and Mythili Sampathkumar. "The Paris climate deal just became law. Now countries must figure out how to make good on their pledges." *Los Angeles Times*. http://1ref.us/p5 (accessed September 6, 2018).

Zimmerman, Eugene. "At It Again." Library of Congress. http://1ref.us/pk (accessed September 6, 2018).

TEACH Services, Inc.
PUBLISHING

We invite you to view the complete
selection of titles we publish at:
www.TEACHServices.com

We encourage you to write us
with your thoughts about this,
or any other book we publish at:
info@TEACHServices.com

TEACH Services' titles may be purchased in
bulk quantities for educational, fund-raising,
business, or promotional use.
bulksales@TEACHServices.com

Finally, if you are interested in seeing
your own book in print, please contact us at:
publishing@TEACHServices.com

We are happy to review your manuscript at no charge.

www.ingramcontent.com/pod-product-compliance
Lightning Source LLC
Chambersburg PA
CBHW070551160426
43199CB00014B/2455